OAKWOOD LIBRARY OF RAILWAY HISTORY OL87

The LYNN & DEREHAM RAILWAY

The Kings Lynn to Norwich Line

by

Stanley C. Jenkins, MA

THE OAKWOOD PRESS

ISBN 0 85361 443 1

Typeset by Gem Publishing Company, Brightwell, Wallingford, Oxfordshire.

Printed by Alpha Print (Oxon) Ltd, Witney, Oxfordshire.

By the Same Author

The Witney & East Gloucestershire Railway (Oakwood Press, 1975)
The Oxford Worcester & Wolverhampton Railway (Oakwood Press, 1977) co-author
The Lakeside & Haverthwaite Railway (Dalesman Publishing Co., 1977) co-author
The Great Western & Great Central Joint Railway (Oakwood Press, 1978)
Branch Lines into the Eighties (David & Charles, 1980) co-author
The Fairford Branch (Oakwood Press, 1985)
The Lynn & Hunstanton Railway (Oakwood Press, 1987)
The Woodstock Branch (Wild Swan Publications, 1987)
The Wells-next-the-Sea Branch (Oakwood Press, 1988)
The Cromer Branch (Oakwood Press, 1989)
The Moretonhampstead & South Devon Railway (Oakwood Press, 1989) co-author
The Northampton & Banbury Junction Railway (Oakwood Press, 1990)
The Watford to St Albans Branch (Oakwood Press, 1990)
The Alston Branch (Oakwood Press, 1991)
The Leek & Manifold Light Railway (Oakwood Press, 1991)
The Rothbury Branch (Oakwood Press, 1991)
The Melton Constable to Cromer Branch (Oakwood Press, 1991)
The Helston Branch (Oakwood Press, 1992)
The Wensleydale Branch (Oakwood Press, 1993)

Dedicated to
Rosemary A. de V. Merriman

Published by
The OAKWOOD PRESS
P.O.Box 122, Headington, Oxford.

Contents

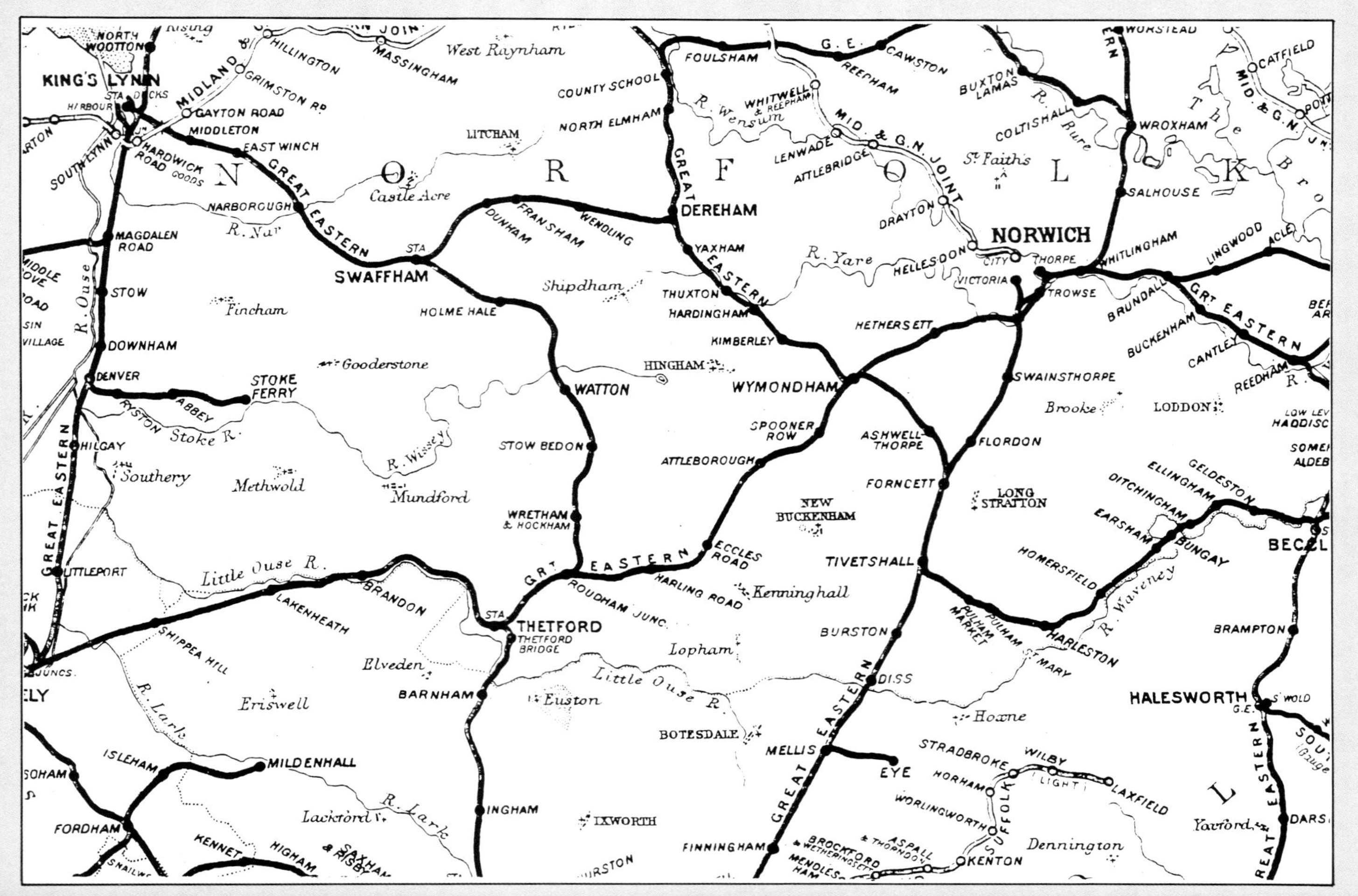
KING'S LYNN
NORTH WOOTTON
MIDLAND
HILLINGTON
GRIMSTON RD
GAYTON ROAD
MIDDLETON
EAST WINCH
MASSINGHAM
West Raynham
COUNTY SCHOOL
NORTH ELMHAM
LITCHAM
FOULSHAM
G.E.
REEPHAM
CAWSTON
WHITWELL & REEPHAM
R. Wensum
LENWADE
ATTLEBRIDGE
MID. & G.N. JOINT
BUXTON LAMAS
COLTISHALL
R. Bure
St. Faith's
WROXHAM
SALHOUSE
WORSTEAD
CATFIELD
The Broads
N O R F O L K
SOUTH LYNN
HARDWICK ROAD GOODS
NARBOROUGH
GREAT EASTERN
Castle Acre
R. Nar
MAGDALEN ROAD
STOW
DOWNHAM
DENVER
R. Ouse
SWAFFHAM
DUNHAM
FRANSHAM
WENDLING
DEREHAM
YAXHAM
THUXTON
HARDINGHAM
KIMBERLEY
DRAYTON
HELLESDON
NORWICH
CITY
THORPE
VICTORIA
TROWSE
R. Yare
WHITLINGHAM
LINGWOOD
ACLE
BRUNDALL
BUCKENHAM
CANTLEY
REEDHAM
GRT EASTERN
Fincham
Gooderstone
HOLME HALE
Shipdham
HINGHAM
WYMONDHAM
HETHERSETT
SWAINSTHORPE
Brooke
LODDON
STOKE FERRY
ABBEY
RYSTON
Stoke R.
R. Wissey
WATTON
STOW BEDON
SPOONER ROW
ATTLEBOROUGH
ASHWELL THORPE
FLORDON
FORNCETT
LONG STRATTON
HILGAY
Southery
Methwold
Mundford
WRETHAM & HOCKHAM
NEW BUCKENHAM
ELLINGHAM
GELDESTON
DITCHINGHAM
EARSHAM
BUNGAY
LITTLEPORT
Little Ouse R.
BRANDON
LAKENHEATH
GRT EASTERN
ECCLES ROAD
HARLING ROAD
ROUDHAM JUNC.
Kenninghall
TIVETSHALL
HOMERSFIELD
R. Waveney
THETFORD
THETFORD BRIDGE
SHIPPEA HILL
Elveden
BARNHAM
Lopham
BURSTON
PULHAM MARKET
PULHAM ST MARY
HARLESTON
BRAMPTON
ELY
Eriswell
R. Lark
Euston
Little Ouse R.
DISS
Hoxne
HALESWORTH
S'WOLD
BOTESDALE
MELLIS
EYE
STRADBROKE
WILBY
HORHAM
LIGHT
LAXFIELD
SOHAM
ISLEHAM
MILDENHALL
WORLINGWORTH
SUFFOLK
FORDHAM
Lackford
R. Lark
INGHAM
IXWORTH
FINNINGHAM
GREAT EASTERN
BROCKFORD & WETHERINGSETT
ASPALL & THORNDON
KENTON
Dennington
Yoxford
DARS
KENNET
HIGHAM
SAXHAM & RISBY
MENDLESHAM
BECCLES

Introduction

Cross-country lines were of particular interest to railway enthusiasts in that they were neither main lines nor branches. Lengthy, often single track routes, they exhibited many branch line characteristics, yet they could (and often did) carry important-looking main line trains. The Lynn & Dereham Railway was a typical cross-country route. Running from west to east across the rural heart of Norfolk, it linked Kings Lynn, Swaffham and Dereham, while serving several much smaller places such as Wendling, Fransham and East Winch. Some trains continued eastwards to reach Norwich, making use of part of the Norfolk Railway branch between Wymondham and Fakenham; if earlier L&DR plans had come to fruition this line would have been part of a much longer Lynn & Dereham-backed line to Yarmouth, but in the event Parliament had dictated that the link to Wymondham would be built by the Norfolk company. By 1862, however, the Lynn & Dereham and Dereham to Wymondham lines had both been absorbed by the newly-created Great Eastern Railway, and, thereafter, a greater degree of integration was possible between these two separate, but closely-linked cross-country routes.

Together, the Lynn & Dereham and Dereham to Wymondham lines formed a useful cross-country link between Kings Lynn in the west of Norfolk and Norwich in the east, and although most local passenger trains from Kings Lynn terminated at Dereham, the 48¼ mile route between Kings Lynn and Norwich filled a useful gap in the GER system – becoming, in effect, an alternative route for through freight and excursion traffic that would otherwise have added to congestion on the main Norwich to Ely line.

The Kings Lynn to Norwich cross-country line served the public for 120 years, but sadly it became a closure victim during the anti-railway purges of the 1960s, and only truncated stubs now remain open (for freight traffic only).

The Great Eastern system has, in recent years, enjoyed considerable popularity among modellers and other enthusiasts, and it seemed appropriate to produce a short history of the Kings Lynn to Norwich line as a companion volume to *The Lynn & Hunstanton Railway*, *The Wells-next-the-Sea Branch*, and other recent Oakwood Press publications.

The present volume follows a generally chronological framework, which starts during the Railway Mania years of the 1840s and finishes in the 1980s; two descriptive chapters are devoted to the route, stations and physical appearance of the railway as it would have appeared around 1960. It is hoped that the completed volume will appeal to both local historians and railway enthusiasts, while at the same time serving as a reminder of one of Norfolk's most attractive rural lines.

The Lynn & Dereham Railway treats the former Norfolk Railway line between Dereham and Wymondham as an 'extension' of the L&DR route, and in view of the inter-related early histories of these two lines, the historical part of the following narrative will give equal weight to both routes. Readers of The *Wells-next-the-Sea Branch* will remember that the majority of the Wells branch trains worked through to Wymondham and thence eastwards to Norwich Thorpe, and as the Wells book contained ample details of the train services between Norwich and Wells-next-the-Sea, this present volume will concentrate primarily on the operation of the Lynn & Dereham section. It is, on the other hand, impossible to treat the L&DR route in complete isolation, and for this reason, some mention of the timetables in force between Dereham and Norwich must also be included in *The Lynn & Dereham Railway*.

The Wells book was first published in 1988 and, since that time, further details have emerged regarding the local stations between Dereham and Wymondham. As the 'route' section of *The Wells-next-the-Sea Branch* concerned itself mainly with details of the Wells & Fakenham Railway stations between Fakenham and Wells-next-the-Sea, there seemed to be scope for a more detailed treatment of the intermediate stopping places between Dereham and Wymondham. Chapter Six of *The Lynn & Dereham Railway* will, therefore, deal with Dereham and the smaller stations *en route* to Wymondham. This chapter will amplify certain points referred to in the Wells book without, however, introducing too much duplication of material – the idea being that *The Lynn & Dereham Railway* and *The Wells-next-the-Sea Branch* should be complementary rather than competing volumes.

A Note on Nomenclature

The correct name of Kings Lynn is 'Bishop's Lynn', although the Victorians usually referred to it simply as 'Lynn'. In modern parlance, the town is usually called Kings Lynn, and this term is used through *The Lynn & Dereham Railway*. Similarly, Dereham should strictly be called East Dereham, but for convenience the town is referred to as Dereham throughout the present work.

Wells-next-the-Sea presents a further problem in that the Great Eastern Railway called this Norfolk coastal port 'Wells', while the London & North Eastern Railway renamed it 'Wells-on-Sea'. In 1957, British Railways belatedly renamed the station Wells-next-the-Sea, and thereby introduced the correct name exactly one hundred years after the railway had been opened. The following narrative will use the full name Wells-next-the-Sea where appropriate, though to prevent repetitious sentences the shorter version of 'Wells' will occasionally be used. Other station name changes will be mentioned in the text, though it is worth noting here that Middleton Towers and Kimberley Park were originally called 'Middleton' and 'Kimberley' respectively.

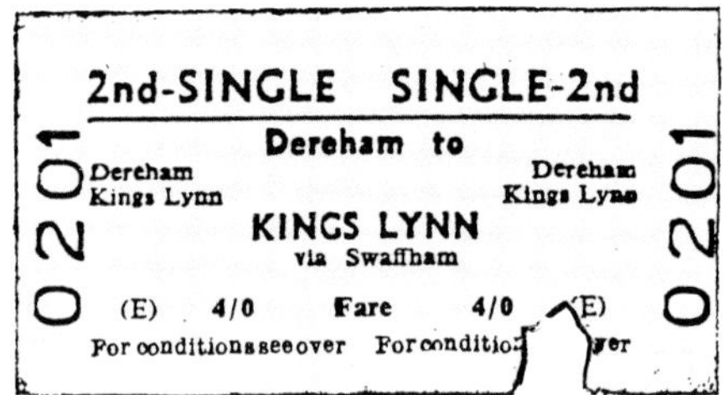

2nd-SINGLE SINGLE-2nd
0201
Dereham to
Dereham
Kings Lynn
Dereham
Kings Lynn
KINGS LYNN
via Swaffham
(E) 4/0 Fare 4/0
For conditions see over
0201

A single ticket from Dereham to Kings Lynn, issued in the BR era. *Courtesy John Strange*

Historical Summary, etc

Companies of Origin

Lynn & Dereham Railway
Formed by Act of 21st July, 1845 (8 & 9 Vic. cap. 126) to build a railway from Dereham to a junction with the Lynn & Ely Railway at Kings Lynn. In 1847, the Lynn & Dereham, Lynn & Ely and Ely & Huntingdon railways were amalgamated to form the East Anglian Railways (EAR), and in 1862 the EAR itself became part of the Great Eastern Railway.

Norfolk Railway
Formed by the amalgamation of the Yarmouth & Norwich Railway (incorporated 18th June, 1842) and the Norwich & Brandon Railway (incorporated 10th May, 1844) by Act of 30th June, 1845. Worked by the Eastern Counties Railway from 8th May, 1848, and amalgamated with the Eastern Counties, East Anglian and other companies to form the Great Eastern Railway in 1862.

Dates of Opening

Kings Lynn to Narborough (L&DR)	27th October, 1846
Wymondham to Dereham (Norfolk Railway)	15th February, 1847
Narborough to Swaffham (EAR)	10th August, 1847
Swaffham to Sporle (EAR)	26th October, 1847
Sporle to Dereham (EAR)	11th September, 1848
Dereham West to Dereham South junctions (GER)	June 1886

Length of Line

Kings Lynn to Dereham (passenger station)	26 miles 43 chains
Dereham (passenger station) to Wymondham	11 miles 33 chains
Wymondham to Norwich Thorpe	10 miles 18 chains
Total distance Kings Lynn to Norwich	48 miles 14 chains

Mode of Operation
Kings Lynn to Dereham; single track with passing places at East Winch, Narborough & Pentney, Swaffham, Dunham and Wendling.
Dereham to Wymondham: double track.
Wymondham to Norwich Thorpe: double track.

Dates of Closure

Kings Lynn to Dereham (passenger & freight traffic)	Saturday 7th September, 1968
Dereham to Wymondham (passenger traffic)	Saturday 4th October, 1969
Dereham to Wymondham (freight traffic)	June 1989

Typical Motive Power
'D15' 4–4–0s, 'D16/2' 4–4–0s, 'D16/3' 4–4–0s, 'D13' 4–4–0s, 'D2' 4–4–0s, 'E4' 2–4–0s, 'F3' 2–4–2Ts, 'J15' 0–6–0s, 'J17' 0–6–0s, 'N7' 0–6–2Ts.

Middleton station, looking east towards Dereham and Norwich during the early 1900s.

Lens of Sutton

Chapter One

Origins of the Line (1840–1849)

Situated in the part of England known as East Anglia, Norfolk is England's fourth largest county. Although in some ways a remote region, East Anglia has never been a backward area; on the contrary, its fertile soils and close proximity to Europe ensured that, throughout the Middle Ages, the region was among the most prosperous in England. In the mid-13th century, for example, Norwich was one of our greatest provincial towns, while Lynn was one of the country's most important ports. In 1377 the tax-paying population of Norwich was 3,952, while the corresponding figure for Kings Lynn was 3,217, and these figures suggest that, at that time, Norwich and Kings Lynn were the fourth and seventh largest towns in England. By the 17th century, Norwich had become England's undisputed second city, its population of about 42,000 being many times greater than that of Leicester, Nottingham or other comparable towns.

Some Early Railway Schemes

Since the Reformation, East Anglia had been a staunchly Protestant region with a long tradition of thrift, sobriety and hard work, and these qualities ensured that East Anglians were able to achieve prominence in many walks of life – including agriculture, banking and the Royal Navy.

Inevitably, the rapid development of railways in other parts of the country during the early 19th century encouraged East Anglians to promote railways of their own, and by the 1840s groups of bankers, landowners and traders were floating a variety of small, regionally-based railway companies. The first East Anglian railway schemes had originated as early as the 1820s, when visionaries such as William James (1771–1837) had dreamed of a possible 'Engine railroad from Bishops Stortford to Clayhithe Sluice with a branch to Waddon'. In 1824–25 an equally-grandiose 'Norfolk, Suffolk & Essex Railroad' had been projected, and if successful, this last-named scheme would have provided a viable nucleus for future East Anglian railway development.

These 1820s projects were hopelessly premature, but in the event, tangible progress was made in the following decade, and on 4th July, 1836 two important schemes – the Eastern Counties Railway (6 & 7 Wllm. cap. 106) and the Northern & Eastern Railway (6 & 7 Wllm. cap. 103) received the Royal Assent.

The Eastern Counties Railway was, in effect, a revival of the earlier Norfolk, Suffolk & Essex scheme, and like its abortive predecessor, this new company hoped to link London with Norwich and Great Yarmouth. Unfortunately, the Eastern Counties company was plagued by financial and other problems, and its promoters were forced to abandon some of their initial aims. Nevertheless, the company was able to make good progress at the London end of the line, and by 29th March, 1843 the ECR was open from London to Colchester, a distance of 51¾ miles.

Meanwhile, further to the west, the Northern & Eastern Railway had also made considerable progress, and a line was open from London to Bishops

Stortford by 1842. On 1st January, 1844 the Eastern Counties Railway took over the Northern & Eastern company on a 999 year lease, and although the original ECR line had still not progressed beyond Colchester, the Northern & Eastern Railway was extended to Cambridge and Brandon on 29th July, 1845. It is interesting to note that the ECR and Northern & Eastern lines were both 5 ft gauge lines, but in September 1844 the combined systems were converted to 4 ft 8½ in. gauge, the work of conversion being accomplished in the commendable time of just one month.

Developments Around Norwich

The apparent failure of the Eastern Counties to reach Norwich caused considerable disquiet in east Norfolk, and when it became clear that the ECR would not be able to serve Great Yarmouth directly, a separate company was formed to link Yarmouth with Norwich. Incorporated by an Act of 18th June, 1842 (5 & 6 Vic. cap. 82), the Yarmouth & Norwich Railway was constructed and opened to public traffic in just 12 months, and on 30th April, 1844 around 200 invited guests were conveyed in a special inaugural train from Norwich to Great Yarmouth. The line was opened to the general public on 1st May, 1844, and *White's History, Gazetteer & Directory of Norfolk* recalled that 'the event was marked with great festivity and rejoicing'. The new railway was served by about half a dozen trains each way on its 20½ mile line, the usual journey time being 50 minutes; at Norwich, the line terminated in a small station which, in later years, became known as Norwich Thorpe.

Encouraged by the success of the Yarmouth & Norwich scheme, local interests lost no time in promoting a railway between Norwich and Brandon, and on 10th May, 1844 the Norwich & Brandon Bill received the Royal Assent (7 & 8 Vic. cap. 15). The Norwich & Brandon Railway was opened at the same time as the ECR's Brandon extension, and thus, on 29th July, 1845, Norwich was physically linked to the Eastern Counties system – thereby creating a continuous chain of communication between Norwich, Brandon, Cambridge, Bishops Stortford and London.

There was, as yet, no direct connection with the earlier Yarmouth & Norwich line, but this problem was rectified on 15th December, 1845 when the opening of Trowse swing bridge provided a through route between Yarmouth, Norwich and London. A few months previous to this, on 30th June, 1845, the Yarmouth & Norwich Railway had combined with the Norwich & Brandon company to form the appropriately-named Norfolk Railway.

The Railway Mania in North Norfolk

Noting the ease with which the Yarmouth & Norwich and Norwich & Brandon lines had been promoted, the people of west Norfolk were eager to promote railways of their own, and there were, by the middle 1840s, several proposals for railways in and around Kings Lynn. Indeed, such schemes were now coming thick and fast, for the 1840s were a time of 'Railway

Mania' in which companies were floated recklessly, with little or no regard for national, or even local planning.

Lines promoted during this period of furious and unco-ordinated expansion included the Lynn & Ely, the Lynn & Dereham, the Ely & Huntingdon, the Newmarket & Chesterford, the Wells & Thetford, the Lynn & Fakenham, the North of Norfolk, and several related schemes for lines to the coast at Wells, Blakeney and elsewhere.

The Lynn & Ely Railway was one of the most important lines promoted in west Norfolk during the 'Mania' years. Authorised by an Act of 30th June, 1845 (8 & 9 Vic. cap. 55), the Lynn & Ely scheme encompassed a 25 mile main line from Kings Lynn to a junction with the Eastern Counties Railway at Ely, together with branches from Watlington (later Magdalen Road) to Wisbech, and from Kings Lynn to Lynn Harbour. Although the new line was of relatively short length, capital of no less than £300,000 was authorised, and the boggy nature of this Fenland route posed many engineering problems.

Meanwhile, various speculators were planning lines running east and westwards from Kings Lynn in the hope that these additional lines would one day form part of a trunk route linking the north and Midlands with the busy ports of Kings Lynn and Yarmouth. Much of this promotional activity stemmed from the efforts of one man – J.C. Williams, a local solicitor – whose range of professional contacts ensured that he was well-placed to organise the disparate schemes that mushroomed during the Mania years of the 1840s. J.C. Williams was involved with both the Lynn & Ely and Ely & Huntingdon railways, and he also played an important part during the promotion of the Lynn & Dereham Railway – a company that was, from its inception, intimately connected with the Lynn & Ely Railway.

The Lynn & Dereham promoters hoped that one day their line would extend east towards Norwich and west towards Nottingham and Manchester, but in the short term the new railway was laid before the public as a purely local line. It was claimed, for instance, that coal would be carried from Kings Lynn to Dereham for only 1*s*. 3*d*. per ton (as opposed to £2 per ton by road), while at the same time the inhabitants of Swaffham and Dereham would be placed into direct contact with London via Kings Lynn and the Lynn & Ely line.

Well supported by the traders and merchants of Kings Lynn and Norwich, a Bill 'for making a railway from Lynn to East Dereham' was presented to Parliament in the early part of 1845, and on 20th March *The House of Commons Journal* reported that petitions in favour of the Bill had been referred to the Select Committee on private Bills.

The Lynn & Dereham Bill was read for the first time on 7th April, 1845, but the scheme faced considerable opposition and on 21st May it was reported that 'the Reverend John Nelson rector of the rectory of Little Dunham, Edward Press of Hingham, and Edward Lombe of Great Melton had petitioned against the Bill.' Despite this unexpected opposition, the committee appointed to consider the Lynn & Dereham Bill eventually decided in its favour, and the Bill was read for the third time on 23rd June, 1845.[1]

Having passed successfully through the Lower House, the Bill was immediately carried up to the Lords, where it was read for the first time on 23rd June. A few days later, on 8th July, the Earl of Shaftsbury reported that the Lords committee appointed to consider the Lynn & Dereham scheme had met, and found everything in order. They recommended, however, that a level crossing should be allowed at Gaywood because the road concerned carried 'scarcely any traffic', and moreover the proposed level crossing would be 'near the station at Lynn' and could be easily supervised.

The House of Commons agreed to this modest amendment, and on 21st July, 1845 the Act 'for making a railway from Lynn to East Dereham' received the Royal Assent.[2]

The Lynn & Dereham Act (8 & 9 Vic. cap. 126) provided for the construction of a 26 mile line from the Lynn & Ely Railway at Kings Lynn to the town of Dereham. Capital of £270,000 (in 10,800 £25 shares) was authorised, together with loans of £90,000. This relatively large share capital was rapidly subscribed, and in an atmosphere of growing enthusiasm the Lynn & Dereham supporters anticipated an early and successful completion of their scheme.

A Rival Scheme

The one cloud on the horizon in the summer of 1845 was the Norwich & Brandon Railway which, in February 1845, had deposited a Bill seeking powers 'for altering the line of the Norwich & Brandon Railway, and for making a branch therefrom to East Dereham in the County of Norfolk'.[3] Aware that this branch would impede any future extensions of their own line, the Lynn & Dereham promoters opposed the Norwich & Brandon Bill and threw their weight behind a rival scheme for an East Dereham to Norwich Railway.

Indeed, the Norwich & Brandon scheme was opposed by a wide range of vested interests, among them 'the Governor and Guardians of the Poor of the City of Norwich . . . two owners of property on the line . . . Richard Ballard and William Peterson of the City of Norwich, and . . . bankers and others of the City of Norwich'. The Bill was, on the other hand, strongly supported by petitions from the merchants of Great Yarmouth, and from the 'occupiers of land and inhabitants of Wendling, Great Fransham, Beeston & Litcham, Fakenham, Witchingham, Reepham, Sparham and neighbourhood, Mattishall, East Dereham, Swaffham, Lyng and North Tuddenham'.[4]

In the event, Parliament decided that the line between Dereham and Norwich would be built by the Norwich & Brandon Railway, and on 31st July, 1845 the Dereham branch scheme received the Royal Assent. The Norwich & Brandon Railway had, by that time, joined forces with the Yarmouth & Norwich Railway to form the Norfolk Railway, but this change of ownership was merely a formality, and the Norfolk Railway Directors were eager to see the proposed Dereham branch in operation.

Norwich & Brandon Railway (Diss & Dereham Branches) Bill. Specially reported.

The Earl *Beauchamp* reported from the Lords Committees appointed a Select Committee to consider of the Bill, intituled " An Act for altering the Line of the " *Norwich* and *Brandon* Railway, and for making a " Branch therefrom to *East Dereham* in the County of " *Norfolk* ;" and to whom were referred the Petitions of the Governor and Guardians of the Poor of the City of *Norwich*, under their Common Seal ; of the Provisional Committee of the proposed *East Dereham* and *Norwich* Railway Company ; of Two Owners of Property on the Line ; of *Richard Ballard* and *William Peterson* of the City of *Norwich* ; and of Bankers and others of the City of *Norwich* ; severally praying to be heard by Counsel against the Bill ; and to whom were also referred the Petitions of Merchants, Traders, and others of *Great Yarmouth* ; of Owners and Occupiers of Land and Inhabitants of *Wendling*, *Great Fransham*, *Beeston*, and *Litcham* ; of *Fakenham*, *Witchingham*, *Reepham*, *Sparham*, and Neighbourhood ; of *Mattishall* ; of *East Dereham* ; of *Swaffham* ; of *Lyng* and *North Tuddenham* ; and of *East Tuddenham* and *Honningham* ; with Leave to the Committee to hear Counsel in favour of and against the said Bill ; " That the Committee had met, and considered " the said Bill, and also the said Petitions, and had heard " Counsel and had examined Witnesses ; and Mr. *Cop-* " *pock* having cross-examined the said Witnesses in support " of the Bill, and there not being any further Opposition " thereto, the Committee had not thought it necessary " to inquire into the Matters required to be reported " upon specially by the First of the Standing Orders with " regard to the Proceedings of Committees on Railway " Bills ; the Committee then found that the Provisions " and Clauses required by the Standing Orders to be " inserted in Railway Bills are contained in this Bill, in " so far as the same are applicable thereto, except in the " following Particular ; (*viz*.) That it is proposed to cross " on the Level the several public Highways mentioned " in the Appendix to this Report ; but the Committee " are of Opinion that the Standing Order prohibiting " such level Crossings should not in the Cases referred " to be enforced, for the Reasons contained in the said " Appendix ; and that the Committee had gone through " the Bill, and directed the same to be reported to their " Lordships, with some Amendments."

An extract from The House of Lords Journal, 17th July, 1845, reporting on the passage of the Norwich & Brandon Railway (Diss & Dereham branch lines) Bill.

Construction Begins

Undeterred by the success of the rival Norwich & Brandon Bill, the Lynn & Dereham supporters lost no time in putting their own plans into effect, and construction work began just a few weeks after the successful passage of the Lynn & Dereham Act.

The authorised route began just a few feet above sea level at Kings Lynn, and it then ran south-eastwards across a low-lying stretch of land for about nine miles towards Narborough. Beyond, the railway builders were faced with a ridge of higher land around Swaffham, but there were no major physical obstacles, and construction of the 26 miles-long railway was expected to be a relatively easy task.

Work was well under way by the early months of 1846, and on 3rd February, 1846 the first consignment of iron rails was delivered under a contract with Messrs Bailey Brothers of Liverpool. This initial contract was for 6,000 tons of rails at a price of £12 2*s*. 6*d*. per ton, and it appears that the new rails were delivered by sea and stockpiled in a makeshift depot at Kings Lynn.

The work of construction was supervised by John Sutherland Valentine (1813–98), a 32-year old civil engineer who had originally trained under John Urpeth Rastrick. A Derbyshire man, J.S. Valentine was responsible for both the Lynn & Ely and Lynn & Dereham lines,[5] though it would seem that the Lynn & Ely (with its troublesome river crossings) warranted more attention than the relatively problem-free Dereham route. The two lines were built simultaneously, and, commencing at Kings Lynn, Valentine built outwards to Downham and Narborough respectively; the first section of the Lynn & Dereham route was soon staked out, and the contract for this first section of line was awarded to Mr J. Walker, who was expected to complete the work within six months.

Rapid progress was made on the Kings Lynn to Narborough contract, and at the half-year meeting held in February 1846 the Lynn & Dereham Directors announced that 'the prospects of the Company with regard to the probable cost of . . . the line' were 'most gratifying'. Arrangements were in hand for the purchase of all the land required for the first contract, and 'the iron rails, chairs and sleepers for the whole of the line' had been purchased. However, the purchase of large quantities of permanent way material had absorbed a large amount of capital, and this outlay 'entailed upon the Directors the necessity of making a .... call of £5 per share upon the proprietors'.

The next item on the agenda was the Engineer's Report, and the assembled shareholders listened attentively as John Sutherland Valentine read out the following paragraphs:

> Gentlemen – In reporting to you the progress made in the works, I must in the first place state to you that, in consequence of the extreme demand during the Autumn of last year for engineering draughtsmen and assistants, I was unable, until the 30th November, to form a sufficient staff for properly commencing operations. Since that time, however, I have been more successful; the whole of the line is staked out, and the levels for the contract sections taken.

> The necessary plans for the purchase of the land required for the first contract are also completed. The contract for the portion of the line from Lynn to Narborough (being a distance of nine miles) is let to Mr James Walker for a sum under my estimate, and the works will be completed by the end of August. The plans and drawings for the next contract are in a state of great forwardness, and may be advertised forthwith.[6]

It was announced that the sum of £3,800 had been expended on 'sleepers and iron for chairs', and a further £9,800 had been spent on 'land and compensation'. These figures did not include the building costs of the Lynn & Ely line, and although rails, timber, bricks and other items were purchased in great quantity for use on *both* lines, the Lynn & Dereham Directors made every effort to keep their accounts entirely separate from those of the Lynn & Ely company.

Construction proceeded apace throughout the summer of 1846, and on 22nd October the Directors gave notice that the portion of line between Kings Lynn and Narborough would be opened to public traffic on Tuesday 27th October. It was confidently expected that the entire line would be open 'by midsummer', and to celebrate the completion of the Lynn to Narborough line the Directors arranged a formal opening on Monday 26th October, with a special train for invited guests. The first section of the Lynn & Ely Railway was also opened on 26th October, and it was agreed that the 'First Day' excursion would traverse both of the new lines – thereby underlining the close links that existed between the Dereham and Ely companies.

Opening to Narborough

Opening Day was celebrated in considerable style, and at 11.30 am the first train left Kings Lynn with some 200 people on board. The special consisted of nine coaches, three of which were first class while the other six were second class vehicles. Travelling outwards via the Lynn & Ely route the inaugural train arrived at Downham around noon, and after a quick reversal, the special returned to Kings Lynn, where the Lynn & Ely and Lynn & Dereham Directors sat down for a formal lunch.

Having eaten their meal the invited guests made their way back to the 'first train' which, in the afternoon, steamed in triumph along the newly-completed Lynn & Dereham line. Although the VIPs had already consumed one substantial meal, a 'cold collation' awaited them at Narborough, and after this second opening day meal, the customary toasts were made to the success and future prosperity of the new railways.

Commenting favourably on the recently-opened lines to Downham and Narborough, *The Railway Chronicle* stated that 'the arrangements for working both lines' were a credit to 'the public spirit of the Directors'. Commentators were particularly impressed by the way in which the Directors seemed determined to 'provide for the humbler classes', and in this context *The Railway Chronicle* noted that third class carriages would accompany each train on the new lines.

On 11th November, 1846 *The Railway Chronicle* printed a further report on the Kings Lynn to Narborough line. This first section of the Lynn &

Dereham Railway was, declared the paper, a 'picturesque' line with favourable curves and gradients. The track had already been laid for about one mile beyond the existing railhead at Narborough, and it was expected that the railway would be open as far as Swaffham by June 1847, and completed throughout to Dereham 'before the end of next year'.

Showing a commendable interest in technical details, the *Chronicle* reporter noticed that the permanent way of the Lynn & Dereham Railway was formed of rails, 'fastened to the sleepers with Ransome & May's chairs'. The carriages, which were made by R. Melling of Manchester and R. Ward of London, were said to be 'superior to those of the Norfolk' in that they were 'fitted up with seats and windows', while the fares on the new railway were 2*d*. for first class, 1½*d*. for second class, and 1*d*. for third class travellers.

Unfortunately, the opening of the Kings Lynn to Narborough line coincided with a social and economic crisis of unparalleled severity, and in common with many other railway companies, the Lynn & Dereham scheme was soon plagued by a host of seemingly-insurmountable problems.

The first hints of trouble came with an unexpected failure of the potato crop at the end of 1845, and when, in the following year, both the corn *and* potato crops failed, the stock market collapsed; at a time when most of the nation's surplus capital was tied-up in expensive railway schemes, the results were catastrophic, and by 1847 prices were spiralling and thousands of people were thrown out of work. In Ireland and western Scotland – even in parts of England – people were starving to death (or dying of disease brought on by malnutrition), and against this background of chaos and disaster, many wild schemes hatched during the railway Mania were abandoned.

Other, more important projects were hurried to completion, and in these critical years several important sections of line were opened, among them the Ipswich & Bury line between Ipswich and Bury St Edmunds (24th December, 1846), the Eastern Union Railway between Colchester and Ipswich (15th June, 1846), and an Eastern Union extension between Haughley and Norwich (12th December, 1849).

Of greater significance, as far as the future Norwich to Kings Lynn line was concerned, were a series of developments around Kings Lynn, notably the completion of the Lynn & Ely Railway on 25th October, 1847. Extending southwards from the existing terminus at Downham, this new main line joined the Eastern Counties system at Ely Junction, thereby placing Kings Lynn in direct contact with Cambridge and London.

The East Anglian Railways

In the meantime the Lynn & Ely, Lynn & Dereham and Ely & Huntingdon Railways had wisely decided to amalgamate, the new, enlarged organisation being called the East Anglian Railways. Unfortunately, this new company soon ran into serious financial difficulties. The struggle to build a relatively expensive main line (and an equally costly branch to Wisbech) during a period of acute economic crisis had hamstrung the Lynn & Ely from its inception, and this financial embarrassment was inevitably passed on to the

Norwich and Brandon Railway.

Length 38 miles. 10 passenger and goods stations. Commences at Norwich, in junction with the Yarmouth and Norwich Railway; and terminates at Brandon, in junction with the extension of the Northern and Eastern Railway, with a branch to Thetford. Passes through the Counties of Norfolk and Suffolk. Gauge of way 4 feet 8½ inches. Royal Assent given to Bill, 16th May, 1844. Half-yearly Meetings, February and August, in London. Opened throughout July, 1845. Fares from London to Norwich, First Class, 22s. 6d. Second Class, 16s. Third Class, 10s. 6d.

Amalgamated with the Yarmouth and Norwich Railway under the title of the Norfolk Railway. Act passed June 30th, 1845, and have also obtained an Act for an extension to Diss and Dereham, 17 miles,

Capital Account.

19,000 Shares, 20*l.* each; 16*l.* Paid. Whole Shares.
19,000 Shares, 10*l.* each; 1*l.* Paid. New Shares.
Total sum authorised to be raised by Shares 380,000*l.*
Ditto ditto by loan or mortgage . 126,000*l*
Total sum expended to June, 1845 . . . . 314,777*l.*

Lynn and Dereham Railway.

Length 26½ miles. Commences at Dereham, in junction with the Norwich and Brandon Railway, and terminates at King's Lynn, in the county of Norfolk. Gauge of way 4 feet 8½ inches; steepest gradient 1 in 100; smallest radius of a curve 80 chains. Royal Assent given to Bill, 21st July, 1845. Estimated nett profit per annum 21,378*l.*, equal to a dividend of 8 per cent. Half-yearly Meetings, March and September, at Lynn.

Capital Account.

10,800 Shares, 25*l.* each; 5*l.* paid. Whole Shares.
Total sum authorised to be raised by Shares . 270,000*l.*
Ditto ditto by loan or mortgage . . 90,000*l.*

Amalgamated with the Lynn and Ely, and Ely and Huntingdon Railways.

Extracts from *Tuck's Railway Shareholders' Manual* of 1845.

East Anglian Railways – a company serving a sparsely-populated rural area, with little scope to develop profitable industrial or residential traffic.

The East Anglian Railways was not officially formed until 22nd July, 1847, but in the interim the associated companies worked in close conjunction with each other. Curiously, many ordinary shareholders seemed unaware that their respective companies were, for all intents and purposes, one and the same, and at a combined meeting held at the end of 1846 an Ely & Huntingdon proprietor asked (apparently in all innocence) if the Ely & Huntingdon Directors 'were distinct and separate' from the Lynn & Ely and Lynn & Dereham Directors. The Ely & Huntingdon Chairman replied that there would be no less than 18 nominal Directors on the East Anglian Railways Board – the idea being that the amalgamated Board would consist of six Directors from each company.[7] In reality, however, there were only eleven Directors because several individuals sat on two or more Boards.

Interestingly, the proposed amalgamation Bill incorporated a provisional agreement for leasing the East Anglian lines to the Eastern Counties Railway, and many Lynn & Dereham proprietors believed that the ECR would happily pay a *guaranteed* dividend of 7½ per cent for the doubtful privilege of working their impoverished system. In reality, the Eastern Counties Directors showed little immediate interest in the financially-embarrassed East Anglian Railways, and the East Anglian company was left to complete the Huntingdon, Wisbech and Dereham lines from its own slender resources.

Meanwhile, the Kings Lynn to Narborough line was working successfully as a branch of the Lynn & Ely line, and with share capital still being subscribed the Lynn & Dereham company appeared at first glance to be a financially viable undertaking. At the half-yearly meeting held on 27th February, 1847, the delighted Dereham shareholders learned that the company's receipts had amounted to £224,909 0*s*. 10*d*., whereas expenditure totalled £149,523 0*s*. 10*d*., leaving a healthy balance of £75,386. Well satisfied with this state of affairs, the shareholders adopted the half-yearly report, and after other matters had been discussed the sum of £600 was voted to the Directors 'for their services during the preceding year'.[8]

It was expected that the Lynn & Dereham Railway would yield a net profit of over £21,000 a year, which would, in turn, enable the company to pay ample dividends of up to 8 per cent. Regrettably, these optimistic predictions had been made before the economic crisis of the mid-1840s, and it soon became clear to all concerned that the company would be hard pressed to pay any dividends at all. Indeed, the completion of the line to Dereham was a more expensive business than had been anticipated, and matters were not helped by the sudden failure of one of the main contractors as a result of the continuing economic crisis.

The unfinished Narborough to Dereham line entailed considerable engineering work, and as early as November 1846 *The Railway Chronicle* had pointed out that the works would be heavy, some of the cuttings being 40 ft deep. At the same time, considerable levelling was necessary at Swaffham and at other places in which stations were planned, but despite these problems, the line was opened between Narborough and Swaffham on

10th August, 1847, and between Swaffham and a temporary railhead at Sporle on 26th October, 1847. A few weeks earlier, on 22nd July, 1847, the Act authorising the formal amalgamation of the Lynn & Dereham, Lynn & Ely and Ely & Huntingdon railways had received the Royal Assent.

East of Dereham

As we have seen, the Lynn & Dereham promoters had intended that their line would one day extend beyond Dereham to reach Norwich, but Parliament had dictated that the Dereham to Norwich branch would be built, not by the Lynn & Dereham but by the Norwich & Brandon Railway. In June 1845 the Norwich & Brandon company joined forces with the Yarmouth & Norwich Railway to form the Norfolk Railway Company, and this new organisation lost no time in completing the projected Dereham branch.

Leaving the former Norwich & Brandon main line at Wymondham, the Dereham branch ran north-westwards towards its destination. Although the authorised route was by no means flat, the Wymondham to Dereham route presented no major problems, and the railway builders' task was made easier by the way in which Parliament had consented to the installation of level crossings in lieu of more expensive bridge works. At Kimberley, for instance, the Lords' committee appointed to consider the 1845 Norwich & Brandon Bill had recommended that a level crossing should be allowed because the proposed crossing would be at 'a first class station at which all trains would stop'. At Thuxton, the Lords' committee had agreed that a crossing would be installed because 'the road could not be raised without great inconvenience to the public', while at Yaxham the committee suggested (somewhat implausibly) that 'the road could not be raised without great inconvenience, and raising it would preclude the opportunity of giving a small station at the spot'.[9]

Work on the Wymondham to Dereham line was well advanced by the closing months of 1846, and in November it was reported that some Norfolk Railway Directors had recently made an experimental trip along the unfinished branch in company with Samuel Morton Peto (1809–89); Mr Peto, who had made his fortune as an engineering contractor, was both a builder *and* a promoter of East Anglian railways – the Norfolk Railway being just one of the many companies in his growing business empire.

Sadly, the work of construction did not proceed without incident, and on 19th December, 1846 *The Railway Chronicle* reported a bizarre accident that had occurred shortly after the Directors' experimental trip to Dereham. The accident, which had taken place on 8th December, was described as follows by the *Chronicle* reporter:

> WYMONDHAM–DEREHAM . . . A bridge over the line, in the parish of Wicklewood, not being safe from a sinking of one of the buttresses, was ordered to be taken down. The men were at work removing it after dark, and two fires were kept burning upon the crown of the bridge. Late at night, from the removal of the chief supporters, the remaining part of the bridge fell in, and about a dozen labourers fell also upon the line beneath and were mingled with the ruin and fires. Great

confusion existed and several of the men, when extricated, were found to be seriously bruised and burnt.

A few weeks earlier, on 14th November, 1846, the same journal had recorded the death and subsequent funeral of an elderly navvy on the neighbouring Lynn & Dereham line. The man, Joe Singleton aged 68, had been found dead in his bed, but his fellow-navvies were determined to give him a decent funeral, and Joe's coffin was followed to the graveside 'by a large body of his comrades on the Lynn & Dereham Railway'.[10]

Completion of the Line

The fact that the Wicklewood bridge collapse had occurred during the hours of darkness suggests that the Norfolk Directors may have been trying to open their line to Dereham before the completion of the Lynn & Dereham route. If this was indeed the case, Samuel Morton Peto and the other Norfolk Railway supporters must have rejoiced when, on 7th December, 1846, their branch was opened for goods traffic between Wymondham and Dereham.

Passenger trains commenced running on 15th February, 1847, though at the half-year meeting held on 23rd February the Norfolk Directors expressed 'much disappointment' at the delays that had prevented a much earlier completion of the Dereham line. These delays were (declared the Directors) 'unavoidable', but their engineers had assured them the works had been retarded by 'causes over which they had no control'.[11]

Although the Wymondham to Dereham line was not opened as quickly as its supporters would have wished, the Norfolk Railway Directors had the undoubted satisfaction of seeing their branch in operation well before the L&DR was opened throughout to Dereham. In fact, the latter route was still far from complete, and from October 1847 until September 1848 East Anglian trains were unable to proceed beyond the temporary railhead at Sporle. Traffic from Kings Lynn to Norwich was, in the meantime, sent southwards to Ely and thence east to Norwich via Brandon and the Eastern Counties Line – a circuitous route involving much time and expense.

Finally, on 11th September, 1848, the Lynn & Dereham route was opened throughout, and East Anglian trains were at last able to reach their eastern destination. Through working to Norwich did not take place, and there was, as yet, no through running connection between the East Anglian and Norfolk Railway systems. Nevertheless, the Lynn & Dereham line was at last complete, and this alone was a source of encouragement for the long-suffering East Anglian Directors, who hoped that a profitable agricultural traffic could soon be developed.

Some Details of the Line

The completed Lynn & Dereham line was worked by a small fleet of eight 2–2–2 passenger locomotives and two 0–4–2 goods engines. Built by Sharp Brothers of Manchester, these diminutive Victorian locomotives were delivered at intervals between 1846 and 1848, Nos. 1 to 4 (*Eagle, Vulture, Ostrich* and *Falcon*) arriving in 1846 while Nos. 5 to 8 (*Hawk, Kite, Raven* and *Heron*) were delivered in the following year. The two 0–4–2 goods engines (No. 13 *Lion* and No. 14 *Tiger*) arrived in 1848. The engines were based in the East Anglian Railways' main depot at Kings Lynn, from where they hauled engineers' construction trains prior to the opening of the Ely and Dereham routes. (The 2–2–2s weighed only 18 tons 12 cwt, and this unusually light weight enabled them to run over lightly-laid contractors' trackwork).

As we have seen, the first Lynn & Dereham coaches were built by outside contractors such as Mellings of Manchester, but the local companies had also built some of their own rolling stock. East Anglian Railways' records reveal that 'two horse boxes, four carriage trucks . . . seven ballast wagons' and six 'plate-layer's lorries' had been completed up to 31st December, 1848 (the company had also made 'forty five luggage wagons', though these were probably small porters' trolleys for use at stations rather than railed-freight vehicles.

Lynn & Dereham architecture was a mixture of good and bad, and although some of the intermediate stations were attractively built in a pleasant 'Tudor Gothic' style, engine sheds and certain other structures were simple wooden sheds. John Sutherland Valentine exercised overall control in matters relating to engineering, but he may have been content to let his subordinates have a free hand in terms of architectural design, It is perhaps significant that the stations between Kings Lynn and Dereham were, in most cases, provided with Tudor or Tudor-Gothic style buildings; Dunham and East Winch were of near-identical design, while Middleton was similar – albeit slightly smaller. Swaffham, in contrast, had a larger, more ornamental station building, while Narborough was equipped with a building which, in some ways, combined the features of Swaffham and the other stations.

Tudor style architecture was also evident on the Norfolk Railway section between Wymondham and Dereham, while Dereham itself boasted a substantial Tudoresque station building.

In contrast to these well-built stations, the original engine sheds at Kings Lynn and Dereham were somewhat lighly-built, timber-framed structures clad in horizontal weather boarding; these sheds were probably intended to be temporary structures which would (hopefully) be replaced as soon as sufficient funds became available. Signal boxes, as such, did not appear until the Great Eastern period, and by analogy with other west Norfolk lines the Lynn & Dereham would have been signalled with the aid of simple semaphores which were operated by station staff rather than specialised signalmen.

The Lynn & Dereham line was laid in conventional fashion, with iron rails resting in Ransome & May's patent iron chairs; these were, in effect, modern-type chairs which were usually secured by two bolts passing through their oval bases. The steepest gradient between Kings Lynn and Dereham was 1 in 100, and the sharpest curve had a radius of 80 chains.

Early train services were modest in the extreme, and there were no more than four trains a day between Kings Lynn and Dereham. As a result of what the East Anglian Directors termed the 'limited passenger traffic' *en route* to Dereham, these trains usually ran as mixed formations carrying 'goods and coals' as well as passengers. The line was worked independently of the Lynn & Ely main line, and a contemporary press report confirms that 'the lines in the Lynn district' were 'worked by three distinct sets of engines and carriages' (i.e. one train for the Lynn & Dereham, one for the Ely line and another for the Wisbech branch).[12]

It should, perhaps, be stressed that the completed Lynn & Dereham line was not yet part of a comprehensive East Anglian railway system, and although the lines from Kings Lynn to Dereham and Ely were now under one management the neighbouring lines were controlled by separate – and sometimes hostile – companies. In the east, for instance, the Norfolk Railway operated a small, localised system comprising the lines from Norwich to Great Yarmouth, Norwich to Brandon and Wymondham to Dereham. To the west, meanwhile, the much larger Eastern Counties Railway provided connecting links between Ely and Brandon and from Ely to Peterborough, while the East Anglian Railways consisted of two entirely separate parts – the short section of track between St Ives and Godmanchester being detached from the main Ely–Kings Lynn–Dereham section; this line (the only part of the Ely & Huntingdon Railway to have been opened) was actually worked by the Eastern Counties Railway.

The following table provides brief details of the lines in operation at the end of the 1840s. It will be seen that the legacy of the 'Railway Mania' was a complex, yet sadly disparate system; there would clearly be scope for consolidation in the years to come, but in the meantime the owners of small companies such as the East Anglian Railways could only struggle against overwhelming odds in an attempt to make their unplanned and inefficient undertakings show some kind of dividend.

Table One

OWNERSHIP OF NORTH NORFOLK RAILWAYS AT THE END OF THE RAILWAY MANIA

Company	*Section of Line*	*Opening Date*
East Anglian Railways	Kings Lynn–Narborough	27th October, 1846
	Kings Lynn–Downham	27th October, 1846
	Downham–Ely	25th October, 1847
	Narborough–Swaffham	10th August, 1847
	Swaffham–Sporle	26th October, 1847
	Sporle–Dereham	11th September, 1848
	St Ives–Godmanchester	17th August, 1847
	Watlington–Wisbech	1st February, 1848
Norfolk Railway	Norwich–Great Yarmouth	30th April, 1844
	Norwich–Brandon	29th July, 1845
	Wymondham–Dereham	15th February, 1847
	Dereham–Fakenham	20th March, 1849

The stations available for public use on the Lynn & Dereham line at (or shortly after) the time of opening included Middleton, East Winch, Bilney, Narborough, Swaffham, Sporle, Dunham, Fransham and Wendling, while the Norfolk Railway stations at the eastern end of the Kings Lynn to Norwich cross-country route included Dereham, Yaxham, Thuxton, Hardingham, Kimberley and Wymondham.

Market Cross, Swaffham

Swaffham market place in the late 19th or early 20th centuries. *Oakwood Collection*

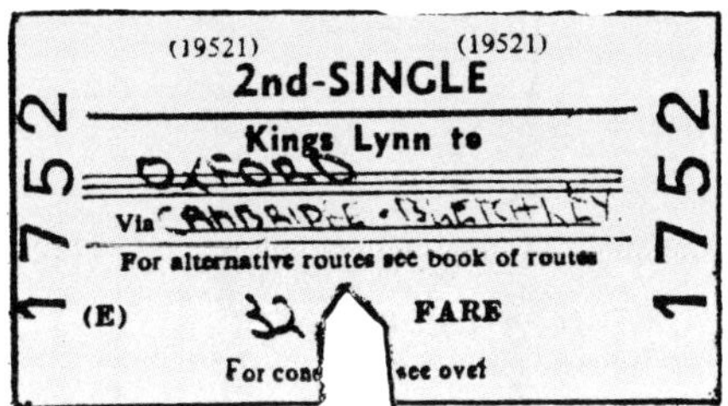

A single ticket from Kings Lynn to Oxford from the author's collection.

414 Town Hall King's Lynn

An Edwardian postcard view of Kings Lynn Town Hall; this distinctive building incorporates a 15th century Guildhall, and a Renaissance porch dating from the late 16th century. *Oakwood Collection*

A panoramic view of Kings Lynn station in LNER days, taken from the open windows of the signal cabin. 'Claud Hamilton' 4–4–0 No. 8790 can be seen to the right, while the new concrete goods shed is visible in the background. *Douglas Thompson*

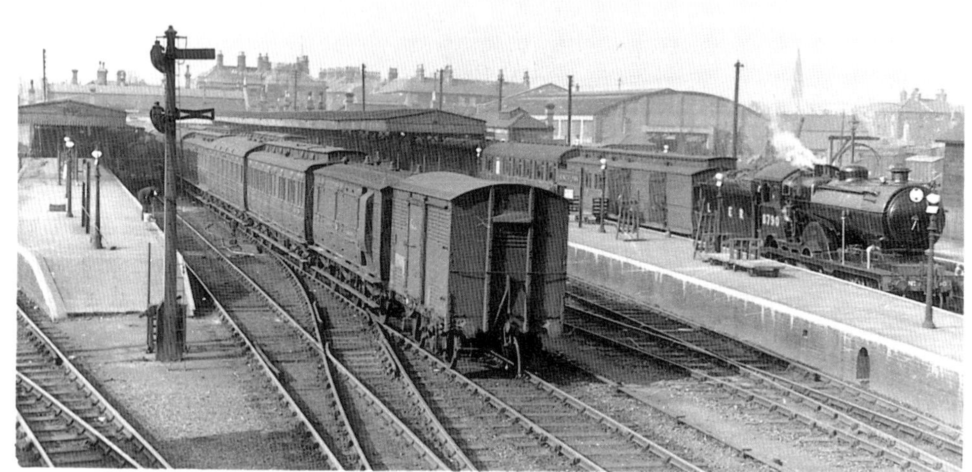

Chapter Two

Early Years of the Lynn & Dereham Line (1849–1862)

Many local railways were promoted by public-spirited landowners who saw rail transport not as a means of making money, but as an essential public service, without which rural areas would stagnate and die. The Lynn & Dereham and its associates were, in contrast, promoted by largely speculative investors with little obvious interest in the transport needs of rural Norfolk. Although some Directors and shareholders lived in Kings Lynn or other parts of Norfolk, many more resided in London, Manchester or other distant places, and it follows that these gentlemen were particularly interested in the concept of a profitable long-distance trunk route which would, one day, link the North and Midlands with East coast ports such as Kings Lynn and Great Yarmouth

An Extension to the West?

As a loyal ally of the Lynn & Ely Railway, the Lynn & Dereham was honour-bound to support a variety of schemes which, if fully implemented, would have elevated both lines to full main line status. In 1846, for instance, the Lynn & Dereham agreed to support a series of grandiose schemes which committed their company to:

> Take such steps, execute such deeds and instruments, and make such payments as they may think fit, for concurring in, promoting, and assisting applications proposed to be made in Parliament in the next session by the Lynn & Ely, for Powers to construct railways from Wisbech to Spalding and Holbeach, and from Ely to Bury St Edmunds, and to construct docks at the port of Kings Lynn, with a navigation or aqueduct from such docks to the River Nar, in the parish of Wormegay, in the county of Norfolk, or so much of such works, and with such modifications, as the Directors may deem expedient.[13]

At the same time, the Lynn & Dereham and its associates promised to give their full support to a group of companies seeking consent for a connecting line from Ambergate to Nottingham, Grantham, Sleaford and Boston. These schemes were later amalgamated to form the grandly-named Ambergate, Nottingham & Boston & Eastern Junction Railway, which, on 16th July, 1846, obtained Parliamentary consent for a main line between Ambergate and Spalding. Sadly, the economic crisis of 1845–49 made it exceedingly difficult for lines promoted during the Railway Mania to raise their authorised capital, and the Ambergate scheme was eventually completed in a modified form as a branch from Grantham to the Midland Railway at Colwick Junction (near Nottingham).

The failure of the Ambergate, Nottingham & Boston & Eastern Junction Railway meant that the East Anglian Railways' Wisbech branch (opened on 1st February, 1848) could not fulfill its intended role as an artery of communication between the Midlands and East Anglia, while, further south, the Huntingdon line had similarly failed to achieve main line status.

Implicit in these schemes was the idea that the East Anglian Railways was

An Edwardian postcard view of Kings Lynn Harbour; the twin towers of St Margarets Church can be seen between the masts of the vessels on the right. Rails and other materials used during the construction of the Dereham and Ely lines were delivered by sea and unloaded at Lynn Harbour. *Oakwood Collection*

The 15th century South Gate at Kings Lynn, as depicted on a turn-of-the-century postcard. *Oakwood Collection*

a natural ally of the Great Northern, but unfortunately the Eastern Counties Railway – which touched the East Anglian at both Wisbech and Huntingdon – had no intention of letting the Great Northern Railway into East Anglia, and in these melancholy circumstances the East Anglian supporters started to fall out among themselves.

A Divided Company

East Anglian Railways' general meetings became lively affairs, and there was, by 1849, every sign that the company had divided along North–South lines, with northern-based shareholders ranged against a mainly local board. On 28th February, 1849 about 45 East Anglian shareholders assembled at the London Tavern to discuss the company's predicament, and it appeared that this meeting would inevitably end in a row. The meeting was fully reported in *The Railway Times* on 17th March, 1849, and it would be of interest to quote some of the proceedings in detail.

The meeting was opened by Henry Bruce, the recently-elected East Anglian Railways' Chairman, and after a summary of financial matters the Chairman said a few words about the company's overall position:

> The length of their line was sixty seven miles – eighteen miles were laid down as double lines, and seven miles of sidings. It had been constructed at the cost of £18,000 per mile, which, although a larger expenditure than it ought to have been, still was not so large as to depress their property to the extent that it had arrived at. Of course he did not include the cost of the plant in the calculation.
>
> The company were in possession of thirty five acres of land close by the harbour of Lynn which, in the course of a few years, must become of immense value, if their line were only to be maintained in its integrity.[14]

Developing his theme, the Chairman suggested that the lines from Ely to Kings Lynn and Dereham were both 'of great value' to the company, though the line between Lynn and Ely had 'to contend with the river for its traffic'. It was hoped, however, that local coal owners and farmers would 'find it in their interests to place traffic on the line', and when that happy day dawned 'the competition would be lessened'.

Turning to other matters, Mr Bruce next raised the subject of the Wisbech branch, which had cost 'not less than £170,000 and . . . was not paying its working expenses'. Furthermore, added the Chairman, the Lynn & Ely Railway had not been able to finance this line, and it had therefore been made out of funds intended for the Lynn & Dereham and Ely & Huntingdon lines. To loud cries of 'shame' from the assembled shareholders, the Chairman proceeded to blame the Eastern Counties Railway for many of the problems that had afflicted the East Anglian Railways:

> What could have induced the Directors of that day to make such an unfortunate line he could not conceive, but he believed it was made under the influence and pressure of the Eastern Counties Company. That Company, he believed, had said that unless the branch was made, the lease to them of the Anglian Company's lines could not go on. Why, no one could conceive, because the Eastern Counties had a line to Wisbech themselves at that very moment.

> The Eastern Counties had succeeded in crippling the resources of the Anglian company so far as the outlay upon the Wisbech branch went; but he saw no reason yet to give it up as hopeless of paying itself. Other lines must yet come into Wisbech, and to either the Midland or the Great Northern their line must yet be valuable. By a line from Stamford to Wisbech the Midland line could command the whole of the Norfolk trade into the Midland counties.[15]

Having raised the possibility of a future sale to the Midland Railway or the Great Northern company, Mr Bruce turned his attention to the Dereham line and other parts of the East Anglian system:

> The Dereham line was an excellent one, and every year it would, he had no doubt, become more and more profitable. It ran through a most rich agricultural country, and if arrangements were made for a more frequent communication with Norwich – which must soon be done – it would yield a handsome profit.
>
> The 4½ miles of the Huntingdon branch had cost no less than £130,000. It joined the Great Northern, and when that great line was opened their line would form the only communication between Ely and Cambridge. It must become of great value either to that line or to the Eastern Counties; one of them would, no doubt, be inclined to purchase, and undoubtedly they must pay cost price at least . . . The Norfolk estuary was now looked upon with much more favour by the farmers in the neighbourhood than it was even last year, and when it was carried out it would greatly benefit their lines.
>
> During the last six months they had carried 159 horses, 2,392 cattle, 14,405 sheep, 5,923 tons of corn, 14,250 tons of coal and coke, 1,639 tons of chalk and gravel and 12,484 tons of merchandise, and any one who knew the trade of their locality must know that such an amount could only be looked upon as the embryo of the traffic they would yet enjoy.
>
> Comparing the first seven weeks of the present year with the corresponding seven of last year, it was evident that their carrying trade was greatly increasing, and he saw no reason why it should not go on increasing.[16]

When the Chairman had finished his report, one of the Directors moved that it be adopted, but at this point a group of proprietors (many of whom were based in the north of England) commenced a barrage of questions and criticisms. One shareholder pointed out that he had recently seen 'not less than 140 ships in the river' at Kings Lynn – and this was clear evidence that traffic existed and could be further cultivated. Other shareholders complained that money that might have been distributed in dividends had been expended on the permanent way, while a Mr Harrison admitted that he had subscribed for upwards of 1,200 shares on the understanding that the line was soon to be leased to the Eastern Counties. What, he asked, had gone wrong? It was all 'a mystery of iniquity'.

At this point several proprietors referred to a committee of enquiry that they hoped would be appointed to investigate the affairs of the East Anglian Railways. Some speakers suggested that all resolutions should be suspended until this committee had reported, while others urged (significantly) that 'they ought to have shareholders from Leeds or Manchester on the Committee'.

As tempers began to fray, one or two shareholders accused the Directors of fraud and malpractice, and when pressed by the Chairman to be more specific, the angry proprietors pointed out that around £300,000 had been expended for no return. Furthermore, some of this money had been 'subscribed for one purpose and applied to another'.

One of the most vociferous critics of the Board was a Colonel Tulloch, who openly advocated a piecemeal sale of assets:

> The Board acknowledged that they had expended £300,000 which realised no return . . . He might find a worse term to be applied to such conduct, but he would find difficulty in finding a better. If they were in such a bankrupt state as was represented by the Chairman, why did they not make the most of the assets in hand – why not sell off land . . . and why not sell off some of their useless first class carriages or exchange them for trucks or wagons, which they wanted. Such would be the conduct of any gentlemen in trade.[17]

In reply, the Chairman stated that it was not as easy to sell second-hand carriages as might be supposed; a neighbouring railway had tried to sell 50, but had been unable to find a purchaser. As for selling land, this would, he thought, be madness – such a policy would be 'the very reverse of prudent' when the land in question might soon be of immense value. With respect to the traffic on the line and the allegedly over-generous expenditure on track and other fittings the Chairman defended himself vigorously:

> The fact was, in summer the traffic was good but in winter it fell off . . . he did not say that the expenditure was to remain for ever at £380 per week; on the contrary, it was most likely that it would vary. But it was to be borne in mind that if their expenses were many their accidents were very few. They had no land slips, no casualties, no compensations to make, which were all prevented by the care bestowed upon the works.
>
> The honourable gentleman had talked of the 140 vessels in the harbour at Lynn, but it was to be remembered that he was there in the very middle of the mart held there by Act of Parliament. Had he been two weeks earlier or two weeks later he would have seen a different state of things.
>
> Their expenditure in coke had been large in consequence of their being obliged to get it from the north, but they were about to make their own on their own premises, and the saving on that item would be very great indeed.

Changing tack, Mr Bruce then attacked those among the shareholders who had declined to take up new shares which might have helped the company to solve at least some of its problems:

> Much saving might have been effected had the proprietors not held their hands in their pockets, had they freely taken up the seven per cent shares. The Directors had been placed in worse than Egyptian bondage, for they had been expected not only to make bricks without straw, but without clay also (laughter). They had no less than three insolvent or very needy contractors to deal with since he joined the direction, and he could assure those who knew nothing about it, that if they only knew the difficulty of dealing with such cases they would have some mercy upon the Board!
>
> The close and unremitting attention of the Directors had been required to save the line for the proprietors, in place of being given wholly to the development of the traffic.[18]

Having listened attentively to the Chairman's remarks the shareholders agreed that the report should be adopted, but further disagreements ensued over the matter of additional capital. Some proprietors felt that all proceedings should be suspended until the committee of investigation had reported, while others argued that such a course of action would be unconstitutional. A compromise solution was eventually suggested, the idea being that the committee of investigation would confer with the Directors 'as to the propriety of the proposal for capitalising the debt', while in the meantime all other matters would be suspended. This, however, failed to satisfy some of the more outspoken shareholders, and in the words of *The Railway Times*:

> A scene of confusion arose, many at one time urging that the Chairman should put the resolution for raising the capital; others protesting against anything being done but appointing the committee. Several proposals were made to pass some of the resolutions but Mr Harrison pressed his resolution for a committee.

In an attempt to restore order, the Chairman magisterially pronounced that the affairs of the company were now in the hands of the committee, but this failed to silence his own supporters who claimed that, by appointing the committee they were in effect passing a vote of no confidence in the Directors. A vote was then taken, with the result that 15 proprietors voted to place matters in the hands of the committee while a majority of 29 voted for an amendment which would allow the Board to raise extra capital immediately (i.e. without waiting for the committee to report).

This failed to satisfy the supporters of the committee of investigation, two of whom – John Harrison and Thomas Kittrick – continued to protest loudly at the conduct of the company's affairs. Matters were finally brought to a conclusion when a Mr Boyd moved that, as the meeting had 'perfect confidence in the Directors' the appointment of a committee of investigation was uncalled for. The motion was promptly seconded, and despite continuing protests from Messrs Harrison and Kittrick the vote of confidence was passed by a large majority.

It is possible that, in trying to appoint a committee of investigation, the 'northern' shareholders were trying to gain control of the company. In the meantime, however, the Chairman and Directors remained London or Norfolk based – Edward Self of Kings Lynn being the principal local Director, while Chairman Henry Bruce appears to have resided mainly in London.

As mentioned earlier, many of the East Anglian shareholders lived in the north of England, and in this context it is interesting to note that a faction known as 'The Liverpool Party' had made its presence felt in a number of other companies (including the Great Western Railway). Although the term Liverpool Party is slightly misleading, there is no doubt that much capital was subscribed by Lancashire-based investors, and moreover some of these investors knew more about railways than one might have expected. After all, much early railway development had taken place in the north of England, and having observed the working of railways at first hand the northern-based shareholders had a distinct advantage *vis-à-vis* their southern counterparts. Moreover, the northerners were major investors, and it is easy to see how a man like John Harrison (who had invested as much as £30,000) should have been dissatisfied with the lacklustre performance of the company.

There was, in retrospect, every reason why the north–south rift should have developed – and in the summer of 1849 that rift showed no sign of disappearing. After leaving the February 1849 East Anglian Railways' meeting the northern proprietors proceeded to appoint their own committee of investigation, and Mr Cope, a Manchester accountant, was called in to prepare a detailed report on the management of the company.

The Committee of Investigation

It is conceivable that Thomas Harrison and his fellow malcontents expected to find evidence of serious financial malpractice, but if this was indeed the case Mr Cope's report must have been something of a disappointment insofar as it identified certain problems but found nothing seriously amiss. Some of the most important sections of the Cope report are given below:

> The accounts, up to the date of the last balance sheet, December 1848, have been subjected to a dissection as minute as could possibly be required in any examination. The books of the Company have been kept with care and neatness, but upon an imperfect system, and in a form so condensed as to render it a matter of some difficulty and labour to arrive at a correct idea of the several accounts – an objection which, in railway accounts, I consider of the gravest character, and requiring immediate attention and reformation, in order to enable your Directors, at the shortest notice, to obtain a more certain estimate of the position of the Company than can at present be accomplished.
>
> I have more particularly to object to the present mode of keeping the stores accounts, the inefficiency of which is manifested by the fact that, out of stores purchased to the extent of £7,289, one half has been distributed for consumption without any distinction between capital and revenue, and, consequently, the whole amount placed to debit of capital, though a considerable portion must necessarily have been appropriated to repairs of various kinds chargeable upon revenue, but which proportion cannot now be determined correctly.
>
> In like manner, an unnecessarily large stock of stationery was purchased at the opening of the line, and has been, up to this time, indiscriminately distributed to capital and revenue, without any charge upon the stores to the latter account. I find also, that in the revenue account for the six months ending the 31st December, 1848, materials for repairs of locomotives, amounting to £230 1s. 5*d*. over and above those drawn from the stores of the Company, and £330 1s. 11*d*. for clothing, have been omitted in the charges against the half year's revenue, reducing the balance or net revenue to £6,573 8*s*. 5*d*., which balance should be further reduced by the amount (unascertained) issued from stores on revenue account.
>
> With these exceptions, I do not find any items improperly charged against capital in favour of revenue, nor do these erroneous charges and omissions appear to have been the result of design, but entirely arising out of the imperfect system of the accounts.
>
> I have also to state that no reserve has hitherto been made for depreciations and renewal of permanent way and plant. I believe the whole of the capital raised has been applied to the purposes for which it was authorised, and is truly accounted for in the books of the Company. With the division of interest between capital and revenue I have not interfered, inasmuch as the whole revenue has hitherto been absorbed in the payment of interest.[19]

In addition to his general examination of the accounts, Mr Cope was asked to make special enquiries into the circumstances surrounding certain controversial contracts that had been entered into by the company – one of these being the purchase of a huge quantity of permanent way materials at a time when iron was said to have been ridiculously over-priced. As far as this rail contract was concerned Mr Cope reported as follows, without commenting on the wisdom of the transaction:

> I find a contract for iron rails existing with Messrs Bailey Brothers of Liverpool, iron merchants, the first delivery of which was made February 3rd, 1846, and the last 30th September, 1848. The original contract appears to have been for 6,000 tons at £12 2*s*. 6*d*. per ton; of which amount £70,919 15*s*. 11*d*. has been paid – leaving a balance due to Messrs Baileys, upon the quantity already delivered, of £1,572 2*s*. 3*d*., and a liability upon the Company for a further delivery of about 118 tons, value at the rate of contract of about £1,430.

Another controversial matter was the so-called 'Brick Account' which, according to the northern shareholders, was said to have been running at a considerable loss. Happily, the Manchester accountant was unable to find any evidence of loss; on the contrary, his report suggested that the brick account had been of some benefit to the company:

> I have examined the account of bricks made by the Company, and although the account shows a balance of loss on the transaction of about £170, I find that nearly a million bricks have been supplied for the use of the Company at the rate of 21*s*. per thousand; which, as compared with the market price of bricks at the time, would have given a profit on this account of about £500.[20]

In general, Mr Cope's report revealed that, apart from the allegedly 'imperfect' system of accounting, the East Anglian Railways and its constituents had been relatively well managed, and any problems that had arisen had occurred mainly through external pressures of one kind or another. The Cope Report was thus of little use as a weapon for the northern faction to use against the Board of Directors, but John Harrison and his fellow-conspirators were determined to press home their attack, and Mr Cope's report was therefore incorporated into a wider-ranging report which was mischievously published immediately before the August 1849 half-yearly meeting of the company.

The report (signed by Thomas Broadbent, John Harrison, Lightly Simpson, William Tinker, John Chadwick and other northern-based proprietors) claimed that the problems afflicting the company were caused by a combination of the following:

1. Excessive capital had been expended on the construction of the lines.
2. The price paid for land had, in most cases, been too high.
3. Too much land had been purchased by the three EAR constituents.
4. The Directors had entered into 'imprudent contracts' for rails, etc.
5. The Wisbech branch had absorbed too much capital.
6. The 'staff and servants for conducting the traffic' was 'beyond the requirements of the Company'.

The members of the Committee of Investigation had, in the interim, 'gone over the lines of railway and examined the permanent way, stations and rolling stock', and they concluded that the railway itself was in such excellent condition that there was 'no necessity for establishing a fund for depreciations'. The general tone of the report was, nevertheless, highly critical, and the committee members concluded their attack on the Directors as follows:

> We do not consider the present amount of traffic any criterion as to the capabilities of the railway; we attribute the extreme smallness of it, to some extent, to the want of amicable arrangements with the neighbouring companies, and to the invariably slow development of railway traffic in agricultural districts, but in a great degree to the want of due business application in the management. An active investigation of the district through which the lines run, instituted by the Directors during our inquiries and conducted by a party competent to work, has convinced us that a large amount of traffic legitimately belonging to this Company is diverted into other channels.
>
> We have to complain that there is a great want of energy and economy pervading the business of the Company, and it is obvious that no radical improvement can be effected without an important change in the Board of Directors, and in the management generally.
>
> The direction is now practically reduced to three gentlemen, two of whom reside in London and one in Lynn. It is impossible for us not to have observed the energy and personal exertions of the Chairman of the Company; we would strongly urge upon the shareholders the importance of soliciting him to retain his office, associating with him Mr Self, who resides in Lynn, and four other gentlemen, three of whom we conceive should be selected from the north, where the stock is extensively held, and whose large interest would insure their attention to the affairs of the Company.
>
> We urge also, as of the utmost importance, the immediate appointment of an able and experienced man to take the entire management of the Company's business, having the control of the servants, and responsible to the Board for due economy and efficiency in every department. We are of the opinion that the appointment of a suitable person, whose remuneration shall be regulated by the net profits of the Company, having full power and authority, and subject to no control except that of the majority of the Board, would give to this railway that unity and efficiency of management which characterises a private business.[21]

Having set out their plan for a complete restructuring of the Board, the northern shareholders added some additional recommendations which, they believed, would be conducive to even greater efficiency:

> We recommend that the accounts should be examined half-yearly by a public accountant employed by the auditors.
>
> We recommend that the old offices in the town of Lynn, the depot for the stores, and the workshops at the harbour branch, be given up, and that suitable buildings be erected at the present Lynn station, as early as the financial position of the Company will warrant the expenditure. The Company possesses almost all the materials requisite, the outlay will not be large, and we think the saving by such a concentration of the various departments will be very great.
>
> We are induced to hope that the recent arrangements for burning coke, and the establishment of a coal depot, by independent parties, on the Company's land, will be a source of considerable advantage.
>
> We regret the necessity for the creation of further capital, as sanctioned by the resolution passed at a general meeting in February last. We conceive that the credit of the Company will be fully established by the calling up of £2 per share of the new issue; and we urge upon the Directors the propriety of not making any further call upon these shares without the consent of the shareholders, to be called

together for that purpose – a proposed resolution to this effect having been placed on the books of the Company at the last meeting.

In conclusion, whilst we admit the difficulties to be encountered, we are of the opinion that a rigid economy and an energetic management will so improve the position of our affairs as to justify the Directors in completing the line of railway between Ely and St Ives, and forming a junction with the Great Northern line at Huntingdon; and we consider the extension of time granted by Parliament for the completion of the line a great advantage to the Company.

Thomas Broadbent
John Harrison
John Chadwick
Wm. Tinker
Thomas Kittrick
T.W. Flint
Lightly Simpson

Manchester, June 30th, 1849.[22]

The report of the committee of investigation was, in some ways, a stroke of genius in that it articulated the complaints of a large proportion of the shareholders without openly criticising the existing Board – indeed, Henry Bruce was actually praised for his 'personal exertions' on behalf of the company. There was also encouragement for Edward Self, who seems to have been a local Director with at least some friends in the northern camp! The discontented northern proprietors were, nevertheless, determined to impose their ideas on the Board, and matters came to a head at the half-yearly meeting of the East Anglian Railways held in August 1849.

This meeting was attended by numerous shareholders, and although several local Directors had apparently resigned, Henry Bruce and Edward Self turned up to hear further tirades against the management of the company. Speaker after speaker attacked the Directors, and, led by the northerners, the meeting decided that the railway would never prosper until 'men of business had been placed on the direction' of the company. The shareholders claimed that the engineering of the existing lines was 'most expensive', and the offices and other facilities at Kings Lynn were said to be costing 'about £1,000 per year'.

Much damage had clearly been done by the northern-based investors and their carefully-orchestrated campaign, and it was perhaps inevitable that, by the end of the meeting, four members of the northern faction had been elected to the Board of Directors. The newcomers included William Tinker of Hyde, near Manchester; John Chadwick of Manchester; T.W. Flint of Hull, and a Mr Bates of Leeds.

The East Anglian Railways thereby passed into northern hands, and in the next few months the company committed itself to a policy of expansion in the west, and an alliance with the Great Northern Railway.

The Directors Defend Themselves

In the meantime, Henry Bruce, Edward Self and the 'rump' of the old Board decided that they could not let the criticisms made by the committee of enquiry pass without a full answer. The local Directors may have conceded control to the northern party, but in a printed counter attack dated 18th August, 1849, they hit back with a strongly-worded defence of their conduct since the formation of the East Anglian Railways.

The Directors could point out, quite legitimately, that until July 1847 the East Anglian lines had been three distinct companies, and it had taken at least a year for the system of accounting to become unified. However, before answering the mildly critical Cope Report in detail the local Directors grasped the opportunity to complain publicly about the circumstances in which the northern faction had launched their attack:

> Gentlemen – On the 2nd instant we, in common with yourselves, received, *for the first time*, a printed copy of the report of the Committee of Investigation, which bears the date the 30th June; though *officially* this document is unknown to us, we think it right, under the circumstances, to reply to it. That Committee, we think it right to inform you, though not appointed at the last general meeting of the shareholders, was nominated immediately afterwards by a number of proprietors resident in and near Manchester; and that nomination was assented to by the registered proprietors of about 22,000 shares. We, therefore, thought it right to receive them as the recognised Committee of the general body of shareholders, and to throw open to them every book, voucher and document relating to the Company's affairs from its first commencement in 1845.
>
> With reference to the commencing paragraphs of the report, which relate to the appointment of a deputation from the Board to meet the shareholders in Manchester, we beg to observe that the statements made at that meeting had reference to the expected traffic of the railways when the resources of the district had been fully developed. That development has been retarded by circumstances over which the Company could have no control, and which are pointedly referred to in the last report of your Directors.
>
> With respect to the statement in the report that a motion for the appointment of a Committee of Inquiry was submitted to the last general meeting of the shareholders but was not carried in consequence of an alleged remark by one of the Directors, we take leave to say that no opposition whatever was offered by any of the Directors to the appointment of a Committee; on the contrary, each member of the Board was willing to defer, in this respect, to the wishes of his co-proprietors, and cordially to concur in the appointment of such a Committee, should it be deemed advisable.[23]

The Directors went on to say that Mr Cope, the Manchester accountant, had been allowed to study, 'for several weeks, all the books of the three companies prior to the amalgamation, as well as those of the East Anglian Company'.

Turning to Mr Cope's claim that the various books had been kept on an 'imperfect system', the Directors pointed out that the system used was the standard 'double entry' method of accounting, and moreover, 'every entry in the journals and cash book' was 'so clear and specific' that any shareholder would have no trouble in understanding the accounts and transactions with 'the utmost facility'.

With regard to the subsidiary books used for stores and other purposes, the Directors believed that the system that had been in operation since 1st January, 1849 was perfectly sufficient to prevent extravagance in every department. If Mr Cope could not understand these matters, they suggested (with more than a hint of sarcasm) that the matter should be examined by 'a competent *London* accountant'.

Having delivered this barbed comment, the Directors addressed themselves to specific matters raised by the Cope Report – notably the claim that the stores account had somehow blurred the important distinction between capital and revenue. This was, they explained, because the original companies had treated the stores account as a general account covering a variety of materials used in the construction of the lines to Dereham and Ely. Rolling stock, for example, had been constructed under this budget heading, while the stores acount had also included the cost of large numbers of items needed during the final stages of construction. These had included the cost of the following equipment:

> Office furniture purchased by the three companies £1,353; tank and timber preserving apparatus ditto, ditto, £941; machinery for the repairing establishment; anvils, bellows etc for the forges; a large number of winches, jack screws, wheelbarrows, pile driving machines etc, used in the construction of bridges; weighing machines, fire-proof boxes, clocks, furniture, ticket cases and other fittings for the stations, gate lodges etc; also cost of labour in landing, storing and delivering rails, chairs, timber, slates, bricks, tiles etc, required for the construction of the works.

The stores account had also covered coke, oil, tallow and other locomotive stores used by engines engaged in the construction of the lines. No credit had been given for revenue prior to 30th June, 1848, but as the work carried out by the engines and rolling stock during the building of the lines to Dereham and Ely had been 'very extensive' the Directors claimed (probably correctly) that 'the work done by the engines and wagons . . . must at least have equalled the cost of the supplies ordered for the locomotives'.

As far as Mr Cope's suggestion that an unnecessarily large supply of stationery had been purchased at the time of opening, the Directors pointed out that there had been *three* companies until 1847, and these three undertakings had ordered their own books, forms, etc on an individual basis. Since 1848, however, the old books had been superseded by others 'costing not one-fourth the original price', and the old stationery was being used only where there was ample stock in hand. Moreover, continued the Directors, the controversial rails contract had been entered into before the amalgamation of the three local companies, and it was therefore unreasonable for the dissatisfied northern proprietors to heap blame upon the present Board of Directors.

Having demolished the Cope Report, the Directors concluded by stating that they were, in many respects, in *agreement* with the northern shareholders insofar as they considered that significant savings could be made if the EAR concentrated maintenance facilities at Kings Lynn station, while they also agreed that a competent General Manager was needed to instill greater efficiency into the company; indeed, they added, a General Manager had actually been appointed, and Mr Wentworth Clay would be taking up his new position on 1st September, 1849. The Directors also reminded their critics that the company had been forced to deal with 'a number of insolvent contractors – and those 'who have had to settle with a number of insolvent contractors' would know the difficulties with which they were surrounded.

The problems with contractors had occurred at a time when there had been 'no accommodation whatever for goods, coal or cattle traffic at Lynn or at any of the other stations, and the utmost quantity of goods that could be landed daily at the harbour station was 50 tons'. Since that time, the company had provided 'accommodation at the principal stations for every description of traffic', while no less than 400 tons of goods could now be landed daily at the harbour. To effect these very real improvements, a considerable outlay had been required, but the Directors had been left with insufficient funds to complete the undertaking, and this had 'entailed upon them a degree of laborious and anxious occupation' over the past two years. The Directors ended their defence with an appeal for unity:

> It has long been our desire to obtain the co-operation, as colleagues, of some desirable parties willing to undertake the duties and responsibilities of the Directorial office. Our wishes in that respect remain unaltered; and we are prepared at any time, when furnished with names, to elect to vacant seats such gentlemen as may be considered best calculated to assist us in developing the resources of the undertaking, and in promoting the interests of the Company.
>
> H. Bruce R.W. Carden
> Thomas Wheeler Edward Self
> 18th August, 1849[24]

The Directors' appeal had, to some extent, been overtaken by events insofar as four northern shareholders had recently joined the Board. Nevertheless, the sentiments expressed by Henry Bruce and his colleagues revealed a real desire to end the differences that had hitherto divided the company, and in retrospect the late summer of 1849 should have been a turning point in the history of the East Anglian Railways.

Continued Difficulties

Sadly, the apparent cessation of hostilities between northern- and southern-based shareholders did not lead to any improvement in the financial state of the company, and by the middle of 1850 the East Anglian Railways were £350,000 in debt. This sorry state of affairs ultimately led to the company being placed in the hands of the Official Receiver; a few months previously, in November 1849, the Directors had introduced a horse-drawn vehicle on the St Ives and Godmanchester line as a means of saving money on this detached portion of the system!

Meanwhile, the lines to Dereham and Ely were somehow managing to operate more or less undisturbed by these problems. The two Sharp 0–4–2 goods engines and the eight 2–2–2 passenger locomotives struggled manfully to work both passenger and goods traffic on the Lynn & Ely and Lynn & Dereham lines, but the 10 EAR engines were maintained fairly successfully in their own depot at Kings Lynn – the East Anglian Railways' locomotive superintendent throughout this difficult period being Mr J. Platt.

On 28th August, 1850 *The Railway Times* reported that an electric telegraph system would be provided on the East Anglian lines when funds permitted, but unfortunately the company did not yet have sufficient funds 'to appropriate to that purpose'!

An Agreement with the GNR

It was, by this time, painfully clear to all concerned that the East Anglian system was a hopelessly uneconomic undertaking with little hope of paying its way as an independent company. Logic dictated that the East Anglian lines should have reached an agreement with the Eastern Counties Railway – which now touched the EAR system at Ely and Dereham (the Norfolk Railway having been worked by the Eastern Counties since 1848).

Unfortunately, the rank and file East Anglian shareholders were highly suspicious of the Eastern Counties company, which had done little to help the EAR in the past – and had in fact already refused to take over the East Anglian system. There was, in truth, no common ground between the supporters of the East Anglian Railways and the owners of the Eastern Counties, and in these circumstances the East Anglian Directors resolved to throw in their lot with the Great Northern Railway.

As we have seen, many East Anglian proprietors lived in Lancashire or other parts of the north, and perhaps for this reason it was always assumed that the EAR would eventually break out of East Anglia in order to reach the populous manufacturing districts of the North and Midlands. In this context the Great Northern Railway seemed to be an ideal ally, and in May 1851 the GNR and East Anglian companies reached an agreement whereby the Great Northern would take over the working of the entire EAR system between Wisbech, Ely, Kings Lynn and Dereham.

The Great Northern hoped to reach East Anglian Railways' metals by means of recently-acquired running powers over the Eastern Counties Railway from Peterborough to Wisbech, but unfortunately these powers did *not* extend through Wisbech ECR station. This inevitably created problems when, in July 1851, the Great Northern attempted to run a through service between Peterborough and Kings Lynn; the Eastern Counties Directors were determined that this Great Northern incursion into Norfolk should be repulsed, and when the GNR tried to exercise its running powers the ECR obstructed the running lines at Wisbech. Legal proceedings ensued, but the Great Northern was unable to obtain an injunction compelling the Eastern Counties to remove the obstruction because the GNR had merely leased the East Anglian system, and until the new arrangements had been ratified by Parliament the courts had no power to interfere.

While the impasse continued at Wisbech, the Great Northern was obliged to transfer passengers between the Eastern Counties and East Anglian stations by horse drawn omnibus, and this tiresome procedure did little to encourage the development of through traffic.

On top of all these problems, the Great Northern shareholders decided that they did not like the deal that had been struck between their own company and the East Anglian – one of the main objections being the fact that the arrangements had been entered into by the GNR Directors without ratification by the shareholders. At the same time, the lease of the East Anglian lines involved a Great Northern guarantee to the EAR shareholders that was costing £15,000 per annum, and the GNR proprietors did not see why they should pay all this money when the East Anglian system was detached, and indeed inaccessible from the Great Northern's own line at Peterborough!

The Eastern Counties Takeover

As frustration mounted on all sides, the hapless East Anglian shareholders again began to question the wisdom of their Directors, and when it became clear that the hoped-for deal with the Great Northern had been thwarted by the Eastern Counties Railway, the EAR proprietors reluctantly concluded that the only course of action open to them was a lease to the hated ECR company. Accordingly, with effect from 1st January, 1852 the Eastern Counties Railway finally assumed control of the East Anglian Railways, all EAR locomotives, rolling stock and other assets being taken over at a valuation. The East Anglian shareholders were to receive a guaranteed net revenue of £17,000 per annum for a period of 21 years, and there was a settlement in shares between the two companies.

Interestingly, the East Anglian company remained in existence as a separate entity for a further 10 years, but this was merely a technicality and it did not alter the fact that the Eastern Counties Railway was now a major force in railway affairs. The company now owned or leased an extensive system throughout the contiguous counties of Norfolk, Suffolk and Essex, and moreover, the ECR had – by fair means or foul – obtained a complete monopoly in a large and geographically-distinct area of Eastern England.

Before dealing with the subsequent history of the former Lynn & Dereham line it would be useful, at this point, to fill in a few details concerning the Norfolk Railway line between Dereham and Wymondham. In general, the story of the Norfolk Railway echoes that of the East Anglian – the underlying theme being one of unequal struggle against the unpopular and potentially-monopolistic Eastern Counties Railway.

Like the East Anglian company, the Norfolk Railway had been beset by financial difficulties following the collapse of the railway stock market in the aftermath of the Railway Mania. One way out of these problems was a policy of union with larger, more successful companies, and in 1848 the Norfolk Railway had been taken over by the Eastern Counties Railway. This takeover was by mutual agreement in the first instance, the assumption being that Parliament would consent to a full amalgamation in due course. Perversely, the final amalgamation was *not* sanctioned by Parliament, and the Norfolk Railway remained in being as a separate organisation. In the interim, the system was worked and managed by the Eastern Counties Railway, and in the next few years the local Norfolk Railway Directors bickered and quarrelled with their ECR counterparts over what was widely seen as an unsatisfactory working agreement.

At one stage, some of the locomotives and rolling stock that had earlier been sold to the Eastern Counties were transferred back to the Norfolk Railway for use on local services, but by 1851, the equipment concerned had been handed back to the ECR as part of a new operating agreement.[25]

As far as the Lynn & Dereham line was concerned, the operating agreement between the Norfolk Railway and the Eastern Counties company was of importance in that, after January 1852, the entire line from Kings Lynn to Dereham and thence to Wymondham and Norwich passed into ECR control.

The Lynn & Dereham and Dereham to Norwich sections were still worked as distinct services – but the way was open for eventual unification in the years to come.

The Formation of the Great Eastern Railway

In 1862 the process by which the Eastern Counties Railway gained control of its smaller neighbours culminated in what was perhaps an inevitable amalgamation, and on 7th August, 1862 at Act to 'amalgamate the Eastern Counties, the East Anglian, the Newmarket, the Eastern Union and the Norfolk Railway Companies' received the Royal Assent. Although in effect the Eastern Counties Railway had simply absorbed lines that it already controlled, the company wisely decided to call itself the 'Great Eastern Railway' – thereby proclaiming a distinct break with the past and underlining the creation of an entirely new organisation which (hopefully) would not be tainted by the unpopularity and abysmal reputation of its immediate predecessor.

The newly-constituted Great Eastern Railway soon earned an improved reputation, and although the stigma of its Eastern Counties Railway origins remained for many years, the reborn company eventually became something of an institution throughout East Anglia – an object of pride rather than derision!

There was, in 1862, still much work to be done before the hitherto disparate parts of the 700 mile Great Eastern system could be welded together, but there can be no doubt that the great amalgamation of August 1862 marked a conscious break with the past; this chapter on the independent years of the Lynn & Dereham line and its connections must, therefore, be brought to a close at this juncture, and the following chapter will deal with the subsequent history of the line under Great Eastern ownership.

A rear view of the attractive Norfolk Railway buildings at Hardingham, on the line between Dereham and Wymondham. *Lens of Sutton*

TIME TABLE FOR MARCH, 1866.

LONDON, ELY, WISBECH, LYNN AND DEREHAM.

UP TRAINS.		Week Days.								S'days.
		Exp. 1, 2 Class.	Parl. 1, 2, 3 Class.	1, 2, 3 Class.	1, 2, 3 Class.	1, 2, 3 Class.	P. 1, 2 Class.	Parl. 1, 2, 3 Class.	1, 2, 3 Class.	1, 2, 3 Class.
		Morn.		Morn.	Morn.	Even.	Morn.	Even.	Even.	Morn.
LOWESTOFT ..	dep.	...		...	...	...	9 10	1 35	...	8 30
YARMOUTH ..	"	...		6 0	...	...	9 25	1 50	...	8 50
NORWICH	"	...		7 0	9 0	...	12 0	3 5	...	10 0
WYMONDHAM ..	"	...		7 27	9 20	...	12 40	3 38	...	10 30
DEREHAM	dep.	...		8 5	9 52	...	1 30	4 20	...	1 20
* Wendling ..	..	...		...	10 2	...	1 40	4 30	...	1 32
* Fransham ..	..	...		...	10 10	...	1 48	4 38	...	1 40
Dunham	..	...		...	10 15	...	1 53	4 42	..	1 46
SWAFFHAM	..	...		8 25	10 25	...	2 3	4 53	...	1 57
Narborough	..	...		...	10 40	...	2 18	5 6	...	2 12
* Bilney ..	..	...		...	10 45	...	2 23	5 11	...	2 17
* East Winch ..	..	...		...	10 50	...	2 30	5 17	...	2 22
* Middleton ..	..	...		...	10 55	...	2 35	5 22	...	2 27
LYNN	arr.	...		8 45	11 5	...	2 45	5 30	...	2 35
Do.	dep.	7 35		8 50	11 30	1 45	5 0	5 45	7 30	2 45
Watlington	..	7 48		9 2	11 42	1 57	5 12	5 57	7 42	2 58
* Magdalen Gate	..	...		...	...	2 2	...	6 2	7 47	...
* Middle Drove	..	...		9 10	...	2 10	...	6 10	7 55	...
* Smeeth Road	..	...		9 15	...	2 14	...	6 15	7 59	...
* Emneth ..	..	...		9 20	...	2 18	...	6 20	8 3	...
WISBECH ..	arr.	...		9 25	...	2 23	...	6 27	8 10	...
Do. ..	dep.	...		9 28	...	2 28	...	6 35	...	...
March	arr.	...		9 40	...	2 45	...	6 53	...	...
PETERBOROUGH ..	"	...		10 15	...	3 30	...	7 35	...	...
*Stow	..	7 54		...	11 48	...	5 18	...	...	3 5
DOWNHAM	..	8 0		...	11 54	...	5 24	...	...	3 12
* Denver ..	..	8 5		...	11 58	...	5 28	...	...	3 17
* Hilgay Fen ..	..	8 14		...	12 5	...	5 35	...	...	3 25
Littleport	..	8 29		...	12 20	...	5 50	...	...	3 40
ELY	arr.	8 45		...	12 35	...	6 5	...	...	4 0
Do.	dep.	8 57	9 4	...	12 50	...	6 17	...	...	4 20
CAMBRIDGE ..	arr.	9 20	9 38	...	1 18	...	6 48	...	...	5 0
LONDON ..	"	11 0	12 50	...	3 40	...	9 10	...	...	7 55½

Third-class carriages by every train between Dereham, Lynn, Ely and Wisbech.
P. Parliamentary from all stations between Middleton and Wendling inclusive to stations beyond (Lynn excepted). Passengers by up train from stations between Lynn and Ely booked at Parliamentary fares by 7.35 a.m. only.

On Tuesdays a composite carriage is attached to the 6.45 a.m. mixed train *ex* Ely to Lynn, and also to the 6.25 p.m. mixed train *ex* Lynn to Ely, calling at all intermediate stations.

* Trains, although noted in the tables to call at these stations, will not do so except there are passengers to take up or set down. Passengers wishing to alight must inform the guard at the preceding *stopping* station. Passengers wishing to be taken up must be at the station five minutes before the time named in the tables.

The timetable in force on the Lynn & Dereham route in March 1866. There were, at that time, just four trains in each direction.

TIME TABLE FOR MARCH, 1866.

LONDON, ELY, WISBECH, LYNN AND DEREHAM.

DOWN TRAINS.		Week Days.								S'days
		1, 2, 3 Class.	Parl. 1, 2, 3 Class.	1, 2 Class.	1, 2 Class.	1, 2 Class.	1, 2 Class.	1, 2, 3 Class.	Exp. 1, 2 Class.	Parl. 1, 2, 3 Class.
		Morn.	Morn.	Morn.	Morn.	Morn.	Even.	Even.	Even.	Even.
LONDON	dep.	...	6 27	8 0	...	10 57	...	...	5 0	1 30
CAMBRIDGE	„	...	10 5		...	1 10	...	...	6 42	5 22
ELY	arr.	...	10 38		...	1 40	...	...	7 5	5 55
Do.	dep.	...	10 48		...	1 50	...	...	7 15	6 0
Littleport	..	...	11 1		...	2 3	...	...	7 28	6 12
* Hilgay Fen	..	...	11 14		...	2 16	...	...	7 41	6 25
Denver	..	...	11 24		...	2 25	...	...	7 51	6 34
DOWNHAM	..	...	11 29		...	2 30	...	...	7 56	6 39
*Stow	..	...	11 36		...	2 37	...	...	8 4	6 46
PETERBORO'	dep.	7 10	...		11 30	...	3 0	5 45	...	...
March	„	7 47	...		12 2	...	3 38	6 32	...	...
WISBECH	arr.	8 3	...		12 20	...	3 55	6 47	...	...
Do.	dep.	8 8	...		12 25	...	4 0	6 50	...	...
* Emneth	..	8 14	...		12 37	...	4 5	...	...	...
Smeeth Road	..	8 18	...		12 41	...	4 9	...	...	...
Middle Drove	..	8 23	...		12 45	...	4 14	...	...	...
Magdalen Gate	..	8 29	...		12 53	...	4 20	...	...	...
Watlington	..	8 35	11 42		12 58	2 45	4 25	...	8 13	6 54
LYNN	arr.	8 50	11 55		1 10	3 0	4 40	7 17	8 30	7 7
Do.	dep.	9 0	12 2		...	...	5 5	7 27	...	7 12
* Middleton	..	9 8	12 10		...	...	5 12	...	...	7 20
East Winch	..	9 13	12 15		...	...	5 17	...	...	7 25
Bilney	..	9 19	12 20		...	...	5 23	...	...	7 30
Narborough	..	9 24	12 25		...	...	5 29	...	...	7 35
SWAFFHAM	..	9 37	12 38		...	...	5 42	7 52	...	7 50
Dunham	..	9 47	12 48		...	...	5 52	...	...	8 0
* Fransham	..	9 52	12 53		...	...	5 57	...	...	8 5
Wendling	..	10 2	1 1		...	...	6 5	...	...	8 13
DEREHAM	arr.	10 12	1 10		...	...	6 15	8 12	...	8 25
WYMONDHAM	arr.	11 3	3 10		...	...	7 2	8 45	...	...
NORWICH	„	11 30	3 48		...	...	7 30	9 5	...	...
YARMOUTH	„	2 35	5 0		...	...	...	10 0	...	...
LOWESTOFT	„	2 55	5 20		...	...	...	10 15	...	...

Third-class carriages by every train between Dereham, Lynn, Ely and Wisbech.

NORWICH MARKET.—On Saturdays a special market train will leave Lynn for Dereham and Norwich at 7.50 a.m., calling at the intermediate stations, returning from Dereham on arrival of the 5.20 p.m. market train from Norwich.

LYNN MARKET.—On Tuesdays a composite carriage is attached to the 6.45 a.m. mixed train *ex* Ely to Lynn, and also to the 6.25 p.m. mixed train *ex* Lynn to Ely, calling at intermediate stations.

* Trains although noted in the tables to call at these stations, will not do so except there are passengers to take up or set down. Passengers wishing to alight must inform the guard at the preceding *stopping* station. Passengers wishing to be taken up must be at the station five minutes before the time named in the tables.

March 1866 (continued).

52 **ELY, LYNN, DEREHAM,** &c.—*Junction with Main Line at Ely.*

Miles from Ely	DOWN TRAINS.	WEEK DAYS.																		SUNDAYS.		
			Mxd.		Parl.	Parl.	A				B				Mxd.	Mxd.				Parl.		
	FROM	morn	morn	morn	morn	morn	morn	morn	morn	morn	even	even		even	even	even				morn		
	LONDON Lpool. St. dep.	...	—	...	—	6 0	7 35	9 10	10 32	11 55	—	2 40	—	5 15	—	Mondays only.	—	—	—	8 0	—	—
	LONDON St. Pancras	...	—	—	—	—	7 33	9 15	10 25	12 3	—	2 35	—	5 5	—		—	—	—	—	—	—
	Newmarket	—	—	...	—	8 15	10 2	10 2	12 23		—	3 58	—	6 12	—		—	—	—	—	—	—
	Cambridge	—	—	...	—	8 28	10 8	10 45	1 38		—	4 17	—	6 40	—		—	—	—	10 14	...	...
	Ely dep.	Mondays only.	Saturdays only.	Not on Mondays.	—	9 15	11 17		2 9		...	4 41	—	7 9	—		—	—	—	10 45	—	—
5¾	Littleport				—	9 32	11 28		2 20		A	C	—	7 20	Wednesdays only.		—	—	—	10 58	—	—
11½	Hilgay Fen				—	9 43	11 38		2 30		[illegible]	C	—	7 30			—	—	...	11 11	—	—
15½	Downham				—	9 55	11 47		2 39		—	5 9	...	7 39			—	—	...	11 22	—	—
18½	Stow				—	•	•		•		...	E	...	•			...	...	...	•	...	...
20½	Magdalen Road				8 23	10 12	12 0		2 51		...	...	—	7 51			...	...	—	11 36	—	...
26½	Lynn arr.				8 36	10 28	12 15		3 5		4 36	5 20	—	8 5			—	...	...	11 50	...	...
	WOLFERTON arr.	...		—	9 33	...	12 40		3 30D		5 4[illegible]	5 49	—	8 38		...	—	...	...	—	—	...
	HUNSTANTON "	..		—	10 0	...	1 6		3 57D		6 15	6 1[illegible]	—	9 [illegible]		...	—	—	—	—	—	—
	Lynn dep.	6 55	8 9	8 8	8 44	—	12 32		4 12		4 40	5 40	Tuesdays only.	8 25		8 45	—	—	—	...	—	—
29½	Middleton	•	•	•	•	...	•		•		—	•		—		•	—	—	—	—	—	—
31½	East Winch	7 5	8 21	8 21	9 4	...	12 45		4 24		...	5 53		8 36		9 6	—	—	—	...	—	—
35½	Narborough	7 17	8 38	8 30	9 14	...	12 54		4 32		B	6 2		8 44		9 20	—	—	—	...	—	—
41½	Swaffham	7 28	8 51	8 41	9 26	...	1 7		4 45		5 6	6 15		8 55	8 50	9 45	—	—	—	—	—	—
45½	Dunham	—	9 0	To Thetford and Bury.	9 35	—	1 16		4 54		B	6 24		9 4	9 5	9 58	—	—	—	—	—	—
46½	Fransham	—	•		•	...	•		•		...	•		...	9 15	•	—	—	—	—	—	—
49½	Wendling	To Thetford.	9 13		9 48	...	1 29		4 6		5 23	6 37		9 15	9 30	10 20	—	—	—	—	—	—
53½	Dereham arr.		9 22		9 56	...	1 38		4 14		5 31	6 45		9 23	9 45	10 30	...	...	...	—	...	...
	Dereham dep.		...		...	—	1 42		4 19		5 31	7 0		—	—	—	—	—	—	..	—	—
	Fakenham arr.		...		...	—	2 14		4 49		6 0	7 30		—	—	—	—	—	—	—	—	—
	Wells "		...		—	—	2 42		5 16		...	7 57		..	—	—	...	—	...	...	...	—
	Dereham dep.		9 36		10 7	—	1 48		4 20		5 40	6 56		9 35	—	—	—	—	—	—	—	—
	Wymondham arr.		10 5		10 22	—	2 17		4 50		5 59	7 26		9 59	—	...	—	—	—	—	—	—
	Norwich "	—	10 35		10 46	—	2 47		5 20		6 20	7 55		10 25	—	—	—	—	—	—	—	—
	Cromer "	—			12 15	—	5 17		7 46		7 46	9 57			—	—	—	—	—	—	—	—
	Lowestoft "	—	—		12 15	—	5 7		6 37		7 57	9 57		—	—	—	—	—	—	—	—	—
	Yarmouth (Vauxhall) "		–		11 57	.	4 50		6 20		7 0	9 40		—		—		—				

A Parliamentary from Stations to Stow, inclusive to Stations below Lynn. D Due at Wolferton and Hunstanton 15 minutes later on Tuesdays.
B Calls at Narborough and Dunham on Tuesdays to set down Passengers. Conveys Hunting Horses between Swaffham and Norwich.
C Calls at Littleport on Mondays and Thursdays, and at Hilgay Fen on Thursdays only to set down Passengers.
Through Carriages are run on all Trains between Lynn, Wisbech, and Peterborough. E Calls at Stow on Fridays only.

The public timetable for the Lynn & Dereham line, in March 1882.

DEREHAM, LYNN, ELY, &c.—*Junction with Main Line at Ely.* 53

Miles from Dereham	UP TRAINS.	WEEK DAYS.																SUNDYS.	
		Exp. Parl.				Mxd.		G										Parl.	
	FROM	morn	morn		morn	morn	morn	morn	morn	morn	even	even	even					even	
	Yarmouth (Vaux.) dep.	—	...	...	6 0	—	8 10	8 10	9 20	10 20	1 0	3 45	From Bury and Thetford.	—	...	—	—	—	—
	Lowestoft "	—	—	—	...	Not on Tuesdays.	7F12	7F12	8 47	10 6	12 40	3 30		—	—	—	—	—	—
	Cromer "	—	—	...	—		6 30	6 30	8 50	10 10	12 30	3 30		—	—	—	—	—	—
	Norwich "	—	—	...	7 0		8 57	8 50	10 20	12 45	3 10	5 55		—	...	—	—	—	—
	Wymondham "	—	...	—	7 27		9 11	9 11	10 41	1 12	3 40	6 25		—	—	—	—	—	—
	Dereham arr.	...	...	...	7 54		9 31	9 31	11 3	1 37	4 8	6 54		—	...	...	—	...	—
	Wells dep.	—	—	...	6 30		—	9 5	10 10	12 50	3 15	6 0		—	...	—	—	—	—
	Fakenham	—	—	—	6 55		9 10	9 33	10 33	1 15	3 40	6 24		—	...	...	—	—	—
	Dereham arr.	...	...	...	7 19	..	9 34	9 58	10 57	1 41	4 8	6 50		—	...	...	...	—	—
	Dereham dep.	...	...	Tuesdays only	7 55	8 2	9 40	10 18	11 6	1 46	4 18	6 58		—	...	—	—	...	—
4	Wendling	—	—		8 3	8‡17	...	10 25	11 16	1 54	4 27	7 7	H	—	—	...	...	—	—
7	Fransham	—	—		—	•	...	•	—	•	—	•	—	—	...	—	—	—	—
8½	Dunham	—	...		8 12	8‡40	—	10 36	11 24	2 5	4 36	7 18	...	—	...	—	...	—	—
12½	Swaffham	—	—		8 20	9 0	10 4	10 45	11 32	2 15	4 45	7 27	8 45	—	—	—	...	—	—
18½	Narborough	—	—		8 30	9 25	...	10 56	11 43	2 27	4 58	7 38	8 57	—	—	—	...	—	—
21½	East Winch	—	—		8 38	9 42	[illegible]	11 5	—	2 36	5 5	7 46	9 6	—	—	—	...	—	—
23½	Middleton	—	—		...	9 50		•	—	•	...	•	•	—	—	—	...	—	—
26½	Lynn arr.	...	...		8 47	10 5	10 33	11 19	12 0	2 50	5 17	8 6	9 20	—	...	—	...	...	—
	HUNSTANTON dep.	—	7 35	...	8 5	—	9 10	10 56	Tuesdays only.	1 55	4 25	...	—	...	—	—	—	—	—
	WOLFERTON "	—	7 54	...	8 30	...	9 34	11 24		2 21	4 45	...	—	...	—	...	...	—	—
	Lynn dep.	7 20	8 15	...	8 50	—	10 38	11 50		3 10	5 25	...	...	—	...	...	...	3 5	—
32½	Magdalen Road	7 32	[illegible]	...	9 2	...	...	12 1		—	5 36	...	—	...	...	...	...	3 17	—
35½	Stow	•		...	Via March.	...	To Peterboro'.	•		—	•	—	—	...	—	...	—	•	—
37½	Downham	7 44	8 23	...		...		12 14		3 30	5 49	—	—	—	...	—	—	3 30	—
42½	Hilgay Fen	7 54	—	...		...		12 23		—	5 58	—	—	—	...	—	—	3 41	—
47½	Littleport	8 5	E	...		...		12 33		—	6 8	—	—	—	—	—	—	3 54	—
53½	Ely arr.	8 17	9 2	...	10 33	...		12 45		4 0	6 20	—	...	...	...	—	...	4 8	—
68½	Cambridge arr.	8 46 / 8 58	9 36	...	11 16	—		1 20	...	4 35	6 55	—	—	—	...	—	...	4 51	—
83½	Newmarket "	9 46 / 9 46	9 46	...	11 17	—		2 12	—	5 15	7 20	—	—	—	—	—	—	5 42	—
135½	LONDON St. Pancras "	10 22 / 12 0	11 14	...	1 5	—		3 0 / 4 3	—	6 13	8 35	—	—	—	—	—	—	—	—
	LONDON Lpool St. "	10 16 / 11 52	11 16	...	1 0	—		2 53 / 4 0	...	6 8	8 30	—	—	...	—	—	...	7 0	—

E Calls at Littleport on Mondays. F From Lowestoft at 7.35 a.m. on Mondays
G Parliamentary from Lynn to St Pancras or Liverpool Street, and from all Stations between Wendling and Middleton inclusive, to Stations beyond Magdalen Road. H On Tuesdays runs 10 minutes later from Swaffham to Lynn. + From Yarmouth on Mondays only.
‡ On Wednesdays leaves Wendling at 8.13 and Dunham at 8.33 a.m., due at Swaffham at 8.43 a.m., in connection with the 8.45 a.m. Train from Swaffham to Thetford. Through Carriages are run on all Trains between Lynn, Wisbech, and Peterborough.

East Anglian Railways 0–4–2 goods engine No. 13 *Lion* (as ECR No. 162).

A GER 'Y' class 2–4–0 as introduced in 1860. Some members of the class possessed cabs and domes placed further along the boiler.

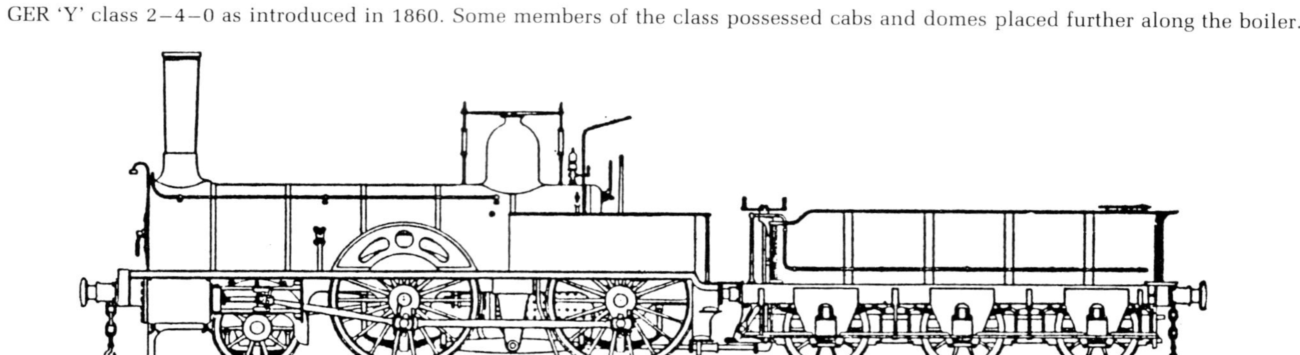

Chapter Three

The Great Eastern Era (1862–1923)

As we have seen, many of Norfolk's railways had been built by a variety of local companies, most of which had been unable to survive as independent undertakings. By the 1850s, however, the great age of railway expansion had ended, and the lines built in the second half of the 19th century tended to be owned by very small, locally-based companies. These modest concerns were, in most cases, formed to connect small towns and villages to nearby main lines – the resulting branch lines being worked by the Great Eastern Railway as part of its now-extensive system. The growth of these branch lines was welcomed by the inhabitants of isolated rural communities which would otherwise have been cut off from the outside world, while the Great Eastern was keen to see local companies brought into existence as a means of providing useful 'feeder' routes for its main lines.

Further Growth of the System

There are, in the case of the Lynn & Dereham route, three such branch lines to consider, and although two of these (the Hunstanton line and the Wells-next-the-Sea route) have formed the subject of companion Oakwood Press volumes, it would be useful to say a few words about the origins of these subsidiary lines insofar as they concerned the 'main line' between Kings Lynn and Dereham.

Although the main line between Kings Lynn, Dereham and Norwich was complete and in operation by 1848, local people still hoped that other branches could be built in order that hitherto neglected towns and villages could be linked to the national railway system. It was clear that such lines would not yield particularly high dividends, and as a general rule these later branches were promoted by landowners such as Thomas William Coke of Holkham Hall (1822–1909) and Henry Styleman le Strange of Hunstanton Hall (1815–62). These gentlemen were wealthy enough to finance the building of railways from their own pockets – but perhaps more importantly, they owned the land upon which the new railways would be built, and by donating land (or selling it at cheap rates) they were able to give immeasurable help to fledgling railway schemes.

The Wells-next-the-Sea Branch

Chronologically, the first branch to be built was the Wells & Fakenham Railway. Authorised on 24th July, 1854 (17 & 18 Vic. cap. 180) this 9½ mile single track route was a lineal descendant of earlier, Railway Mania schemes that had sought to link Wells-next-the-Sea to Dereham and Norwich.

Supporters of the Wells & Fakenham Railway included the above-mentioned Thomas Coke, together with local traders such as Joseph Southgate, and Norfolk Railway Directors such as Sir Samuel Morton Peto and Richard Till. The line was engineered by George Berkely, and when opened on 1st December, 1857, it was worked by the Eastern Counties Railway as an extension of the existing Fakenham line.

The Lynn & Hunstanton Railway

The neighbouring Lynn & Hunstanton Railway was slightly later than the Wells & Fakenham, and although a series of promotional meetings had been held in Kings Lynn and the surrounding area in 1856, the scheme did not receive Parliamentary consent until 1st August, 1861.

The Lynn & Hunstanton Act (24 & 25 Vic. cap.199) authorised the construction of a 15 mile branch commencing 'by a junction with the East Anglian Railways at or near the Almshouse Lane in the parish of Gaywood, near to the terminus of the East Anglian Railways in the borough of Kings Lynn', and terminating 'in or near a field in the parish of Hunstanton . . . near to the hotel there called The Golden Lion'. The first Directors included Henry Styleman le Strange, Major Humphrey John Hare of Docking, Lightly Simpson, Edward Self, and other representatives of the East Anglian company.[26] The Hunstanton scheme was, in effect a subsidiary of the East Anglian Railways, and its Engineer was none other than John Sutherland Valentine – who had already built much of the surrounding railway system in his capacity as Engineer to the Lynn & Ely and Lynn & Dereham companies.

Construction began in the Autumn of 1861, and the first sod was ceremonially cut by the Mayor of Kings Lynn on 13th November. Thereafter, progress was rapid, and the branch was substantially complete by the following summer. Meanwhile, work was proceeding on a new seaside resort which the Lynn & Hunstanton Directors had laid out on a green field site near the station at Hunstanton; when completed, this new holiday and residential town would provide a lucrative source of traffic for the new railway.[27]

The Hunstanton branch was opened on Friday 3rd October, 1862, with an initial train service of three return workings between Kings Lynn and Hunstanton. The new line diverged from the original Lynn & Dereham route near the junction of the Dereham and Ely lines, the resulting triple junction being sited a few yards to the east of the busy Gaywood Road level crossing. At Hunstanton the branch terminated in a small station with a barn-like overall roof and a turntable near the very end of the line, and there were intermediate stations at North Wootton, Wolferton, Dersingham, Snettisham and Heacham. As first built, the Lynn & Hunstanton route was single track throughout, with passing places (though a section of double track was later added between Kings Lynn and Wolferton).

The Hunstanton line was an immediate success – its popularity being enhanced by the rapid development of Hunstanton as a residential resort, and by the purchase, in February 1862, of a country estate at nearby Sandringham as a private residence for Edward, the Prince of Wales (later King Edward VII). Sandringham was only 2¼ miles from Wolferton station, and in later years the Hunstanton line would see many Royal specials – thereby becoming, in the public eye, very much a 'Royal' branch.

By a quirk of history the Hunstanton branch could also claim, quite by chance, to have been the first railway opened by the newly-formed Great Eastern Railway (the opening day of the line coming just two months after the passage of the GER Act of Incorporation).

The Hunstanton branch was, in many ways, peripheral to the Lynn & Dereham line, though it contributed much extra traffic to the neighbouring Lynn & Ely route and made Kings Lynn station a much busier place. The Wells-next-the-Sea branch, in contrast, was closely associated with the Lynn & Dereham route in that it brought additional traffic to the former Norfolk Railway line between Dereham and Wymondham. (In fact, there was always some indecision regarding the status of the Wymondham to Dereham route, and although timetables treated this section of line as an integral part of the Wells branch, it also formed part of the cross-country route between Kings Lynn and Norwich).

The Watton & Swaffham Line

The third line to be considered in this section was, like the Wells-next-the-Sea branch, closely connected with the Lynn & Dereham route. Incorporated on 12th July, 1869, the Watton & Swaffham Railway was designed as a link between the Lynn & Dereham route at Swaffham and the authorised route of the Thetford & Watton Railway at Watton. The Thetford & Watton company had itself been incorporated by an Act of 16th July, 1866, and it was envisaged that, when completed, the Thetford & Watton Railway and the Watton & Swaffham Railway would form one continuous, 18¼ mile line between Swaffham and Roudham Junction (near Thetford).

The Thetford & Watton line was opened in 1869, with an initial train service of four up and four down workings on the nine mile route between Watton and Roudham Junction. The line was, from its inception, worked by the Thetford & Watton company – earlier plans for a working agreement with the Great Eastern Railway having been abandoned.

The Watton & Swaffham Railway had, in the interim, been unable to raise sufficient capital, and the company's promoters were obliged to seek Parliamentary consent for an extension of time to complete the works. A new Act was, accordingly, obtained in 1872, and having surmounted these initial difficulties the Watton & Swaffham supporters were able to proceed with their modest, but entirely feasible railway scheme.

Construction was soon under way, and in September 1875 *The Railway Times* reported that the work was 'proceeding very rapidly'. The earthworks and bridges were in a forward state, and part of the permanent way was already in place. The intermediate station at Holme Hale was 'nearly completed', while the 'greater part of the rails' had been delivered; the Directors expected that the railway would be open for traffic by the end of the year,[28] though in fact the route was brought into use for freight traffic as early as 20th September, 1875.

Passenger trains commenced running on 15th November, 1875, the Watton & Swaffham line being worked as a 9½ mile extension of the existing branch from Roudham Junction. All trains were worked by the Thetford & Watton Railway under operating agreements between the Thetford & Watton and Watton & Swaffham companies.

For a time, some trains ran through to Bury St Edmunds over the metals of the Bury St Edmunds & Thetford Railway, but this arrangement was never entirely satisfactory and, after a few years of independent existence, the local companies were sold to the Great Eastern Railway – the first to be sold being the Bury St Edmunds & Thetford company, which was wound up in 1878. The Thetford & Watton and Watton & Swaffham companies were leased to the GER in the following year, and finally, in 1897, both companies were formally vested in the Great Eastern Railway.

There were, for many years, just four up and four down passenger trains between Swaffham and Thetford, together with one up and one down goods working that usually ran to and from Kings Lynn. Roudham Junction, the original 'terminus' of the Thetford & Watton line, saw little use in later years, being served by one or two branch trains but very few main line services. In emergencies, it was sometimes used for interchange purposes, but otherwise Roudham Junction was used mainly for freight trains.

The line from Swaffham to Roudham Junction was single track throughout, with an intermediate crossing loop at Watton. Watton, in fact, was a comparatively large station with several goods sidings and an old engine shed that had originally served as the locomotive and carriage sheds of the Thetford & Watton Railway. The other intermediate stations at Holme Hale, Stow Bedon and Wretham & Hockham were, in contrast, merely single-platform, wayside stations.

As far as the Lynn & Dereham route was concerned, the Swaffham line was of some importance in that it brought additional freight traffic onto the line between Kings Lynn and Swaffham. Passenger trains usually worked a localised service between Swaffham and Thetford, though there were, at various times, one or two through workings to Kings Lynn or elsewhere.

A Rival Scheme

The lines described above were all planned in conjunction with the Great Eastern, but mention should also be made of a rival scheme which, from its very inception, was designed to break the Great Eastern's monopolistic position in East Anglia. We have seen how, in the early 1850s, the rival Great Northern Railway had attempted to gain control of the East Anglian Railways – while at around the same time the East Anglian Directors had also raised the possibility of some form of sale or working agreement with the Midland Railway. Although these tentative plans failed to produce lasting results, there was always a chance that the Midland or Great Northern companies would one day renew their advance into Great Eastern territory, and in the 1870s the formation of a company known as the Lynn & Fakenham Railway opened the way for such an attack.

The Lynn & Fakenham was another descendant of the speculative schemes that had sought to build competitive east-to-west cross country lines across north Norfolk during the heady days of the Railway Mania, and its appearance heralded the start of a further flurry of promotional activity in the Kings Lynn area.

The Lynn & Fakenham Railway (L&FR) was incorporated on 13th July, 1876, with Powers to construct an 18¾ mile line from Gaywood Junction, on the Lynn & Hunstanton Branch, to the town of Fakenham. Capital of

£150,000 was authorised, together with loans of £50,000, and the supporters of the scheme included local landowners such as Sir W.A. Browne-Folkes and Mr W. Walker of Little Massingham. After many vicissitudes, the Fakenham line was opened between Kings Lynn (GER) and Massingham Road on 16th August, 1879, and the L&FR route was completed throughout to Fakenham on 16th August, 1880.

In its original form, the Lynn & Fakenham line was little more than a branch, but in the next few years its promoters successfully extended their original line south-eastwards to Norwich (2nd December, 1882) and east to North Walsham (5th May, 1883). At North Walsham, the line made an end-on connection with the Yarmouth & North Norfolk Railway in open defiance of the GER. In the west, meanwhile, a series of Great Northern and Midland-backed lines had resulted in the creation of a further system of lines which, by linking-up with the parent Midland and Great Northern companies, opened the way for through running between Great Yarmouth and the industrial Midlands.

Events were now moving fairly rapidly, and in the next few years these disparate local lines were progressively brought under unified control, the lines east of Kings Lynn being amalgamated to form the Eastern & Midlands Railway, while the earlier lines to the west of Kings Lynn had joined forces to create the Midlands & Eastern Railway.

In a subsequent development the confusingly-named Eastern & Midlands and Midlands & Eastern companies were merged to form a much enlarged Eastern & Midlands system, and by 1893 the entire undertaking had been reborn as the Midland & Great Northern Joint Railway – a competitive cross-country route which effectively smashed the Great Eastern's coveted monopoly in north Norfolk.

In its final guise, the Midland & Great Northern Railway was wholly owned by the GNR and Midland companies, though day-to-day management of the system was placed in the hands of a fully devolved joint committee. In its completed form the M&GN was a well-managed undertaking and a formidable competitor for the Great Eastern Railway. Having started as little more than a branch, the original Lynn & Fakenham route had expanded in all directions – one of the last lines to be built being the Cromer branch from Melton Constable to Cromer Beach (see *The Melton to Cromer Branch* (The Oakwood Press) for further details).

Another important section of the M&GN system was the Lynn avoiding line between South Lynn and Bawsey Junction – this 4 mile 45 chain 'cut-off' being particularly important in that it enabled the M&GN to avoid the embarrassing necessity of reversing into and out of the rival GER station at Kings Lynn (though M&GN local services continued to serve the latter station).

Running from east to west across the very centre of Norfolk, the Midland & Great Northern line posed a major threat to the Lynn & Dereham route. These two, more or less parallel lines competed for the same local traffic, while in terms of longer distance traffic they were also in competition as cross-country routes between the Midlands and Norfolk resorts such as Great Yarmouth and Lowestoft. As holiday traffic increased in importance during the later years of the 19th century this competition intensified, and there is no doubt that traffic that would otherwise have been sent via the former Lynn & Dereham route was carried by the Midland & Great Northern line – and to that extent the M&GN route exerted an important, though entirely negative effect on the Great Eastern lines between Kings Lynn and Norwich.

Improving the Kings Lynn to Norwich Route

Although the appearance of the Midland & Great Northern Railway had obviously been a blow for the Great Eastern company, the threat of competition may have encouraged the GER to improve its own system in order to compete more effectively with the newcomer. There were, at the same time, instances of the Great Eastern co-operating with the Midland and Great Northern companies in order to improve local railway facilities. An example of this co-operation could be seen at Kings Lynn, where the three companies joined forces to build a new terminus that replaced the original East Anglian Railways' structure. The new station, with its distinctive brick buildings, was completed in 1871.

The nearby Kings Lynn Dock was another example of co-operation between the rival companies. Built by the Kings Lynn Dock Company under Powers obtained on 19th June, 1869 (28 & 29 Vic. cap. 88), the Docks branch was opened on 10th June, 1870. It diverged from the Great Eastern Railway in the parish of Gaywood, and although worked mainly by the GER, the Midland and Great Northern companies had running powers over the dock system.

Elsewhere, though the GER was a comparatively poor railway, the GE company did not shirk from investing in rural lines when existing equipment or facilities needed improvement. There was no sudden, large scale replacement of time-expired equipment, but many improvements were nevertheless put into effect during the later 19th century. On 31st December, 1873, for example, the GER Way and Works Committee authorised the construction of a new 200 ft platform at Wendling at a cost of £110, while in November 1897 the committee agreed to the building of an additional bedroom in the station master's house at Hardingham at a cost of £90.

On a more ambitious level, the company decided that the Wymondham to Dereham section was busy enough to justify the cost of doubling, and this work was put in hand during the early 1880s. The additional track (and associated signalling) was inspected in November 1882,[29] and the new works were brought into use shortly afterwards. In connection with this scheme, the GER rebuilt the intermediate stations at Kimberley, Hardingham, Thuxton and Yaxham, new up platforms being provided in each case. At the same time the existing (down) platforms and buildings were altered and adapted, each station receiving new, glass-fronted passenger accommodation and extensive platform canopies. Happily, these Great Eastern additions left most of the original Norfolk Railway station buildings intact, and few ordinary travellers could have guessed that the rebuilt stations incorporated two distinct periods of construction.

Similar rebuildings took place on the former Lynn & Dereham line where, as a general rule, the GER erected improved passenger accommodation alongside the original L&DR buildings – new platform canopies being the most obvious features of the rebuilt stations. In some cases, stations that had originally been single platform stopping places were given crossing loops and second platforms, the new platforms being equipped with simple brick waiting rooms.

Of greater significance in terms of the development of long distance passenger and freight traffic was the decision to install an avoiding line at Dereham. The arrangements at this important local traffic centre were far from ideal, the main problem being the way in which the station was aligned on a north-south axis to suit trains between Norwich and Wells-next-the-Sea, rather than on an east-to-west alignment – which would have been preferable in relation to the Kings Lynn–Dereham–Norwich route. The layout functioned adequately so long as trains continued to operate as two distinct services between Norwich and Wells-next-the-Sea and from Kings Lynn to Dereham, but if the Great Eastern wished to compete with the Midland & Great Northern line in any meaningful way the awkward layout at Dereham would have to be modified.

The GER operating authorities decided that the situation could be improved by the provision of a west-to-east avoiding line which would, in effect, comprise the third side of a triangle. New signal boxes had recently been installed at Dereham South and Dereham West[30] (then known as Dereham 'A Box' and Dereham 'D Box' respectively), and it was resolved that the new avoiding line would be built between these two points – the new boxes being used to control the west-to-east curve that would thereby be formed.

The curve, which was double track throughout, was inspected by the Board of Trade in June 1886[31] and brought into use shortly afterwards. The new section of line left the original Lynn & Dereham route at Dereham West Junction and joined the former Norfolk Railway at Dereham South. Dereham West box had a 32-lever frame at that time while Dereham South had a 26-lever frame; both frames had four spare levers at the time of the BoT inspection.[32]

With the new curve in operation, the Kings Lynn to Wymondham line could, at long last, function as a unified cross-country route. Local passenger trains continued to run into and out of the station, but the avoiding line was soon being used by excursion trains, freight workings and diverted main line traffic. The route between Wymondham and Kings Lynn was now double-tracked for much of its length, with continuous up and down lines all the way from Wymondham to Dereham West Junction. The Lynn & Dereham section remained single, but there were crossing loops at Dunham, Wendling, Swaffham, Narborough and East Winch, and these provided ample capacity on the single line between Dereham West Junction and Kings Lynn Junction.

At the eastern end of the Kings Lynn to Norwich route, the GER opened a 6 mile 20 chain 'cut-off' line between Wymondham, Ashwellthorpe and Forncett on 2nd May, 1881, and the Great Eastern also completed a major redevelopment scheme at Norwich Thorpe, where the original Norfolk

Railway terminus was superseded by a new station with many improved facilities. The Ashwellthorpe cut-off was double track throughout, and it formed a useful short cut between the Ipswich and Ely main lines. Passengers between Dereham and London were, by changing at Forncett, able to avoid Norwich entirely, and in the next few years a number of Dereham line trains were run to and from Forncett rather than Norwich Thorpe – although Norwich was always regarded as the primary destination for through workings from Kings Lynn.

Kings Lynn to Norwich Train Services

Train services, though modest, were sufficient for the needs of an agricultural area in which few people had need to travel more than a few miles from their native villages. There were, in general, around four trains each way during the mid-Victorian period, average journey times for the 26½ mile trip between Lynn and Dereham being from 65 to 70 minutes. The 1862 passenger timetable shows four up and four down workings, with an extra train on Mondays and one service in each direction on Sundays. One of the daily trains was, apparently, a through working from London, and this service left Bishopsgate at 6.27 am and arrived in Swaffham by 12.57 pm – having covered the intervening 110 miles in 6½ hours.

This pattern of services persisted, with little modification, throughout the middle years of the 19th century. In March 1866, for example, daily operation began with the departure of a fast up train from Dereham at 8.05 am, which reached Kings Lynn in just 40 minutes, having called *en route* only at Swaffham. Further trains left Dereham at 9.52 am, 1.30 and 4.20 pm, while in the opposite direction corresponding down workings left Kings Lynn at 9.00 am, 12.02, 5.05 and 7.27 pm. On Sundays, a train left Dereham at 1.20 pm, and arrived in Kings Lynn by 2.35 pm, while a return working left Kings Lynn at 7.12 pm and reached Dereham at 8.25 pm.

It is unclear which (if any) trains continued beyond Dereham to Norwich at this time, but on balance it seems likely that some at least of the daily trains were through services which may have combined with Wells–Norwich trains at Dereham. At other times, good connections were available at Dereham, and through travellers could easily reach Norwich by changing into a Wells branch train. Significantly, the Wells to Norwich service also consisted of four up and four down trains, and study of the relevant timetables suggests that there was a high degree of integration between the Kings Lynn–Dereham and Wells–Dereham–Norwich lines – indeed, the Kings Lynn to Norwich line eventually came to be regarded as the 'main line', while the Dereham to Wells section was inevitably relegated to 'branch' status.

A point which might be made here is that, whereas Norwich–Dereham–Wells trains were, quite naturally, designated 'down' workings, the former Lynn & Dereham route was treated as an extension of the East Anglian main line, and for this reason trains from Dereham to Kings Lynn or beyond were regarded as 'up' services. Thus a train from Norwich to Kings Lynn would be considered a down working until it reached Dereham, but it would, thereafter, become an *up* working for the remainder of the journey to Kings Lynn.

Although the change from 'up' to 'down' at Dereham was somewhat inconvenient, it made sense in relation to trains which continued through from Kings Lynn to Ely or beyond, and in this context it is worth mentioning that the early morning departure from Dereham to Kings Lynn ran through to Peterborough, while the 1.30 pm afternoon train was advertised as a 'Parliamentary' service for passengers 'between Middleton and Wendling inclusive to stations beyond (Lynn excepted)'.

On Saturdays a special market train left Kings Lynn at 7.50 am, and according to a note at the bottom of the timetable, this working was for 'Dereham and Norwich'. Confusingly, the return service that left Norwich at 5.20 pm did *not* run through, and intending passengers were advised that a connecting service left Dereham for Kings Lynn 'on the arrival of the 5.20 pm market train from Norwich'.

The 1882 public timetable was somewhat more ambitious than its 1862 predecessor, and intending travellers between Norwich, Dereham and Kings Lynn were offered a choice of seven up and five down trains between Dereham and Kings Lynn – the apparent disparity between eastbound and westbound workings being balanced by two further down workings that worked complicated diagrams involving trips on the Swaffham to Thetford route.

In the up (westbound) direction, trains left Dereham at 8.02 (7.55 on Tuesdays), 9.40, 10.18, 11.08 am, 1.45, 4.18 and 6.58 pm, while in the down (eastbound) direction there were departures from Kings Lynn at 8.53 am, 12.32, 3.12, 4.40 and 5.40 pm. Additional trains ran on Tuesdays and Saturdays, but there were no Sunday trains on the Lynn & Dereham section.

Peculiarities of the 1882 timetable included a working that left Fakenham (on the Wells branch) at 9.10 am and then formed the 9.40 am working from Dereham to Kings Lynn. Travellers prepared to study the timings more closely would, moreover, have discovered that this circuitous through service eventually formed the 10.38 am from Kings Lynn to Peterborough! Another curious through working was the 4.40 pm departure from Kings Lynn, which had earlier started its journey at Peterborough, and later formed the 5.40 pm evening service from Dereham to Lowestoft; this train also conveyed a portion for Ipswich, which was detached at Wymondham, going forward at 6.47 pm and travelling via Forncett and the Colchester main line.

The overall pattern of train services on the former Norfolk Railway section between Dereham and Wymondham Junction was similar to that in operation on the Lynn & Dereham line. In 1882 there were nine up and nine down workings on the line east of Dereham including a handful of services that ran through to Forncett via the Ashwellthorpe cut-off line. In general, most of the trains between Dereham and Wymondham were Wells-next-the-Sea branch workings, which operated on a Norwich–Wymondham–Dereham–Wells axis.

Although the direct west-to-east curve at Dereham was not yet built, there were several through workings between Norwich and Kings Lynn during the early 1880s, and in addition to the above-mentioned evening train from Peterborough to Lowestoft there was also a morning through train from

Lowestoft to Dereham, Kings Lynn and Peterborough, together with an additional through train to Kings Lynn on Tuesdays only.

A further point which might be made in connection with these 19th century train services concerns the status of some of the smaller intermediate stopping places on the Norwich to Wells and Dereham to Kings Lynn routes. The concept of the unstaffed 'halt' did not really develop until the turn-of-the-century, but many smaller stations on these Norfolk lines were nevertheless treated as 'request stops' at which trains called only when required to pick up or set down passengers. Travellers wishing to alight at these stations were asked to 'intimate the same to the guard at the preceding stopping station', while people wishing to join trains at such stations were told to 'be at the station five minutes before the time named in the tables' (i.e. to inform the station master or senior porter that they wished to get on a train).

In 1882, the stations regarded as request stops included Middleton and Fransham on the Lynn & Dereham line, and Kimberley, Thuxton and Yaxham on the Dereham to Norwich section. These stations, which were fully staffed and handled goods traffic, were not unstaffed halts in the modern sense; it is, nevertheless, a sobering thought that, even in the Victorian era, the amount of passenger traffic handled at Middleton, Fransham and the other stations was not large enough to justify a full service of stopping trains.

While on the subject of smaller stopping places one might add that two of the original Lynn & Dereham stations were closed as long ago as the 19th century. The stations concerned were Sporle, which had disappeared from the timetables as early as the 1860s, and Bilney – which was shown as a request stop in the 1862 timetable but had fallen into disuse by 1882.

Narborough was one of the more important intermediate stations on the Lynn & Dereham line. This September 1955 view shows the main station buildings, on the up side of the line. *Douglas Thompson*

Victorian Motive Power

The original East Anglian Railways locomotives passed into Eastern Counties ownership on 1st January, 1852, but, as non-standard locomotives, their subsequent history was destined to be somewhat short. The attractive 'bird' names that had been carried in EAR days were soon removed, and the 10 former East Anglian engines were renumbered in sequence from 108 to 115, with the two 0–4–2s becoming ECR Nos. 162 and 164.

Engine No. 108 was reboilered in 1862, but its companions were scrapped in the next few years without being rebuilt. Details of these original EAR engines, with their years or withdrawal, are given in *Table Two* (below).

Table Two

EAST ANGLIAN RAILWAYS LOCOMOTIVES 1846–75

EAR No.	*ECR No.*	*Type*	*Name*	*Cylinders*	*Scrapped*
1	108	2–2–2	*Eagle*	15 in. × 20 in.	July 1875*
2	109	2–2–2	*Vulture*	15 in. × 20 in.	June 1867
3	110	2–2–2	*Ostrich*	15 in. × 20 in.	January 1870
4	111	2–2–2	*Falcon*	15 in. × 20 in.	September 1868
5	112	2–2–2	*Hawk*	15 in. × 20 in.	October 1869
6	113	2–2–2	*Kite*	15 in. × 20 in.	October 1869
7	114	2–2–2	*Raven*	15 in. × 20 in.	March 1870
8	115	2–2–2	*Heron*	15 in. × 20 in.	January 1870
13	162	0–4–2	*Lion*	16 in. × 22 in.	
14	164	0–4–2	*Tiger*	16 in. × 22 in.	

* No. 108 survived as a stationary boiler until about 1890.

On a footnote, it is perhaps worth mentioning that these early Victorian engines were all coke burners, and for this reason it was necessary for the East Anglian Railways to import stocks of coke, or else make their own in the depot at Kings Lynn (locomotives did not burn coal until the development of the brick-arched firebox).

The East Anglian engines were, in many respects, normal-looking locomotives, but their replacements exhibited many unusual features. The Eastern Counties Railway and its constituents favoured a type of locomotive known as the Stephenson 'long boiler'. These curious engines had very short wheelbases and (presumably to counteract inherent instability) their boilers were often very low pitched. This, in turn, meant that long boiler engines often had disproportionately-tall chimneys and boiler fittings – the overall effect being (to modern eyes) decidedly quaint and picturesque!

Precise details of the type of engines used on the Kings Lynn to Dereham line during the 1860s and 1870s are exceeedingly scarce, though it is tempting to conclude that former Norfolk Railway locomotives would have been employed to at least some extent. The Norfolk Railway owned just 37 engines when it placed itself under Eastern Counties control in 1848, and

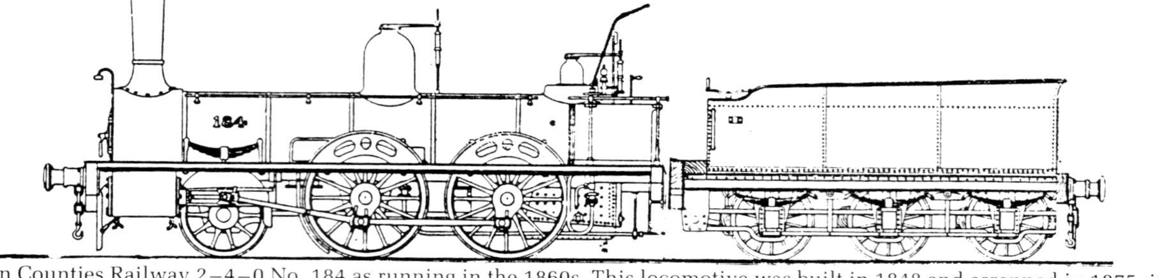

Former Eastern Counties Railway 2–4–0 No. 184 as running in the 1860s. This locomotive was built in 1848 and scrapped in 1875, it had 5 ft diameter coupled wheels.

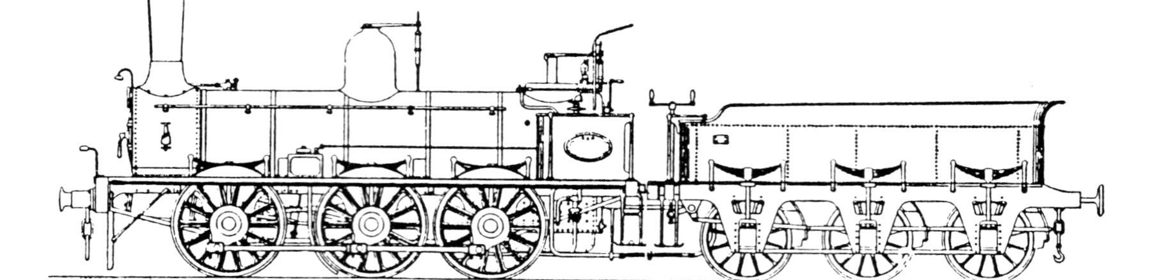
Norfolk Railway 0–6–0 goods locomotive No. 17 (as GER No. 220). This engine was built in 1846 and scrapped in 1881.

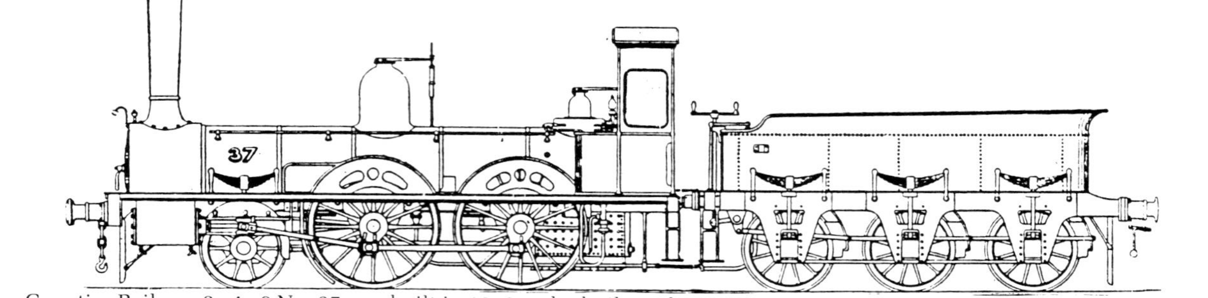

Eastern Counties Railway 2–4–0 No. 37 was built in 1846 and rebuilt as shown in 1863; it was withdrawn in 1878. The curious stovepipe

most of these were 0–6–0 or 2–4–0 long boilers from Stephensons, Jones & Potts and other specialist engine manufacturers. It is reasonable to assume that most of these engines remained on their own section long after the ECR takeover – the usual practice being for elderly locomotives to spend their last years pottering about on undemanding secondary duties when they became too old or decrepid for main line work.

Former Norfolk Railway 2–4–0s Nos. 30–39 were typical examples of the engines used on the Norwich–Wells and Lynn & Dereham routes during the 1860s. Renumbered from 130 to 139 by the Eastern Counties Railway, they had 15 in. × 22 in. outside cylinders and 5 ft 7 in. coupled wheels; they weighed about 24 tons and had a boiler pressure of 110 lb. per square inch.

Some of these engines were later rebuilt by the ECR, receiving new boilers, stove pipe chimneys and simple weather boards in place of the original open cabs. Nos. 137 and 139 were the first to be withdrawn, both engines being taken out of service in 1866; further withdrawals took place at intervals throughout the 1870s, and the last survivor – No. 131 – was scrapped in 1882.

Recorded locomotive history really begins with the advent of Robert Sinclair's versatile 'Y' class 2–4–0s. Although originally intended for fast goods work, the 'Y' class engines were also used for local passenger duties, and at a time when modern engines were in short supply on the Great Eastern Railway, these 2–4–0s were increasingly used as 'mixed traffic' engines on rural lines throughout East Anglia. Built by a variety of different manufacturers, the 'Y' class 2–4–0s were delivered in batches between 1859 and 1866, and there were eventually no less than 100 of these useful locomotives. They had 17 in. × 24 in. outside cylinders and 6 ft 1 in. diameter coupled wheels, some further particulars being as follows:

Coupled wheelbase	9 ft
Total wheelbase	15 ft 1 in.
Diameter of leading wheels	3 ft 7 in.
Overall length	24 ft 4½ in.
Boiler diameter	4 ft
Length of firebox casing	4 ft 8 in.
Grate area	approx. 13¾ square ft
Water capacity	1,600 gallons
Weight (engine only)	approx. 30 tons
Weight with tender	approx. 52 tons

The engines were numbered in sequence from 307 to 416, one of the locomotives used on the Lynn & Dereham line being No. 328 which, according to Ernest Ahrons, 'worked from Norwich to Hunstanton and back via Dereham and Lynn'.

The 'Y' class engines were rebuilt and modified in a variety of ways, some becoming 4–4–0s while others remained 2–4–0s. The 4–4–0 rebuilds were intended for main line use, but the remaining engines remained at work on local GER passenger and freight services in Norfolk and elsewhere. Ahrons recalled that they were even pressed into service as shunting engines – this expedient being necessary because the Great Eastern Railway had few shunting engines during the Victorian period.[33]

Another 2–4–0 type used on the Kings Lynn to Norwich route during the later years of the 19th century was the celebrated 'No. 1 class' of 2–4–0. Originally intended for use on the North British Railway, the first five 'No. 1 class' (or 'Little Sharpie') 2–4–0s were delivered to the GER in 1867. Built by Neilson, Reid & Co., the initial batch had 6 ft coupled wheels and 16 in. × 22 in. inside cylinders. These engines were so successful in GER service that a further three engines were built at Stratford in 1868, and these became the prototypes of the 'No. 1 class' proper, of which 40 were constructed between 1867 and 1872. Thirty of the new engines were built by Sharp, Stewart & Co., and a further ten were built by the GER at Stratford.

The 'No. 1 class' proper weighed 47 tons in working order, and they had a boiler pressure of 140 lb. per square inch. They had 5 ft 7 in. coupled wheels and 16 in. × 22 in. inside cylinders. The first five engines were numbered in sequence from 125 to 129, and the remaining 40 'No. 1 class' 2–4–0s were numbered in random batches between 1 and 161.

Like the slightly earlier 'Y' class 2–4–0s (which they eventually superseded) the 'No. 1 class' engines were widely used on local passenger and freight duties throughout East Anglia, and in this capacity they enjoyed a long association with the Lynn & Dereham and Norwich–Wells lines. Engine No. 115 was stationed at Dereham for most of its working life, while 'No. 1 class' 2–4–0s Nos. 2, 4, 35, 44, 45, 46, 50, 107, 108, 110, 112, 113, 114, and 115 were all stationed at Kings Lynn at various times. Nos. 30, 117 and 126 were based at Wells-next-the-Sea, and Nos. 6, 26, 31, 33, 34 and 49 were some of the Norwich-based 'No. 1 class' engines.[34]

On 21st January, 1881 'No. 1 class' 2–4–0 No. 126 (one of the original five engines) was involved in an accident while working an early morning train from Wells-next-the-Sea to Norwich. This mishap took place outside Norwich Thorpe station after No. 126 had overrun its signals; the Wells train was thereby brought into the path of a Yarmouth to Norwich passenger train headed by 'Y' class 2–4–0 No. 375, with the result that No. 126 struck No. 375 between the leading and driving wheels.

Although it would probably be true to say that the 'Y' class 2–4–0s and the 'No. 1 class' engines were among the most widely-used locomotives on the Kings Lynn to Norwich route during the later 19th century, it is worth noting that other types also appeared. These other classes included the distinctive 'G14' class 2–4–0s, which had originally been designed by T.W. Worsdell for fast express work. Dating from 1882, the 'G14s' had 7 ft diameter coupled wheels and 18 in. × 24 in. inside cylinders. Visually, their most noticeable features were their stovepipe chimneys and massive 'double' splashers; to late Victorian locomotive enthusiasts these 2–4–0 engines must have seemed huge, but, sadly, their performance did not match their impressive appearance, and by the 1890s they had been relegated to branch line and local duties. Nos. 562, 563, 564, 565 and 567 were stationed at Kings Lynn by 1889, and although they were initially employed on main line duties, they also appeared on the Lynn & Dereham line; in 1894, 'G14' class 2–4–0 No. 567 was involved in a spectacular derailment incident at Swaffham (*see Chapter Five*).

The Edwardian Years

When first built, railways such as the Lynn & Dereham line had been new and revolutionary, but with the passage of time they became part of the fabric of British life. By the end of the 19th century the railway system had reached into every corner of the land, and few people could remember the days when long distance passenger and freight traffic had travelled no faster than the speed of a horse. Railways were, in fact, at their very peak during the late Victorian and Edwardian periods; great companies such as the Midland and London & North Western railways held an undisputed monopoly of land transport, and railway engineering was at the 'leading edge' of Britain's world-beating industrial technology.

Although by no means the most profitable railway company in the British Isles, the Great Eastern Railway shared at least some of the prosperity experienced by British railway companies at the end of the 19th century. In technical matters, the company could hold its own with other, much larger organisations, and the development of new locomotives such as the 'T19' 2–4–0s and the famous 'Claud Hamilton' 4–4–0s ensured that the GER was frequently in the limelight as far as turn-of-the-century locomotive enthusiasts were concerned.

In terms of publicity, the GER gained considerable advantage by the adoption of an unusual dark blue locomotive livery. Until the later years of the 19th century most Victorian locomotives had been adorned (if that is the right word) in a drab green livery; the 'No. 1 class' 2–4–0s, for example, had originally been painted dark green with brown underframes. In the 1880s, however, improved paint technology had increased the range of paints available for engineering use, and although many companies retained their traditional green engine liveries, the Great Eastern Railway opted for the use of 'royal blue' lined in red and black. This new livery struck a chord with the travelling public, and by the turn-of-the-century the dark blue Great Eastern locomotives, with their trains of varnished teak coaches, had become an accepted part of the East Anglian scene.

The train services provided during the early 1900s were similar to those offered to the travelling public during the 1880s. The Kings Lynn to Norwich route was still worked in two parts – albeit with a high degree of integration between the Lynn & Dereham and Norwich to Wells-next-the-Sea routes. There were, in general, around half a dozen trains each way between Kings Lynn and Dereham, and in 1901 the main down services left Kings Lynn at 8.51 am, 12.30, 3.10, 5.43 and 8.25 pm. In the up direction, westbound services departed from Dereham at 7.03 (Mondays Only), 7.33 (Mondays excepted), 9.03, 10.14 am, 1.53 and 4.41 pm. Additional trains ran on Thursdays and Saturdays, and (as in 1882) some of the trains on the Lynn & Dereham line were in fact through workings. The 4.41 pm up service, for instance, actually started its journey at Great Yarmouth, and having reached Kings Lynn at 5.30 pm it then continued to Peterborough.

The timings outlined above remained more or less the same throughout the early 1900s, though by 1911 a number of additional trains had been introduced. There were, by that time, seven up and seven down workings

NORWICH, DEREHAM, FAKENHAM AND WELLS.

Junction with Cambridge Main Line at Wymondham.

Ref. Page	DOWN TRAINS.	morn	morn	morn (Via Forncett)	morn	morn	morn	noon (Via Forncett)	S even	even (To Lynn & Peterboro')	even (Saturdays only)	even (Tuesdays only. From Lynn)	even (Saturdays only)	even	even (Via Forncett)	even (To Lynn)	even (Via Forncett)	even	even (Via Lynn)	SUNDAYS even
102	Yarmouth (Vaux.) dep.		7 33			9E8		12 0	12 57	3 15	3 15		3 40	5 8		6 5		7 22		6 0
	Lowestoft (Central) "		7 0			8 43		11 19	12 48	2 53	2 53		3 30	3 30		5 48		6 48		5 47
104	Cromer "		8 23			8Y45		10 0	2 25	2T58	2 54		2 54	5U20		5Z55		5Z55		5D10
78 to 82	NORWICH (Thorpe) dep.	6 36	8 17			10 35		12 55	3 20	4 2	4 2		5 22	6 17		7 5		8 12		7 0
	Trowse	6 41	8 22			10 40		1 0	3 25	4 7	4 7		5 27	6 22				8 17		7 6
	Hethersett	6 51	CC			10 50		1 10	3 35				5 37	6 32				8 27		7 16
	Wymondham arr.	7 0	8 38			10 59		1 19	3 44				5 46	6 41		7 23		8 36		7 25
71 77 & 132	LONDON (Liverpool St. dep.			5 5	5 23		9 10	10 0	12 0					2 35	3 20		4 55	5 12		3 30
	LONDON (St. Pancras "						9 15		12 20					2 40				5 5		
132	Ipswich "			7 1		9 8		12 0							5 5					
74-77	Cambridge "		6 45		8 15		10 52		1 37					4 6			6 28	6 36	E	5 0
94	Peterborough dep.				7 14		9 30		12 52					3 30				4 58	7 2	4 40
85	YORK "								10 25					12 50					4 0	
	Doncaster "						8 9		11 16					1 42					4 47	2 35
	Lincoln "						9 5		12 9					2 37					5 45	3 35
74-77	Ely "		7 8		8 47		11 18		3 6					4 37				7 9		5 33
	Wymondham arr.		8 25	8 25	10 16	10 48	12 37	1 10	3 27					6 15	6 32		7 47	8 20		6 58
	Wymondham dep.	7 3	8 40		11 1		1 21		3 49				5 47	6 46		7 25	7 49	8 39		7 28
	Kimberley	7 10			11 8		1 28		3 56				5 51	6 53				8 47		7 36
	Hardingham	7 15	8 50		11 13		1 33		4 1				5 59	6 58			H	8 52		7 41
	Thuxton	7 19	H		11 17		1 37		4 5				6 3	7 2				8 56		7 45
	Yaxham	7 25			11 23		1 43		4 12				6 10	7 8			F	9 3		7 52
96	Dereham arr.	7 30	8 59		11 28		1 47		4 17	4 38	4 39	6 46	6 15	7 12		7 42	8 6	9 8	9 11	7 57
	Dereham dep.	7 33	9 7		11 31		1 52		4 23	4 41	4 43	6 50	6 18	7 16		7 47	8 9	9 16		8 0
	North Elmham	7 42	9 16		11 40		2 0		4 32		4 52	6 59	6 27	7 25			8 18	9 25		8 9
	County School	7 48	9 21		11 44		2 4		4 36		4 57	6 4	6 33	7 29			8 22	9 29		8 14
	Ryburgh	7 55	9 28		11 51		2 11		4 43		5 4	6 11	6 40	7 36			8 29	9 36		8 21
	Fakenham	8 0	9 34		11 57		2 19		4B49		5 10	6 16	6 48	7 42			8 35	9 42		8 27
	Walsingham		9 45		12 8		2 30		4 59		5 27		7 0	7 52			8 45	9 53		8 38
97	WELLS arr.		9 58		12 22		2 43		5 13		5 37		7 15	8 6			8 58	10 6		8 52

Ref. Page	UP TRAINS.	(Mondays only)	morn	morn (Mondays only)	morn (Not on Mondays)	(Via Forncett)	morn (Via Lynn)	morn		morn	(Via Forncett)	even	G even (Via Forncett)		J even	(Via Lynn)	even (Thursdays only)	even (From Peterborough and Lynn)	(Via Forncett)	even	even (From Lynn)	SUNDAYS even
98	WELLS dep.		6 15	7 15	8 5		8 5	9X5		10 0		12 50	1 58		3 25					5 58		5 0
	Walsingham		6 25	7 25	8 15		8 15	9X15		10 11		1 0	2 8		3 35					6 8		5 11
	Fakenham		6 35	7 35	8 25		8 25	9 38		10 21		1 10	2 30		3 46		5 10			6 18		5 22
	Ryburgh		6 40	7 40	8 30		8 30	9 43		10 26		1 15	2 35		3 51		5 15			6 23		5 27
	County School		6 47	7 47	8 38		8 38	9 50		10 33		1 22	2 42		3 58		5 22			6 30		5 34
	North Elmham		6 53	7 53	8 43		8 43	9 55		10 39		1 27	2 46		4 3		5 28			6 37		5 41
96	Dereham arr.		7 1	8 1	8 51		8 51	10 3		10 47		1 35	2 54		4 11		5 36	5 46		6 45	9 11	5 49
	Dereham dep.		7 4	8 4	9 1		9 3	10 8		10 50		1 40	2 57		4 17	4 41		5 51		6 51	9 16	5 53
	Yaxham		7 9	8 9				10 13		10 55		1 45			4 22					6 56		5 58
	Thuxton		7 15	8 15				10 19		11 1		1 51			4 28					7 2		6 4
	Hardingham		7 19	8 19	9 11			10 23		11 5		1 55			4 32			H		7 7	R	6 9
	Kimberley		7 24	8 24				10 28		11 10		2 0			4 37					7 12		6 14
	Wymondham arr.		7 30	8 30	9 20			10 31		11 16		2 6	3 13		4 43			6 7		7 18	9 32	6 20
78-82	Wymondham dep.	7 42	8 1	8 58		9 52			11 25	11 36	11 53	2 35	3 17		5W5				6 50	7 32	10 53	6 37
	Ely arr.		9 6	10 34			10 42			12 48		4 2			6 26					8 58	12 19	7 41
83	Lincoln "		10 57				12 17		2 21			8 7			9 53	8 7						
	Doncaster "		11 48				1 19		3 26			9 2			11 5	9 2						
	YORK "		12 35				2 12		4 25			9 54				9 54						
93	Peterborough "		10 5	11 41			11 23		1 45			5 53			7 28	6 41					1 43	
78-82	Cambridge arr.		9 40	11 4			11 14			1 16		4 34			6 55					9 27	12 45	8 11
132	Ipswich "	9 4				11 54					1 16		4 47		8 35				8 35			
78-82 & 132	LONDON (St. Pancras "		11 15	1 50			1 50			2 43		6 10			8 35					+		9 44
	LONDON (Liverpool St. "	10 45	11 10	12 40		2 25	12 40			2 49		6 6	6 40		8 26						3 0	9 37
74 to 77	Wymondham dep.		7 35	8 34	9 22			10 39		11 19		2 8		3 27	4 46			6 9		7 21	9 35	6 23
	Hethersett		7 43	8 43	B			10 48		11 27		2 16		3 36	4 54			L		7 29		6 32
	Trowse		7 52	8 51	9 37			10 59		11 37		2 26		3 46	5 4			6 24		7 39	9 50	6 42
	NORWICH (Thorpe) arr.		7 57	8 56	9 42			11 7		11 42		2 31		3 50	5 9			6 29		7 44	9 56	6 47
103	Cromer arr.		10 0	10 0				12 13		2 9		4 56		4 56	6 58			7 42		8 48		7 45
101	Lowestoft (Central) "		10P2	10P3	11K14			12 13		2 31		5M19		5 19	6 36			7 54		10 17		8 30
	Yarmouth (Vaux.) "		8 53	9 57	10 30			12 8		1 8		4V50		4 50	6 13			7 18		8 50	10 47	8 34

NOTES.

A Arrives at Fakenham at 2.17 p.m.

B Calls at Hethersett at 9.30 a.m. when required to take up Passengers.

CC Calls at Hethersett at 8.29 a.m. on Tuesdays when required to take up Passengers.

D During October will leave Cromer 5.45 p.m.

E Commencing 2nd November will leave Yarmouth at 9.15 a.m.

F Calls at Yaxham at 8.0 p.m. on Mondays when required to set down Passengers.

G Passengers for Trowse, Norwich, Cromer, Yarmouth, and Lowestoft by this Train change at Wymondham.

H Horses and Private Carriages not conveyed by these Trains.

J Horses and Private Carriages are not conveyed by this Train for Stations between Wymondham and London.

K To Lowestoft on Mondays only, and will run during October only.

L Calls at Hethersett at 6.16 p.m. on Tuesdays when required to set down Passengers.

M On Saturdays arrives at Lowestoft 4.32 p.m.

N From Lowestoft on Saturdays only.

P During October will arrive at Lowestoft 9.55 a.m.

R Calls at Thuxton at 9.23 p.m. when required to set down Passengers from March and Stations beyond.

S Fakenham Market.—On Thursdays this Train will leave Fakenham for Wells at 5.0 p.m.

T On Saturdays leaves Cromer at 2.51 p.m.

U On Saturdays leaves Cromer at 5.24 p.m.

V On Mondays, Thursdays, and Saturdays during October will arrive at 3.30 p.m.

W On Saturdays leaves Wymondham at 5.21 p.m.

X From Wells and Walsingham on Saturdays only.

Y During October will leave Cromer at 8.50 a.m.

Z On Saturdays leaves Cromer at 5.52 p.m.

Train services on the Norwich–Dereham–Wells line, as shown on the 1908 GER public timetable; note that the 8.05 am up service from Wells divided at Dereham – one portion going on to Wymondham while the other worked through to Kings Lynn. Study of the timetable between Kings Lynn and Dereham, the basic times of arrival and departure being as shown below:

DOWN

		am	am	pm	pm	pm	pm	pm
Kings Lynn	dep.	8.06	8.51	12.30	3.11	4.53	5.43	8.18
Dereham	arr.	8.55	9.52	1.33	4.07	5.46	6.40	9.13

UP

					TO				
		am	am	am	am	pm	pm	pm	pm
Dereham	dep.	7.08	9.03	10.14	11.30	1.52	4.21	4.41	7.47
Kings Lynn	arr.	8.03	9.52	11.15	12.30	2.48	5.17	5.30	8.45

TO = Tuesdays Only

The Wymondham to Dereham line was served by eight or nine trains in each direction, including two up and two down through workings to or from Kings Lynn and a limited number of services between Wells-next-the-Sea and Forncett. The latter trains continued southwards over the Ashwellthorpe cut-off line, and travellers for Norwich were advised to change at Wymondham.

For people wishing to travel from Dereham to London the Forncett line provided some reasonably-timed services – the 'best' train being an early afternoon working from Wells which ran non-stop between Dereham and Wymondham and reached Forncett by 3.08 pm. This service connected with the 2.55 pm express from Norwich, and allowed through travellers to reach London by the early evening.

With luck, the through journey between Dereham and London could be accomplished in about 3¾ hours on the Dereham–Forncett–Chelmsford route; the 1908 timetable, for example, reveals that a traveller leaving Dereham on the 2.57 pm to Forncett would arrive at Liverpool Street by 6.40 pm. However, similar timings could be achieved via the Kings Lynn route; for instance, the 7.08 am from Dereham provided a connection at Kings Lynn with the 8.28 am (ex-Hunstanton) restaurant car express to London. This service reached Liverpool Street by 10.56 am – giving an overall journey time between Dereham and London of 3 hours 48 minutes.

It should, perhaps, be stressed that the number of people wishing to travel from Dereham to London would have been comparatively small, and although many Edwardian businessmen and professional people regularly commuted to and from north Norfolk and London, these gentlemen tended to live in prosperous residential resort towns such as Cromer or Hunstanton. The Hunstanton branch was, indeed, an important commuter route in the days before World War I, and for this reason the Hunstanton–Kings Lynn–London route was served by some of the Great Eastern's most prestigious business expresses. The Lynn & Dereham route, in contrast, remained primarily a local branch throughout its life, and none of the small towns and villages served by the line developed as residential centres during the Great Eastern or LNER eras.

Many of the passenger bookings between Kings Lynn, Dereham and Wymondham were merely for short distance journeys to Kings Lynn or Norwich, though (in common with all Victorian and Edwardian railways) the line was also used by people wishing to make occasional or 'one-off' journeys to more distant destinations. In this context it is important to remember that railways were the only form of long distance land transport available for passenger traffic; motoring was in its infancy during the early 1900s, and for this reason commercial travellers, businessmen, and a whole range of travellers who would today travel by motor car travelled by rail as a matter of course. There were also, in those days, groups of more exotic passengers such as travelling concert parties, music hall performers and circus entertainers – all of whom needed rail transport as part of their everyday working life. With large numbers of young women and girls in domestic service the Victorian and Edwardian railways were widely used by servants travelling home on their rare days off (or perhaps moving to new jobs in some distant part of the country). Soldiers used the railways when travelling to or from leave, while the rifle or artillery 'volunteers' (of which there were many in the 19th century) needed a means of transport to and from their summer training camps.

Mention of the volunteers serves as a reminder that Victorian England had been a land at peace. The struggle against Napoleonic France had culminated in the great victory at Waterloo in 1815, and, thereafter, the United Kingdom had no real enemies. Wars were small in scale and fought in remote and distant places such as the Sudan, Afghanistan or the Crimea; there was simply no need for Britain to pay for a large national army, and in these happy circumstances the Victorians had maintained a small professional force of about 180,000 men. By European standards this force was diminutive, though in time of war or other emergency it could be swelled by the calling up of volunteer and militia units (the predecessors of the Territorial Army).

The Boer War of 1899–1902 tested the army to its limit, no less than a quarter of a million men being mobilised to defeat just 30,000 Boer irregulars. The railways were kept busy throughout this period, and the site of khaki-clad soldiers soon became a familiar sight at stations such as Swaffham, Wendling and Dereham. A few years later, in August 1914, stations throughout the land were again thronged with men in khaki – on this occasion, however, the railways were called upon to transport men, horses and equipment to the horrific battlefields of an immeasureably greater conflict.

World War One

On 4th August, 1914, the German army invaded neutral Belgium, and in response to this brutal and entirely unprovoked attack on a small and inoffensive country the British government declared war on the aggressors; the ensuing conflict cost 1,114,789 British lives – and ended for ever the settled, Edwardian world in which railways such as the Lynn & Dereham line had quietly flourished.

With motor transport in its infancy, the railways were needed to rush hastily-mobilised men to the front, and the whole system was immediately placed on a war footing. Government control was enforced at the very start of the war, a Railway Executive Committee being formed to direct railway operations on the British mainland (Irish railways were not brought into government control until 1st January, 1917).

In common with other East Anglian lines, the Kings Lynn to Norwich route was intimately connected with the war by reason of its geographical position on the North Sea coast. It was thought that the outcome of the struggle against Imperial Germany would be decided by a sudden attack on the flat beaches and open spaces of East Anglia. For this reason Norfolk was heavily garrisoned throughout the 1914–18 war, not only by soldiers but also by naval airmen of the Royal Naval Air Service, who were stationed at several makeshift aerodromes along the supposedly-threatened coast.

On 3rd November, 1914, German warships ineffectively shelled Great Yarmouth, but in the event the main threat to East Anglia came, not from the sea, but from the air. With the opposing armies bogged down on the Western Front the German High Command hoped that their new weapons – the gas filled airships invented by Count Ferdinand von Zeppelin – could be used to strike a series of blows against the British homeland. Accordingly, on the night of 19th January, 1915 Zeppelin No. L4 nosed its sinister way inland, and having dropped three bombs in a field near Hunstanton the raider released four more high explosive bombs above Kings Lynn. This first aerial attack on England resulted in the deaths of two people, and a further 14 civilians were injured.

Further airship raids followed at intervals throughout the war. On 31st January, 1916, for example, Zeppelin L20 crossed the North Sea coast near Sheringham, and after wandering aimlessly around the countryside it eventually dropped its bomb load on an East Midlands town. In the following August an airship dropped an incendiary bomb on Wroxham, and in a subsequent raid on the night of 2nd–3rd September, 1916 a large force of Zeppelins raided eastern England, dropping their bombs in random patterns over a wide area.[36]

It remains a matter of conjecture why the German airship commanders should have expended their lethal cargoes in such a wasteful fashion, but the most plausible explanation is that they were simply lost! Lacking navigational aids for accurate night operations, the airships were forced to rely on dead reckoning, chart reading and other traditional methods. However, the British defenders soon realised that the enemy aviators were relying on visual navigation, and a strict blackout was quickly imposed as a means of further confusing the nocturnal raiders. Furthermore, as the British air defence measures became more sophisticated the Zeppelins were forced to fly at hitherto unknown altitudes of 20,000 ft or more; this took them well above the ceilings obtainable by pursuing aeroplanes, but at the same time the raiders were unable to spot their targets, and navigation became a matter of complete guesswork.

For these reasons the Zeppelin offensive was only partly effective – although the psychological effect produced by the raiders may (in German minds) have justified their employment as a 'Terror' weapon against civilian targets. The Great Eastern Railway was, from 1915 onwards, called upon to play an important role in the anti-Zeppelin campaign. Railways made good landmarks for Zeppelin navigators – especially on moonlit nights when the burnished rails provided a reflective path for the raiders. Signal lights were used by the enemy for sighting purposes, the clusters of red and blue-green lights at important junctions such as Kings Lynn or Ely being particularly noticeable from the air. To mitigate this problem signals lights were fitted with hooded shields which masked them from the air without obscuring them from the ground. Railwaymen were also expected to keep a sharp look for nightly raiders, and when a 'Zepp' was spotted its position was immediately telegraphed to London. With reports coming in from every station on an airship's path it was possible for a clear picture of the enemy's movements to be built-up, and this information was of vital importance to defending aircraft – which could be sent up to intercept the vulnerable airships before they returned to their bases across the North Sea.

Zeppelin raids continued until the end of the war, and the Kings Lynn to Norwich line was often involved in these raids. On the night of 19th–20th October, 1917, for instance, three German airships crossed the North Sea coast between Cromer and Wells-next-the-Sea. One of the raiders parted company with its companions near County School and, flying southwards towards Dereham, it then dropped at least three bombs on the blacked-out countryside between Dereham and Hardingham before turning east towards Norwich.

Meanwhile, the Kings Lynn to Norwich route was continuing to play an active part in the war effort, and in addition to transporting large quantities of men and equipment, the line was patrolled, on several occasions, by an armoured train. Based upon the kind of armoured trains that had been used in the Boer War, this unusual ensemble consisted of a Great Northern Railway 0–6–2T locomotive marshalled between two bogie infantry vehicles (adapted from Great Western Railway 40 ton coal wagons) and two gun-carrying vehicles. The train was protected by armour-plating, and for offensive armament it was equipped with rapid-firing Maxim machine guns and naval-type 12-pounders.

The armoured train was stationed, for much of the war, at North Walsham, from where it regularly patrolled the jointly-owned Great Eastern–Midland & Great Northern coastal line between Cromer and Mundesley-on-Sea. However, for security reasons it was felt that regular patrols should sometimes be interrupted, and for this reason the train occasionally visited other GER or M&GNJR lines such as the Wells-next-the-Sea or Lynn & Dereham routes.

In physical terms, the Great War produced few obvious changes on the Kings Lynn to Norwich route, although deferred maintenance and lack of regular cleaning had an adverse effect on the once-smart Great Eastern Railway locomotives. Some engines retained their royal blue liveries throughout the war, but, as an economy measure, the GER started to paint many of its locomotives in an austere, dark grey colour scheme that needed less cleaning and polishing than the flamboyant colour schemes of earlier years.

There appear to have been few alterations in terms of trackwork or other infrastructure on the Lynn & Dereham or Dereham to Norwich routes, though one or two minor changes were effected at Dereham and elsewhere. In February 1916, for example, a new siding was installed on the direct west-to-south curve at Dereham,[37] while in May 1917 the junction arrangements at Wymondham (north end) were altered.[38]

Apart from these minor alterations, the most significant result of the Great War concerned the staffing of stations, goods yards, motive power depots and other departments. The struggle against Germany and its allies called for vast increases in the size of Britain's armed forces, and as casualties on the Western Front mounted inexorably, more and more men were needed to fill the places of those who had been killed or maimed. Railwaymen were exempted from conscription when that measure was introduced in 1916, but large numbers of men from the GER (and other companies) willingly volunteered for service in HM forces. Many others had been pre-war reservists – and these individuals were of course among the first to go into action.

With so many men serving in the war, the Great Eastern was obliged to employ female staff in jobs that had hitherto been regarded as men's work, and in this capacity several female booking clerks served on the Lynn & Dereham line during the four years of conflict. Older man were brought out of retirement while, in a further attempt to keep stations fully staffed, elderly employees were allowed to remain in Great Eastern service long after their normal retirement dates; one of these veteran railwaymen was porter William Ellis, who continued working at Dunham station although he was over 70 years old (*see Chapter Five*).

The Great War ended on 11th November, 1918, but sadly, the cost of victory had been appalling, not only in financial but also in human terms. No town, village or hamlet was spared, and the long lists of names on countless war memorials remain to this day as mute reminders of those who died in the so-called 'War to End Wars'.

A number of local railwaymen died in the war, including John Neale, who had worked as a porter at Dunham and Wroxham prior to joining the Norfolk Regiment, and Harry Minns who had also joined the Norfolk Regiment after working as a porter at Dunham and elsewhere; John Neale was killed in action on 29th September, 1918. Another local casualty was porter-gateman Edwin Ward of Swaffham, who died of wounds in October 1918 while serving with the Royal Field Artillery. Several Dereham-based railwaymen were killed in the war, together with significant numbers of men from Kings Lynn, Norwich and other local GER stations.

The Last Years of the GER

World War One left all railways in a run-down condition, and recovery was not helped by a damaging coal strike in 1920–21. In spite of these problems, the Kings Lynn to Dereham and Norwich route was still served by about half a dozen trains each way between Kings Lynn and Dereham, and eight workings each way on the eastern portion of the line between Dereham and Norwich.

Examination of the 1921 GER passenger timetable reveals that there were, at that time, seven up and six down trains on the Lynn & Dereham section, together with eight trains in each direction between Dereham and Norwich. The Wells branch was served by five up and six down trains between Wells, Dereham and Norwich, and all of these workings connected with Kings Lynn services at Dereham. There was one through train in each direction on weekdays, with an additional Kings Lynn to Norwich service on Saturdays only; the weekday train left Norwich at 3.09 pm and reached Kings Lynn at 5.23 pm, while in the reverse direction the corresponding down service departed from Kings Lynn at 8.50 pm and reached Norwich by 10.33 pm.

The timings in force in 1921 were similar to those in 1911, the basic times of arrival and departure being as follows:

DOWN				SO				
		am	am	am	pm	pm	pm	pm
Kings Lynn	dep.	7.15	9.03	10.18	12.15	3.06	5.32	8.50
Dereham	arr.	8.18	10.04	11.12	1.17	4.05	6.34	9.47
Dereham	dep.	8.23	10.13	11.20	1.38	4.11	6.42	9.52
Norwich	arr.	9.16	11.10	*12.04*	2.33	5.04	7.41	10.33

UP								SO	
		am	am	am	am	pm	pm	pm	pm
Norwich	dep.	6.17	7.52	8.20	10.35	12.59	3.09	3.54	6.22
Dereham	arr.	7.12	8.46	9.05	11.30	1.52	4.09	4.38	7.17
Dereham	dep.	7.22	8.51	9.10	11.43	1.57	4.17	4.55	7.23
Kings Lynn	arr.	8.23	9.40	10.10	12.42	2.56	*5.23*	5.57	8.22

SO = Saturdays Only

The Sunday service consisted of one train in each direction between Norwich, Dereham and Wells-next-the-Sea – though, as in previous years, there were no Sunday workings on the Lynn & Dereham section between Kings Lynn and Dereham.

Motive power, at the end of the Great Eastern period, consisted mainly of Holden's 'T26' class 2–4–0s, which had replaced the veteran 'No. 1 class' engines in the years preceding World War One. The 'T26s' had 5 ft 8 in. coupled wheels and 17½ in. × 24 in. inside cylinders. Introduced in 1891, the 'T26' class engines were built at Stratford, and the class eventually totalled 100 engines. Numerous members of the class worked on the Kings Lynn to Norwich route at various times, though the regular engines, at the end of World War One, included the following examples:

Shedded at Norwich (sub sheds at Yarmouth, Dereham, Cromer, etc):
438/440/441/442/443/445/446/447/448/449/450/452/487/488/489/490/491/492/493/494/495/496

Shedded at Kings Lynn (sub sheds at Hunstanton etc):
477/478/479/480/481/482

The Norwich-based engines worked local services to Cromer and Great Yarmouth as well as those to Wells-next-the-Sea, while the six Kings Lynn-based locomotives were employed mainly on the Lynn & Dereham and Hunstanton routes.[39]

Goods services were typically worked by Worsdell 'Y14' class 0–6–0s. These engines had first been introduced in 1883, and although designed primarily for goods duties, they were also used on mixed traffic duties. The 'Y14s' had 17½ in. × 24 in. inside cylinders and 4 ft 11 in. coupled wheels. Some of the 'Y14' 0–6–0s had higher-pitched boilers than their companions, though the 81 high boiler engines were usually regarded as part of the all-embracing 'Y14' class.

Larger engines such as the famous GER 'Claud Hamilton' 4–4–0s may have appeared on long distance excursion duties, but in general the 'T26' 2–4–0s and 'Y14' class 0–6–0s seem to have been the types most widely used on the Kings Lynn to Norwich route at the very end of the Great Eastern period.

Tank engines, in the form of Holden 5 ft 8 in. 2–4–2Ts, had started to appear on the Kings Lynn to Hunstanton and Norwich to Wells-next-the-Sea routes towards the end of World War One, and it is likely that these large 2–4–2Ts also worked – at least occasionally – on the Lynn & Dereham route around 1918–23. Designed originally for main line stopping services, the 5 ft 8 in. tanks were mechanically similar to the 'T26' 2–4–0s, having the same 17½ in. × 24 in. cylinders and 5 ft 8 in. coupled wheels.

Another class which may have appeared around 1920 were the Holden 'T19' 2–4–0s, some of which had been rebuilt with leading bogies to become 4–4–0s. However, these 'large' engines were comparatively rare on the Kings Lynn to Norwich line during the later GER and early LNER periods, and their occasional forays from Kings Lynn or Norwich caused considerable excitement among youthful 'spotters'!

Rebuilt 'T19' class engine No. 8029, seen at Kings Lynn on 27th May, 1937; in LNER days these locomotives were designated class 'D13'. These engines were originally 2–4–0s, and they first appeared in the Dereham area around 1920. *H.C. Casserley*

Rebuilt Great Eastern 'T19' class 2–4–0 (as LNER 'D13' class 4–4–0) No. 7756 is prepared for duty at Kings Lynn shed on 30th June, 1936. 'Claud Hamilton' 4–4–0 No. 8792 can be seen to the right. *H.C. Casserley*

Worsdell 'J15' class 0–6–0 No. 5470 stands beside the engine shed at Kings Lynn on 15th April, 1947. These locomotives were widely used for freight work throughout East Anglia. *H.C. Casserley*

Chapter Four

The London & North Eastern Railway Period (1923–1947)

In Victorian days, successive governments had resisted calls for large-scale railway amalgamation on the grounds that competition would (in theory) lead to greater efficiency. In 1909, for example, the Great Northern, Great Eastern and Great Central companies had sought Powers for an amalgamation, but Parliament refused to countenance such a union, and the scheme was rejected in its entirety. Official opposition to railway amalgamations lessened considerably after World War One, and in 1921 Parliament itself imposed a comprehensive 'grouping' scheme – this measure being seen as an alternative to outright nationalisation. Thus, on 1st January, 1923, the Great Eastern Railway found itself forced into a union with the Great Northern, Great Central, North British, Great North of Scotland and other companies – the resulting East Coast group being known as The London & North Eastern Railway.

Effects of the Grouping

For administrative purposes the Great Eastern, Great Northern and Great Central systems became the LNER Southern Area, and this geographically-distinct area was placed under its own General Manager. Otherwise, the former Great Eastern system was left more or less undisturbed, and ordinary travellers would probably have been blissfully unaware that a significant change of ownership had in fact taken place!

The one obvious change put into effect in the months following the 1923 grouping concerned the liveries of locomotives and rolling stock. Each of the 'Big Four' companies was keen to foster a distinctive corporate image, and railway enthusiasts were soon able to enjoy the spectacle of familiar locomotive types appearing in a range of new and unexpected liveries. The London Midland & Scottish group, for instance quickly adopted a Midland Railway-style red livery for its engines and passenger vehicles, and this striking colour scheme was soon being applied to former London & North Western and Lancashire & Yorkshire locomotives (which had been painted black in the pre-grouping era). The Great Western revived its traditional chocolate and cream coach livery,[40] while the Southern group introduced an overall green coach livery. These changes placed the LNER in a difficult position in that, with overall red or green already selected by other companies, the East Coast group would need to find some other colour for its passenger rolling stock. Great Northern-style varnished teak was therefore adopted as the LNER standard coach livery, and by this means the desired corporate identity was maintained.

Unfortunately, GER coaches had been painted crimson in the immediate pre-grouping period, and it was very difficult to restore these painted vehicles to a varnished wood finish. Similar problems were experienced with former North Eastern and North British railway vehicles (which had also been painted red), and for this reason most LNER coaches were painted in a drab overall brown livery which was sometimes known as 'teak brown';

The Worsdell 'Y14' class 0–6–0s (later LNER class 'J15') worked on local freight duties in the Norfolk area for many years. No. 5367 was photographed by Mr Casserley at Kings Lynn on 15th April, 1947. *H.C. Casserley*

Ex-Great Eastern 'E4' class 2–4–0 No. 7477 simmers gently at Kings Lynn on 27th May, 1937. The long shed visible in the background housed the LNER Royal Train. *H.C. Casserley*

true 'varnished teak' (either real or 'scrumbled') was confined, in the main, to new or main line passenger rolling stock.

The coaches used on local services between Norwich, Dereham and Kings Lynn were still exclusively six-wheelers, but as new bogie stock was progressively introduced during the 1920s and 1930s displaced North Eastern Railway vehicles began to appear in increasing numbers on East Anglian local services. This process was, nevertheless, spread out over many years, and in 1934 it was reported that the LNER owned 54 per cent of the non-bogie stock operated by the 'Big Four' companies. Two years later, in June 1936, a survey published in *The Railway Magazine* revealed that the LNER was still operating 2,596 six-wheel coaches and 310 four-wheelers out of a total carriage fleet of 11,066 vehicles.[41]

A small change initiated under LNER auspices concerned the system of class notation used for locomotives. A new, standardised system was introduced, and this system was both logical and simple in that large Pacific engines became 'As', 4–6–0s became 'Bs', 4–4–2s became 'Cs', 4–4–0 engines received a 'D' prefix, and so on. As there was usually more than one engine type with a particular wheel arrangement these basic notations were further sub-divided by the addition of numerals denoting each class. As far as the Lynn & Dereham route was concerned the rebuilt 'T19s' became LNER class 'D13', the 'T26' 2–4–0s became class 'E4', Worsdell's 'Y14' 0–6–0s became LNER class 'J15', and Holden's 5 ft 8 in. 2–4–2Ts became class 'F3'.

The above-mentioned locomotive classes remained hard at work on the Kings Lynn to Norwich route during the mid- to late-1920s, together with a variety of other types including former GER 'J17' 0–6–0s, and 'Claud Hamilton' 4–4–0s.

In LNER days, local passenger and freight locomotives were painted in an overall black colour scheme, and although the company adopted an attractive apple green livery for large main line engines, this green livery was not applied to engines with driving wheels of less than 6 ft 6 in. diameter. Most of the engines employed on the routes between Norwich, Dereham, Wells and Kings Lynn were, therefore, painted in black livery during the LNER period, and this sombre colour scheme did little to enhance the drab brown coach livery that had been adopted by the London & North Eastern Railway.

Train Services in the LNER Era

The train service provided during the LNER period was similar to that provided at the end of the Great Eastern period. There were normally around half a dozen trains each way between Kings Lynn and Dereham, with a similar number on the eastern portion of the line between Norwich and Dereham. The Norwich to Dereham services continued through to Wells-next-the-Sea, while some Kings Lynn to Dereham trains worked through to Norwich or Yarmouth; good connections were provided between the Kings Lynn and Wells routes at Dereham, and some workings conveyed portions for both Kings Lynn and Wells-next-the-Sea.

In July 1925 the Kings Lynn to Dereham section was served by six up and

'Claud Hamilton' 4–4–0 No. 2558 shunts passenger stock at Kings Lynn on 15th April, 1947. The engine shed is visible in the background. *H.C. Casserley*

Immaculate 'Claud Hamilton' 4–4–0 No. 8792 stands outside the engine shed at Kings Lynn on 30th June, 1936. *H.C. Casserley*

six down trains, with up workings from Dereham at 7.22, 9.06, 11.33 am, 1.57, 4.16 and 7.36 pm and down services from Kings Lynn at 7.15, 9.00 am, 12.32, 3.09, 5.28 and 8.54 pm. On Saturdays, an additional up train left Dereham at 4.50 pm, and an extra down service departed from Kings Lynn at 10.20 am. At least two up and one down trains ran to or from Norwich, and the remaining services connected with Norwich workings at Dereham.

The July 1932 timetable was similar to its 1925 predecessor, with a basic pattern of operation involving six up and six down workings between Kings Lynn and Dereham. As in 1925, some of these services were in fact through workings, and although the remaining trains started or terminated their journeys at Dereham, the connecting Wells–Dereham–Norwich workings ensured that through travellers were able to reach a range of destinations beyond Dereham.

The main services in the up direction from Dereham in July 1932 were as follows:

Time of Dep.	*From*	*To*
7.22 am	Dereham	March via Kings Lynn
9.06 am	Yarmouth	Peterborough North via Kings Lynn
11.33 am	Dereham	Kings Lynn
2.02 pm	Norwich Thorpe	Kings Lynn
4.16 pm	Yarmouth Vauxhall	Doncaster Central via Kings Lynn
7.33 pm	Dereham	Kings Lynn

In the down direction, corresponding services left Kings Lynn at the following times:

Time of Dep.	*From*	*To*
7.15 am	Kings Lynn	Dereham
9.00 am	Kings Lynn	Dereham
12.35 pm	Kings Lynn	Dereham
3.09 pm	Kings Lynn	Dereham
5.40 pm	Kings Lynn	Dereham
8.50 pm	Peterborough North	Yarmouth Vauxhall via Dereham

Additional trains ran on Tuesdays and Saturdays, and it is interesting to note that the extra Tuesday services were worked by a Sentinel steam railcar. This vehicle (which also worked on the Wells-next-the-Sea branch) left Dereham at 1.33 pm and arrived in Kings Lynn at 3.02 pm; at 3.30 pm the steam car returned to Dereham, and having reached the latter station at 4.32 pm, the vehicle then reversed in the branch bay in order to form the 4.34 pm (TO) service to Norwich Thorpe.

As a general rule, most Kings Lynn to Dereham trains accomplished the 26½ mile journey in about one hour, while through services to Norwich usually took a little over two hours for their 48½ mile journeys. Sunday services were not provided on the Lynn & Dereham line, but there was, for many years, a service of one up and one down Sunday train on the Norwich to Wells-next-the-Sea route, and these workings called intermediately at Kimberley, Hardingham and the other stations between Wymondham and Dereham.

KING'S LYNN AND DEREHAM.

WEEKDAYS

Page				SO	SO				
		a.m.	a.m.	a.m.	a.m.	a.m.	a.m.	p.m.	p.m.
211	**LONDON** (Liverpool St.) ... dep.	...	...	5 50	...	8 30	11 50	2 34	5 49
	Cambridge — — — „	—	—	8 12	—	10 6	1 24	4 4	7 21
	Ely .... „	...	...	...	8D55	10 36	1 48	4 27	7 50
	King's Lynn — — — arr.	—	—	9 34	10D17	11 16	2 39	5 10	8 42
211	Peterborough (East) .... dep.	...	7 5	...	...	9 24	1 10	3 34	7 15
	March — — — „	—	7 35	—	9 34	10 6	1 54	4 5	7 44
	Wisbech .... „	...	7 52	...	9 50	10 23	2 12	4 19	7 59
	King's Lynn — — — arr.	—	8 25	—	10 17	10 59	2 46	4 53	8 32
216	Hunstanton .... dep.	...	7 50	...	8 46	10R58	2 25	4 43	8 10
	King's Lynn — — — arr.	—	8 27	—	9 23	11R36	3 3	5 20	8 46
	KING'S LYNN .... dep.	7 15	9 0	...	1020	12 32	3 9	5 28	8 54
	Middleton Towers — — — „	7 22	9 7	—	—	12 39	3 16	5 35	9 1
	East Winch .... „	7 27	9 12	...		12 44	3 21	5 41	9 6
	Narborough and Pentney — — „	7 35	9 19	—	10 36	12 51	3 28	5 48	9 13
	Swaffham A .... „	7 52	9 35	...	10 49	1 5	3 42	6 4	9 27
	Dunham — — — „	8 0	9 43	—	10 58	1 13	3 50	6 12	9 35
	Fransham .... „	8 4	9 47	...		1 17	3 54	6 16	
	Wendling — — — „	8 10	9 53	—	11 6	1 23	4 0	6 22	B
	DEREHAM .... arr.	8 17	10 0	...	1113	1 30	4 7	6 29	9 50
218	Dereham — — — dep.	9 9	11 34	...	11 34	1 56	4H21	7 33	—
	Wells-on-Sea .... arr.	10 0	12 24	...	12 24	2 47	5H10	8 23	
218	Dereham — — — dep.	8 23	10 9	—	11 18	1 38	4 13	6F45	9 55
	Wymondham .... arr.	8 49	10 39	...	...	2 4	4 39	7F17	10 16
	Norwich (Thorpe) — — — „	9 13	11 5	—	12 0	2 30	5 5	7F41	10 38

WEEKDAYS

Page									SO	
		a.m.	a.m.	a.m.	p.m.	p.m.	p.m.	p.m.	p.m.	p.m.
218	Norwich (Thorpe) .... dep.	6 19	8 17	10 35	...	12 59	...	3 9	3 54	6 31
	Wymondham — — — „	6 46	8 42	11 2	—	1 25	—	3 38	4 15	6 58
	Dereham .... arr.	7 14	9 2	11 29	...	1 52	...	4 9	4 42	7 29
218	Wells-on-Sea — — — dep.	5MO55	7 28	9 6	...	12 48	...	3 13	—	5K43
	Dereham .... arr.	6MO40	8 19	10 3	...	1 35	...	4 3	...	6K39
	DEREHAM — — — dep.	7 22	9 6	11 33	—	1 57	—	4 16	4 50	7 36
	Wendling .... „	7 30	9 14	11 41	...	2 5	...	4 25	4 58	7 44
	Fransham — — — „	7 36	9 20	11 47	—	2 11	—	4 31	5 4	7 50
	Dunham .... „	7 41	9 25	11 52	...	2 16	...	4 36	5 9	7 55
	Swaffham A — — — „	7 51	9 34	12 1	—	2 25	—	4 46	5 19	8 4
	Narborough and Pentney .... „	8 2	9 44	12 11	...	2 35	...	4 57	5 29	8 14
	East Winch — — — „	8 10	9 52	12 19	—	2 43	—	5 8	5 40	8 22
	Middleton Towers .... „	8 15	9 57	12 24	...	2 48	...	5 13	5 45	8 27
	KING'S LYNN — — — arr.	8 22	10 4	12 31	—	2 57	—	5 23	5 52	8 34
216	King's Lynn .... dep.	8 36	10 22	12SO38	1N19	3 20	...	6N16	6N16	8 47
	Hunstanton — — — arr.	9 12	10 57	1 SO15	1N54	3 56	—	6N51	6N51	9 22
211	King's Lynn .... dep.	8 45	10 9	1 52	...	3E12	4 15	5 37	7 9	10 25
	Wisbech — — — arr.	9 17	10 34	2 25	—	—	4 48	6 11	7 41	10 56
	March .... „	9 35	10 47	2 43	...	4E39	...	6 31	8 2	11 12
	Peterborough (East) — — — „	10 4	11 12	3 18	—	5E12	—	7 25	9 3	1 17
213	King's Lynn .... dep.	8 34	10 25	1L41	...	3 12	...	5 30	7Z46	10D25
	Ely — — — arr.	9 27	11 16	—	—	4 7	—	6 21	8Z29	11D51
	Cambridge .... „	9 56	11 45	2L40	...	4 36	...	6X46	8Z59	12D45
	LONDON (Liverpool St.) — „	11 27	2 7	L	—	6 10	—	8X22	10Z30	2D50 a.m.

A For service between Swaffham and Thetford, see page 207.
B Calls at Wendling 9.43 p.m. to set down passengers only.
D Via March.
E Via Ely.
F On Saturdays leaves Dereham 6.56 and arrives Wymondham 7.27 and Norwich 7.51 p.m.
H On Saturdays leaves Dereham 4.46 and arrives Wells 5.37 p.m.

K On Saturdays leaves Wells 5.56 and arrives Dereham 6.50 p.m.
L Runs 20th July to 12th September inclusive. Arrives London (King's Cross) 4.10 p.m.
MO Mondays only.
N Third class only.
R On Wednesdays leaves Hunstanton 11.31 a.m. and arrives King's Lynn 12.10 p.m.

SO Saturdays only.
SX Saturdays excepted.
TO Tuesdays only.
X On Tuesdays, Wednesdays and Thursdays arrives Cambridge 7.0 and Liverpool Street 8.33 p.m.
Z Not after 12th September.

The 1925 LNER public timetable for the Lynn & Dereham section.

DEREHAM.

WORKING OF DOWN TRAINS.

Down passenger trains for Wells are to be brought to a stand at Dereham Station, with the front brake van of the Wells portion under the covered way. If the engine requires to take water, and the raised disc near the water tank on the down platform, applicable to engines drawing down the main line to the water column, has been turned to "Clear," the engine is to be detached and run ahead to the water column, the driver afterwards returning to his train with great care.

SIDINGS ADJOINING MESSRS. FISON & SON'S MALTINGS AND PREMISES.

When traffic is being loaded to and unloaded from trucks at these sidings, a red flag by day and a red light after dark is to be exhibited by Messrs. Fison's people, from the second story of the Malting, in such a manner as to be clearly visible to the shunters and others engaged in shunting operations.

Whenever a red flag or red light is exhibited, the greatest care must be exercised during shunting by all concerned, to prevent any vehicles running down on to those being loaded or unloaded, or on to any trucks standing on the siding immediately next the cattle pens, as the slightest movement of the trucks may result in personal injury.

SOUTH JUNCTION SIGNAL BOX.

Working of Bell during shunting operations.

A loud sounding bell is provided on a post about 100 yards on the Yaxham side of the Dereham South Junction Box.

The plunger, to sound this bell is fixed in a small box placed on a post near the signal applicable for leaving the siding and this bell is to be sounded by the man in charge of the shunting operations, in accordance with the following code :—

One sound	...	**"Move Forward."**
Two sounds	...	**"Move Back."**
Three sounds	...	**"Stop."**
Four sounds	...	**"Ease Couplings."**

Enginemen when shunting to or from the sidings and the shunting spur at Dereham South Junction must act on the sounds given on the bell.

The small box covering the plunger, when not in use, must be locked and the key kept in the signal box.

FRANSHAM.

The siding connections are worked from a ground locking frame and controlled by the tablet for the Wendling and Dunham section.

Whenever the siding connections are required to be used, the train tablet must be obtained from the driver by the man in charge of the shunting operations, who must place the tablet in the lock provided for that purpose in the signal box to enable the siding connections to be released.

After the shunting operations have been completed the lever in the signal box must be restored to its normal position and the train tablet handed back to the driver.

MIDDLETON.

The siding connections are worked from the signal box and controlled by the tablet for the King's Lynn and East Winch section.

Whenever the siding connections are required to be used, the train tablet must be obtained from the driver by the man in charge of the shunting operations, who must place the tablet in the lock provided for that purpose in the signal box to enable the siding connections to be released.

After the shunting operations have been completed the lever in the signal box must be restored to its normal position and the train tablet handed back to the driver.

An extract from an LNER Sectional Appendix showing operating instructions for freight traffic at Dereham, Fransham and Middleton.

DEREHAM, SWAFFHAM AND KING'S LYNN.

Single Line between Dereham West Junction and King's Lynn Junction.

UP — WEEK DAYS.

Miles from Dereham			1	2	3	4	5	6	7	8	9
			Trks.	Eng.	Pass.	H.B's &c.	Gds.	Pass.	Pass.	Gds.	
	from		4.20 a.m. ex Norwich.			District Supt. to arrange.		8.38 a.m. ex Thetford.	7.5 a.m. ex Yarmouth.	7.40 a.m. ex Dereham.	
	See page		36					31	36		
			WB	MFO		WR					
M. C.			a.m.	a.m.	a.m.	a.m.	a.m.	a.m.	a.m.	a.m.	
— —	Dereham	arr.	....	....	....	....	....	....	9 2	....	....
		dep.	—	6 50	7 22	—	7 40	—	9 6	—	—
— —	Dereham West Junc. Ⓣ	"	5 25	6 52	7 23	....	7 42	....	9 7	....	....
4 8	Wendling Ⓣ	arr.	—	—	7 29	—	7 50	—	9 13	—	—
		dep.	5 35	6 59	7 30	....	8 15	....	9 14	....	....
6 64	Fransham (NB)	"	—	—	7 36	—	* *	—	9 20	See	—
8 8	Dunham Ⓣ	arr.	....	....	7 40	....	8 45	....	9 24	Col.	....
		dep.	5 50	7 7	7 41	—	9 5	—	9 25	5	—
12 6	Swaffham Ⓣ	arr.	6 0	7 15	7 49	....	9 15	9 26	9 32	9 15	....
		dep.	6 30	—	7 51	8 10	9 50		9 34	9 50	—
17 71	Narboro' and Pentney Ⓣ	arr.	....	....	8 0	* *	See	....	9 43	10 5	....
		dep.	6 45	—	8 2	8 27	Col.	—	9 44	10 20	—
21 28	East Winch Ⓣ	arr.	....	....	8 9	* *	8	....	9 51	10 30	....
		dep.	6 55	—	8 10	8 39	—	—	9 52	10 45	—
23 29	Middleton Towers ... (NB)	arr.	....	....	8 14	* *	....	....	9 56	10 53	....
		dep.	—	—	8 15	8 48	—	—	9 57	11 5	—
— —	King's Lynn Junc. ... Ⓣ	"	7 10	....	8 21	8 56	....	....	10 3	11 16	....
26 44	King's Lynn	arr.	7 12	—	8 22	8 57	—	—	10 4	11 18	—
		dep.		....	8 44		....	....	10 9		....
	To				March.		King's Lynn.		Peterboro' North.		
	See page				28				28		

Station		10	11	12	13	14	15	16	17	18
		Pass.	Pass.	Gds.	Gds.	Stm. Car.	Pass.	Gds.	Pass.	Gds.
from			11.43 a.m. ex Thetford.				1.5 p.m. ex Norwich T.	2.15 p.m. ex Roudham Junc.	2.55 p.m. ex Thetford.	
See page			31				36	31	31	
				NS	SO	TO		SO		NS
		a.m.	p.m.	p.m.	p.m.	p.m.	p.m.	p.m.	p.m.	p.m.
Dereham	arr.	....	....	....	....	....	1 57	....	....	....
	dep.	11 33	—	—	—	1 32	2 2	—	—	2 30
Dereham West Junc.	"	11 34	....	....	....	1 33	2 3	....	....	2 32
Wendling	arr.	11 40	—	—	—	1 40	2 9	—	—	2 40
	dep.	11 41	....	....	....	1 41	2 10	....	....	3 6
Fransham	"	11 47	—	—	—	1 47	2 16	—	—	*
Dunham	arr.	11 51	....	....	....	1 51	2 20	....	....	3 40
	dep.	11 52	—	—	—	1 52	2 21	—	—	4 15
Swaffham	arr.	11 59	12 33	....	....	2 0	2 28	3 35	3 48	4 25
	dep.	12 1		—	—	2 1	2 30	4 0		7 45
Narboro' and Pentney	arr.	12 10	....	....	....	2 13	2 39	4 15	....	See
	dep.	12 11	—	—	—	2 14	2 40	4 35	—	Col.
East Winch	arr.	12 18	....	....	....	2 22	2 47	....	....	25
	dep.	12 19	—	1 0	1 30	2 23	2 48	4 45	—	—
Middleton Towers	arr.	12 23	....	1 5	1 35	2 27	2 52	....	....	....
	dep.	12 24	—	2 0	2 20	2 28	2 53	....	—	—
King's Lynn Junc.	"	12 30	....	2 10	2 28	2 34	3 1	4 58	....	....
King's Lynn	arr.	12 31	—	2 12	2 30	2 35	3 2	5 0	—	—
	dep.		....						....	....
To										To King's Lynn.

Station		19	20	21	22	23	24	25	26	27	28
		Pass.	Pass.	Gds.	Gds.	Pass.	Pass.	Gds.	Pass.	Pass.	
from		2.9 p.m. ex Yarmouth Vx.	3.55 p.m. ex Norwich T.	2.15 p.m. ex Roudham Junc.	12.50 p.m. ex Norwich.	5.33 p.m. ex Thetford.	5.33 p.m. ex Thetford.	2.30 p.m. ex Dereham.		8.50 p.m. ex Thetford.	
See page		37	37	31	36	31	31			31	
			SO	NS	SO	NW	WO	NS			
		p.m.	p.m.	p.m.	p.m.	p.m.	p.m.	p.m.	p.m.	p.m.	
Dereham	arr.	4 9	4 42	....	3 35	....	....	....	....	....	....
	dep.	4 16	4 47	—	4 25	—	—	—	7 33	—	—
Dereham West Junc.	"	4 17	4 48	....	4 27	....	....	....	7 34	....	....
Wendling	arr.	4 23	4 54	—	4 37	—	—	—	7 40	—	—
	dep.	4 24	4 55	....	5 20	....	....	....	7 41	....	....
Fransham	"	4 31	5 1	—	5 40	—	—	See	7 47	—	—
Dunham	arr.	4 35	5 5	....	5 45	....	....	Col.	7 51	....	....
	dep.	4 36	5 6	—	6 0	—	—	18	7 52	—	—
Swaffham	arr.	4 43	5 13	5 45	6 12	6 25	6 30	4 25	7 59	9 41	....
	dep.	4 46	5 15	6 15	6 50			7 45	8 1		—
Narboro' and Pentney	arr.	4 55	5 24	* *	7 8	....	....	8 0	8 10	....	....
	dep.	4 57	5 25	6 35	7 20	—	—	8 25	8 11	—	—
East Winch	arr.	5 4	5 32	* *	7 30	....	....	8 35	8 18	....	....
	dep.	5 6	5 33	6 55	7 45	—	—	9 10	8 19	—	—
Middleton Towers	arr.	5 10	5 37	* *	7 50	....	....	9 20	8 23	....	....
	dep.	5 11	5 38	—	8 0	—	—	9 28	8 24	—	—
King's Lynn Junc.	"	5 19	5 44	7 43	8 8	....	....	9 36	8 30	....	....
King's Lynn	arr.	5 20	5 45	7 45	8 10	—	—	9 38	8 31	—	—
	dep.	5 37				....	....			....	....
To		Doncaster Cent.									
See page		29									

5 Calls at Fransham to attach. Engine to perform shunting at Swaffham. 8 Calls Middleton to attach cattle and for brake goods only. —15 Allowed 2 minutes extra between Middleton Towers and King's Lynn for recovery. 16 Calls at Narboro' and Pentney to attach cattle for Tufnell Park, which is to be sent forward from King's Lynn by 8.20 p.m. train. 18 On Tuesdays to work down road traffic from Wendling, Fransham and Dunham into Swaffham, which is to be attached there to 5.50 p.m. ex King's Lynn. Engine to perform shunting at Swaffham. To work from Swaffham only empties including those off 2.15 p.m. ex Roudham Jc. and also sugar beet traffic from stations on the Dereham side of Swaffham. The empties to be kept together. —19 Due Fransham 4.29 p.m. 21 To work from Swaffham loaded traffic only, including that off 2.30 p.m. ex Dereham and call at Narboro', East Winch and Middleton to attach and for brake goods only. 22 Due Fransham 5.28 p.m. To shunt at Wendling for 20. To call at Middleton to detach empties for Boam & Co. 25 To shunt at Narboro' for 25. —26 May work fitted trucks of cattle from Dereham to King's Lynn.

The July 1932 Working Timetable for the Kings Lynn to Dereham line.

KING'S LYNN, SWAFFHAM AND DEREHAM.

Single Line between King's Lynn Junction and Dereham West Junction.

Miles from King's Lynn	DOWN. WEEK DAYS.		1	2	3	4	5	6	7	8	9	10	11	12	13	14
			Eng.	Gds. Class B		Pass.	Pass.	Gds.		Pass.	Pass.	Pass.	Gds. Class D	Eng. and Brke	Pass.	Pass.
	From															
	See page															
			MFO									SO	NTS	NS		WO
M. C.			a.m.	a.m.		a.m.	a.m.	a.m.		a.m.	a.m.	a.m.	a.m.	a.m.	p.m.	p.m.
— —	King's Lynn	arr.														
		dep.	—	5 15	—	—	7 15	7 45	—	9 0	—	10 23	11 55	11 55	12 35	—
— —	King's Lynn Junc. (T)	"		5 17			7 16	7 47		9 1		10 24	11 57	11 57	12 36	
3 15	Middleton Towers (NB)	arr.	—	—	—	—	7 21	—	—	9 6	—	—	—	—	12 41	—
		dep.					7 22			9 7					12 42	
5 16	East Winch (T)	arr.	—	—	—	—	7 26	8 5	—	9 11	—	—	12 15	12 15	12 46	—
		dep.		5 30			7 27	8 15		9 12		10 32	12 25		12 47	
8 53	Narboro' & Pentney (T)	arr.	—	—	—	—	7 34	8 25	—	9 18	—	10 38	12 35	—	12 53	—
		dep.		5 40			7 35	8 35		9 19		10 39	1 10		12 54	
14 38	Swaffham (T)	arr.	—	6 0	—	—	7 47	8 55	—	9 31	—	10 51	1 33	—	1 6	—
		dep.	6 0	6 10		7 30	7 52	10 15		9 35	10 5	10 52	1 50		1 8	1 17
18 36	Dunham (T)	arr.	—	* *	—	—	7 59	—	—	9 42	—	10 59	2 0	—	1 15	—
		dep.	6 8	6 25			8 0			9 43		11 0	2 30		1 16	
19 60	Fransham (NB)	"	—	—	—	—	8 4	—	—	9 47	—	—	* *	—	1 20	—
22 36	Wendling (T)	arr.		* *			8 9			9 52		11 7	2 51		1 25	
		dep.	6 16	6 40	—	—	8 10	—	—	9 53	—	11 8	3 20	—	1 26	—
— —	Dereham West Junc. (T)	"	6 23	6 48			8 16			9 59		11 14			1 32	
26 44	Dereham	arr.	6 25	6 50	—	—	8 17	—	—	10 0	—	11 15	3 30	—	1 33	—
		dep.										11 20				
	To			On Sats. runs to Norwich T.		Thetford.		Roudham Junc.			Thetford.	Norwich Thpe.				Thetford.
	See page			38		31		31			31	38				31

Miles from King's Lynn	DOWN. WEEK DAYS.		15	16	17	18	19	20	21	22	23	24	25	26	27	28
			Pass.	Eng & Brke.	Gds. Class D	Pass.		Stm. Car	Pass.	Pass.	Pass.	Gds. Class B	Pass.		Pass.	
	From														6.40 p.m. ex Peterboro' N.	
	See page														27	
			NW	SO	SO			TO		NS	SO	TO				
M. C.			p.m.	p.m.	p.m.	p.m.		p.m.	p.m.	p.m.	p.m.	p.m	p.m		p.m.	
— —	King's Lynn	arr.													8 33	
		dep.	—	12 45	12 45	3 9	—	3 30	—	5 40	5 50	5 50	—	—	8 50	—
— —	King's Lynn Junc. (T)	"		12 47	12 47	3 10		3 31		5 41	5 51	5 52			8 51	
3 15	Middleton Towers (NB)	arr.	—	—	* *	3 15	—	—	—	5 46	5 56	—	—	—	8 56	—
		dep.			1 10	3 16				5 47	5 57				8 57	
5 16	East Winch (T)	arr.	—	1 15	1 15	3 20	—	—	—	5 51	6 1	—	—	—	9 1	—
		dep.			1 25	3 21		3 42		5 52	6 2	6 0			9 2	
8 53	Narboro' & Pentney (T)	arr.	—	—	1 35	3 27	—	—	—	5 58	6 8	* *	—	—	9 8	—
		dep.			1 45	3 28		3 49		5 59	6 9	6 30			9 9	
14 38	Swaffham (T)	arr.	—	—	2 5	3 40	—	4 2	—	6 11	6 21	6 45	—	—	9 21	—
		dep.	1 30		2 29	3 42		4 3	4 10	6 13	6 23	7 0	7 10		9 23	
18 36	Dunham (T)	arr.	—	—	2 39	3 49	—	4 11	—	6 20	6 30	* *	—	—	9 30	—
		dep.			2 55	3 50		4 12		6 21	6 31	7 15			9 31	
19 60	Fransham (NB)	"	—	—	* *	3 54	—	—	—	6 26	6 35	—	—	—	* *	—
22 36	Wendling (T)	arr.			3 15	3 59		4 22		6 30	6 40	* *			* *	
		dep.	—	—	3 35	4 0	—	4 24	—	6 31	6 41	7 25	—	—	9 39	—
— —	Dereham West Junc. (T)	"			3 43	4 6		4 31		6 37	6 47	7 33			9 45	
26 44	Dereham	arr.	—	—	3 45	4 7	—	4 32	—	6 38	6 48	7 35	—	—	9 46	—
		dep.						4 34							9 51	
	To		Thetford.					Norwich Thp.	Thetford.				Thetford.		Yarmouth V.	
	See page		31					39	31				31		39	

2 When 4 up runs, King's Lynn to attach brake for same. To call at Dunham when required to detach or attach cattle. On Tues. may work traffic for Dunham & Wendling when required. To call at Wendling on Sats. to attach cattle for Trowse. To leave King's Lynn marshalled engine, Wells Line traffic, Aylsham Line traffic, South Dereham traffic brake. —8 No extra vehicles to be attached without District Supt's. authority. 11 To call at Fransham when reqd. to detach trucks or leave brk. gds. only. 12 Runs attached to 11 (NT). 16 Runs attached to 17. 17 To call at Middleton & Fransham when required to detach trucks or leave brk. gds. only. —18 May work from King's Lynn to Swaffham 3 piped trucks of cattle for Bury, to go forward on 21.

—22 On Tuesdays may work 2 piped trucks of cattle from King's Lynn to Swaffham. 24 To be worked by engine of 7.40 a.m. ex Dereham. To work cattle, also through traffic from King's Lynn to Swaffham and Dereham. Brake goods for Dunham to be loaded at King's Lynn into the Wendling pick up truck. Calls at Narboro' and Pentney to attach only, at Wendling for brake goods and at Dunham to leave brake goods.

—27 Not to work empty stock. For exceptional working arrangements when 5.49 p.m. ex London running late, see page 56. To call at Fransham when required to set down passengers only and at Wendling for electric token purposes and set down passengers only.

July 1932 (continued).

Freight Trains and Traffic

Freight traffic between Norwich, Dereham and Kings Lynn was conveyed by a number of pick-up goods services which, between them, provided a comprehensive web of services throughout north Norfolk. The line was worked in two parts, with trains running from Norwich to Wells-next-the-Sea, and from Kings Lynn to Dereham. However, this basic pattern of operation was augmented by the provision of through services from Kings Lynn to Norwich, and by the running of local goods services from Kings Lynn to Swaffham and Roudham Junction.

The July 1932 Working Timetable provides a useful glimpse of these diverse goods services in operation. The eastern portion of the line was served by two up and two down goods workings between Wymondham, Dereham and Wells-next-the-Sea, while the western half of the line was served by one up and one down working between Kings Lynn and Roudham Junction, and one up and one down service between Kings Lynn and Dereham. A further train ran between Kings Lynn and Dereham on Mondays, Wednesdays, Thursdays and Fridays, while on Tuesdays and Saturdays this service was replaced by special (TO) or (SO) workings.

Traffic between Kings Lynn and Wells-next-the-Sea could also be carried by separate Kings Lynn to Wells workings which were routed via the Hunstanton branch to Heacham, and thence along the West Norfolk route to Wells-next-the-Sea. (See the *The Lynn & Hunstanton Railway*, published by The Oakwood Press, for further details of the West Norfolk branch.)

Operations began, on the western part of the line, with the departure of an early morning down goods service from Kings Lynn to Dereham at 5.15 am. This service called at Dunham to attach cattle wagons if required, and on Tuesdays it called as necessary at Dunham and Wendling. A note appended to the working timetable reveals that this working left Kings Lynn with Wells-next-the-Sea traffic at the front, Aylsham traffic[42] in the centre and Dereham traffic at the rear. The train reached Dereham at 6.50 am, and the various portions were then shunted and re-marshalled as required; on Saturdays, the service continued to Norwich, but on other days the train returned to Kings Lynn at 7.40 am.

Another daily goods working left Kings Lynn at 7.45 am, and this service reached Swaffham by 8.55 am. Twenty minutes later, at 9.15 am, the 7.40 am up goods service from Dereham also arrived at Swaffham, and the engine of the latter working performed any necessary shunting operations before the 7.40 am resumed its journey to Narborough, East Winch, Middleton and Kings Lynn at 9.50 am. The down train, meanwhile, remained at Swaffham until 10.15 am, and it then continued along the Watton & Swaffham line to Roudham Junction.

A third pick-up working departed from Kings Lynn at 11.55 am (Saturdays and Tuesdays excepted). This train was usually double-headed as far as Middleton – the reason being that it also conveyed an engine and brake van which would later work an early afternoon short-distance goods service from East Winch to Kings Lynn. The 11.55 am usually ran as far as Dereham, and having called at most of the intermediate stations it reached its destination at 1.33 pm. On Saturdays, a similar working left Kings Lynn at the slightly later time of 12.45 pm, while on Tuesday, the 11.55 am was replaced by a 5.50 pm service from Kings Lynn to Dereham.

In the up direction, goods trains left Dereham at intervals throughout the day, and in addition to the above-mentioned 7.40 pm service, there were up goods services at 2.30 pm (SX), and 3.35 pm (SO), together with up workings from East Winch at 1.00 pm (SX), and 1.30 pm (SO), and from Swaffham at 9.15 am and 4.00 pm (SX). The Swaffham workings were through services from Roudham Junction via the Watton & Swaffham line, while the East Winch services were worked by the engine and brake van that had earlier left Kings Lynn attached to the 11.55 am down train. On the days when the latter train did not run (i.e. Tuesdays and Saturdays) the engine and brake ran to East Winch as a separate working.

It will be seen that the goods services provided on the Lynn & Dereham line were surprisingly complex – and when one considers that these services were augmented by further trains on the Norwich, Dereham and Wells-next-the-Sea route, the scope and complexity of local goods operation becomes even more apparent.

In the days in which most of the nation's freight traffic was moved by rail it was quite common for small consignments to be sent over very short distances; a trader might wish, for example, to send a load of animal feed from Kings Lynn Docks to Fakenham. In this case the consignment would be loaded and taken first to Dereham, from where the loaded wagon would be collected by a Wymondham to Wells pick-up working for the short journey from Dereham to Fakenham. Similarly, a load might be sent from Kings Lynn to Yarmouth (or some other point beyond Norwich), and in this case the wagon would probably have been shunted at Dereham, Wymondham and Norwich stations. Such journeys were only possible where scheduled freight trains ran to and from recognised trans-shipment points such as Dereham or Swaffham – each local goods train being part of an overall pattern of operation that provided a service throughout East Anglia and indeed the whole nation.

The types of freight carried on the Kings Lynn to Dereham and Norwich routes reflected the local economy. Agricultural traffic was of particular importance, although there were, in addition, a number of engineering works at Kings Lynn, Dereham and elsewhere. At the same time, Kings Lynn, and (to a lesser extent) Wells-next-the-Sea were busy coastal ports, and this was an important factor in terms of traffic flows.

Dereham was clearly the most important intermediate station on the Kings Lynn to Norwich route in terms of originating freight traffic. The opening of the Lynn & Dereham and Norfolk lines had stimulated the development of local industry, and by 1860 this Norfolk town could boast an iron works, a brewery, saw mills, maltings, a coach works and at least four light engineering works specialising in the repair and manufacture of agricultural machinery. Some of these factories and maltings were situated beside the railway, and a number of private sidings were installed so that railway vehicles could be loaded or unloaded directly. One of the most important of these sidings served Fison's extensive maltings, while others served

Dereham gas works and H.C. Stammers & Co.'s mill.

Private sidings were also provided at Swaffham, Narborough & Pentney, Hardingham, Wymondham, and at various stations on the Wells-next-the-Sea branch. A list of sidings available in the 1930s is given in *Table Four*, and it will be seen that most of these served maltings or granaries. There were, also, sand and quarry sidings at Wymondham and Middleton, and these sidings enabled the railway to handle sand and other forms of mineral traffic as well as bulk agricultural products such as grain and animal feedstuffs.

It may be worth adding that the word 'corn' was used in Victorian times to describe a range of crops, of which wheat was probably the most important. In East Anglia, wheat was usually grown on heavier soil whereas barley was the chief crop on lighter, poorer soils. These crops were planted in rotation with 'clearing' crops such as turnips or potatoes, so that fields could be used more or less continuously without fear of exhaustion, while in the 20th century sugar beet became increasingly important. All of these crops provided traffic for the railway, and at times – particularly during the sugar beet season – extra trains were run to and from Dereham to prevent the goods yard from becoming filled to capacity with loaded wagons.

Coal was a major source of incoming freight traffic, and most of the intermediate stations were equipped with coal wharves at which local traders received bulk consignments for bagging and re-sale to domestic users. There were, in addition, one or two industrial users – notably the rail-connected gas works at Dereham.

Up and down workings pass each other in the crossing loop at East Winch during the LNER period. *H.C. Casserley*

Other freight-handling facilities at intermediate stations included cattle pens, end loading docks (for vehicles or heavy machinery) and fixed yard cranes.

Some stations, such as Narborough, Swaffham and Hardingham had a full range of facilities, while others had only minimal provision for coal class traffic in wagon loads; the following table (compiled with reference to the 1938 *Railway Clearing House Handbook of Stations*) will give some indication of the varied freight facilities available between Kings Lynn & Norwich Thorpe.

Table Three

GOODS AND PASSENGER ACCOMMODATION ON THE KINGS LYNN TO NORWICH LINE, 1938

Name of Station	*Miles from Kings Lynn* m.	c.	*Facilities*	*Crane Power*
Kings Lynn	0	0	P G F L H C	5 ton (station), 15 ton (docks)
Middleton Towers	3	15	P G F L H C	n/a
East Winch	5	15	P G F L H C	n/a
Narborough & Pentney	8	52	P G F L H C	1 ton
Swaffham	14	37	P G F L H C	1 ton
Dunham	18	36	P G F L H C	1 ton
Fransham	19	59	P G	n/a
Wendling	22	35	P G F H C	2 ton
Dereham	26	43	P G F L H C	6 ton
Yaxham	28	35	P G L H	1.5 tons
Thuxton	31	04	P G	n/a
Hardingham	32	34	P G F L H C	1 ton
Kimberley Park	34	17	P G	n/a
Wymondham	37	76	P G F L H C	1 ton
Herthersett			P G H	n/a
Norwich Thorpe	48	14	P G F H C	15 tons

KEY
P = passenger and parcels traffic; G = goods and mineral traffic; F = furniture vans, portable engines, etc; L = livestock traffic; H = horse boxes and prize cattle vans; C = carriages and motor cars.

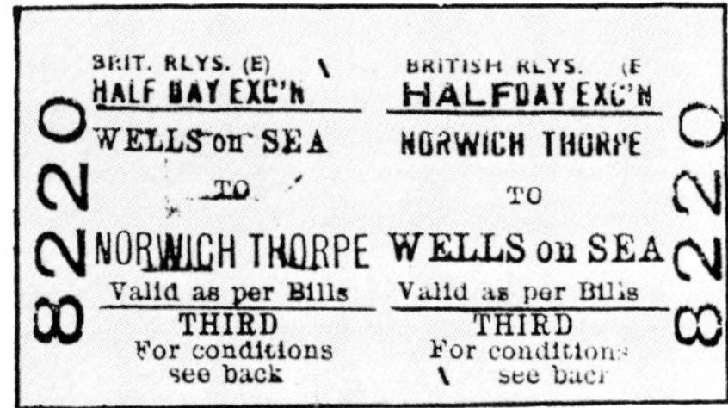

Table Four

SOME RAILWAY-LINKED INDUSTRIES (1938)

Station	*Name of Firm*	*Position*
Kings Lynn	Anglo American Oil Company	Docks branch
	Bristow & Copley's siding	Docks branch
	Kings Lynn Electricity Works	Docks branch
	Kings Lynn Co-operative coal depot	Docks branch
	J.H. Finch & Co.	Docks branch
	Central Electricity Board	Docks branch
	Chapman & Co.'s siding	Docks branch
	Fison & Sons	Docks branch
	Pattrick & Thompson's siding	Docks branch
	Savage's siding	Docks branch
	Stanton & Co.'s siding	Docks branch
Middleton Towers	J. Boam & Son	Middleton station, down side
Narborough	Vynne & Everitt Ltd	Narborough station
Swaffham	Chamberlayne & Co.	Swaffham station
	Kenny Co.	Swaffham station
	Vynne & Everett	Swaffham station
	W. Preston	Swaffham station
	Jeffry & Co.	Swaffham station
Dereham	Dereham Gas Works	Dereham South Junction
	Dereham Urban District Council	Dereham station
	Fison & Sons	Dereham station
	H.C. Stammers & Co.	Dereham station
	Hobbies Ltd siding	Dereham station
Hardingham	J. Baly & Sons	Hardingham

Livestock traffic, in the form of cattle or sheep, was handled at most of the intermediate stations between Kings Lynn and Norwich, while all of the stations dealt with appreciable amounts of milk traffic. Milk was, for many years, conveyed in ponderous metal cans or churns which were delivered to the stations by local farmers at least once a day for despatch by passenger train.

The growth of road transport in the years following World War One resulted in a reduction in the levels of livestock and milk traffic handled at local stations, but the progressive introduction of bulk milk tankers enabled the railways to offer an improved service to dairy farmers. Rail-connected dairies were established at a number of places, and these became a focal point for the collection and despatch of milk traffic by rail; farmers were encouraged to bring their churns to the dairies, and rail transport was then able to concentrate on bulk haulage by scheduled trains. One of these new dairies was built on the Wells-next-the-Sea branch at North Elmham (to the north of Dereham) and, thereafter, loads of up to six or seven milk tanks were conveyed between North Elmham, Dereham and Norwich by passenger train. From Norwich, the tank wagons were sent to Ilford for distribution in the London area.

Although dairies such as the one at North Elmham speeded-up the despatch of milk by train, they led to a further reduction in the carriage of milk in churns, and for this reason smaller stations such as Fransham or Wendling ceased to handle milk traffic during the LNER period.

The freight vehicles seen on the Kings Lynn to Norwich line were predominantly open wagons, seven-plank vehicles being used for the carriage of coal or minerals, while five- or three-plank wagons were typically used to carry loads of timber, building materials or general merchandise. Timber or other long loads could also be conveyed on special flat trucks or bolster wagons, and similar flat-topped wagons were also available for the conveyance of motor cars or portable engines.

Photographic evidence suggests that most loads were carried in open wagons during the Great Eastern period, though covered vans of various kinds were sometimes used for general merchandise traffic. Cattle were carried in special cattle wagons, while horses were usually sent in horse boxes (which also contained a small passenger compartment for the grooms). It is likely that local Great Eastern wagons were the types of vehicle most commonly seen on the Kings Lynn to Dereham route, even during the LNER era, though loads from more distant destinations would sometimes bring 'foreign' rolling stock from the other 'Big Four' companies onto the line.

General Developments in the 1920s and 1930s

As we have seen, the 1923 grouping did not produce any immediate changes, but in the next few years the LNER initiated one or two minor improvements and innovations. In February 1926, for example, *The Railway Magazine* reported that the company intended to erect a new brick and concrete goods shed at Kings Lynn for the convenience of local traders, the cost of this structure being £10,000. At the same time, the LNER authorities announced that they intended to build 'new offices at Kings Lynn to accommodate the whole of the company's dock and harbour clerical staff at a cost of £4,000'.

On a more mundane level, the LNER introduced improved platform lighting at a number of local stations, including Kings Lynn and Dereham – although most of the smaller stations between Kings Lynn, Dereham and Norwich retained their traditional oil lamps until closure.

The LNER also made one or two small changes in terms of station nomenclature – Middleton being renamed 'Middleton Towers' to prevent confusion with Middleton in Lancashire, Middleton in Northumberland and Middleton in Cumberland. Kimberley was, similarly, renamed 'Kimberley Park' in 1923 to prevent confusion with a station in Nottinghamshire. A further name change took place at Wells-next-the-Sea, where the station (hitherto known merely as 'Wells') was designated Wells-on-Sea.

Other changes effected during the period 1923–1939 included the erection of a new, brick-built engine shed at Dereham, together with the introduction of various small economies *vis-à-vis* signalling and other infrastructure. At Thuxton, for instance, the signal box was reduced to ground frame status, while at Dereham the West signal box was moved to a new position to the west of Dereham West Junction; these changes took place in 1933. Meanwhile, as part of a longer-term programme, the LNER started renewing wooden-posted Great Eastern signals as they became life-expired. There was, however, no sudden removal or GER signalling components, and at the end of the LNER period many stations sported an assortment of original GER lower quadrants, LNER steel-posted upper quadrants, and GER-LNER 'hybrids' – many of which consisted of upper quadrant semaphore arms mounted on ancient wooden posts of indeterminable vintage!

On the locomotive front, the 1920s and 1930s saw the progressive introduction of 'Claud Hamilton' 4–4–0s onto the Lynn & Dereham and Norwich–Dereham–Wells routes, and by 1939 it was possible to see 'D15', 'D16/2' and 'D16/3' 4–4–0s at work on these rural lines. In general, however, the majority of local passenger services seem to have been worked by 'D13' 4–4–0s or 'E4' 2–4–0s, while goods traffic was still handled by 'J15' 0–6–0s.

Other classes, including 'J17' 0–6–0s and 'F3' 2–4–2Ts also appeared, while further variety was provided by the occasional appearances of former Great Northern Railway 'D2' 4–4–0s, or even North Eastern Railway 'J21' 0–6–0s. A sample day's observation at Dereham in June 1936, for example, revealed that Norwich to Wells services were then being worked by 'E4' 2–4–0s Nos. 7415 and 7492, and by 'D13' 4–4–0 No. 8030, while former NER 'J21' 0–6–0 No. 300 was noted at the head of a Norwich to Dereham (via County School) passenger working.

The passenger rolling stock seen on the Kings Lynn to Norwich line in the later 1930s exhibited a curious mixture of panelling, waist heights and roof details. In an attempt to eliminate the large number of short wheelbase vehicles in use on East Anglian local services the LNER had transferred numerous former North Eastern Railway bogie coaches to the GER section. However, these ex-NER vehicles were by no means uniform, and although many of the NER's characteristic 'high-roof' coaches were sent to Norfolk, some NER clerestory roof stock was also transferred. Moreover, Great Eastern six-wheelers were retained for strengthening and emergency purposes, and these veterans were still included in the formation of many trains on the eve of World War Two – along with Great Eastern bogie coaches of various kinds and the transferred NER vehicles. A typical formation might, therefore, have included clerestory vehicles, arc-roofed coaches and elliptical roof vehicles, some coaches being six-wheelers while others were bogie vehicles. (The varied passenger rolling stock used on the Kings Lynn to Norwich route would have delighted present-day enthusiasts, though most contemporary travellers would have paid little attention to the external appearance of their trains.)

World War Two

On Sunday 3rd September, 1939, the people of Norfolk heard on their 'wireless' sets that Britain had declared war on Nazi Germany following

Hitler's brutal invasion of Poland. For the second time in a little over 20 years, the British people found themselves engaged in a major European (later world) conflict, but despite fears of a major air attack, the first months of the war were so quiet that they became known as 'The Phoney War'.

For railway travellers, the sight of uniformed servicemen hurrying to their ships or units was a reminder that 'there was a war on', while at night blackout regulations were strictly enforced. The threat of a massive air strike was taken very seriously, and with memories of World War One Zeppelin raids still fresh in many minds, it was feared that the German *Luftwaffe* would drop no less than 950 bombs a day during the first months of the war. Whole cities were expected to be knocked out in a series of 'knock-out blows', with poison gas and fire bombs adding to the chaos and destruction wrought by hundreds of tons of high explosives. London and other major cities were thought to be so dangerous that thousands of children were immediately evacuated to the relative safety of country areas such as East Anglia. There were, in fact, two waves of evacuees – one of which occurred at the very start of the war, while the other took place at the start of 'The Blitz' on London and other major cities.

The great evacuation is a story in itself; many of the children sent to Norfolk or other rural areas had never seen cows or other farm animals, while many of the middle class farmers or professional families who were ordered to provide homes for the evacuees had never before met working class children on a 'social' level. Among the evacuated children was a group of orphans from a Doctor Barnardo's home, who were given accommodation in a large house in Narborough; one of these children was Leslie Thomas who, in later years, would become famous as a best-selling author.

Happily, pre-war fears of a 'knock-out blow' were wildly inaccurate, and although, at certain periods during the war, the *Luftwaffe* did indeed turn its full attention onto London or other centres of population, it emerged that the dreaded Nazi airforce had been greatly over-estimated. Ironically, at a later stage in the war, the Royal Air Force and allied bomber forces were able to inflict massive damage on German military and civilian targets, the employment of heavy, four-engined bombers such as the British Lancaster and the American Flying Fortress being used to devastating effect in a series of cataclysmic raids on enemy cities such as Cologne, Hamburg and Dresden.

The gigantic allied bomber offensive called for an unprecedented expansion of the Royal Air Force, and by 1944 much of Lincolnshire and East Anglia had been covered by a dense network of aerodromes, from which the Lancasters, Flying Fortresses and other heavy bombers could take off to wreak vengeance and destruction throughout the German Reich. Many of these airfields were situated in north and mid Norfolk, and local railways such as the Lynn & Dereham line became intimately connected with the bomber offensive through the presence of important aerodromes such as Swanton Morley, near Dereham, and Marham, near Swaffham.

Other local airfields included North Pickenham, (to the south-east of Swaffham), Shipham (to the south of Dereham) and Wendling – many of these aerodromes being 'bases' for the United States Army Air Force.

The building of these aerodromes was an epic of construction, calling for vast amounts of cement, tarmac and other building materials. Many of these materials were brought into the area on the Lynn & Dereham line or other local railways – Dereham itself being a major centre for the reception of airfield construction traffic. At the height of the aerodrome building boom, at the end of 1943 and the beginning of 1944, Dereham was handling an average of 75 wagon loads of building materials a day; on one day in March 1944 the station dealt with no less than 95 wagons containing 1,000 tons of cement and aggregates. Some idea of the scale of the operation will become apparent when one realises that each new airfield consumed about 640,000 square yards of concrete – in other words enough material to build a road 18 ft wide and 60 miles long.

Airfield construction traffic declined as, one by one, the new aerodromes were brought into use, but there was, thereafter, a heavy traffic in men and equipment to and from Dereham and neighbouring stations.

Wartime traffic was probably at its peak in the weeks before D-Day in May and June 1944, when East Anglian aerodromes such as Swanton Morley and Marham played an important part in the invasion. RAF Swanton Morley, for example, was part of the Second Tactical Air Force, and it served as a vital support unit for the invading forces; aircraft allocated there in June 1944 included RAF Mosquitoes, Bostons and Mitchell bombers.[43]

The railways had been taken into government control at the start of the war, and every effort was made to restrict unnecessary civilian travel. Timetables were drastically cut, and although there were large numbers of special freight and passenger trains for military purposes, ordinary travellers were offered a severely reduced train service. On the Lynn & Dereham line, the pre-war train service of six workings in each direction was cut to just four trains each way – though it is interesting to note that services to and from Wells were less severely affected; in May 1939, for instance, the branch had been served by half a dozen trains in each direction on weekdays, whereas in May 1943 the Wells line was still being served by five up and five down trains.

Normal weekday passenger services between Norwich and Dereham were, in contrast, reduced from 10 up and 9 down trains in 1939 to six up and six down workings by May 1943. Most of these services were through workings between Norwich and Wells, and study of the timetables suggests that through services between Kings Lynn and Norwich had all been withdrawn. It was, on the other hand, still possible to find good, cross-platform connections at Dereham, and it appears that an additional train that ran on Tuesday only continued to work through from Norwich to Kings Lynn (rather than Wells). The basic train service, in May 1943, was as follows:

DOWN						TO		
		am	pm	pm	pm	pm	pm	pm
Kings Lynn	dep.	6.48	–	12.53	3.05	4.13	5.50	–
Dereham	arr.	<u>8.00</u>	–	<u>1.57</u>	<u>4.05</u>	<u>5.08</u>	<u>6.50</u>	–
Dereham	dep.	8.09	10.53	2.08	4.12	5.13	6.55	8.28
Norwich	arr.	9.03	11.44	3.03	5.06	5.53	7.42	9.18

UP					TO				
		am	am	am	am	pm	pm	pm	pm
Norwich	dep.	–	7.25	10.05	10.45	12.00	3.12	4.45	6.38
Dereham	arr.	–	8.12	10.58	11.25	12.51	4.09	5.34	7.29
Dereham	*dep.*	*6.55*	*8.19*	*11.01*	*11.32*	*1.00*	*4.16*	–	–
Kings Lynn	*arr.*	*7.59*	9.20	11.53	*12.25*	2.00	5.24	–	–

It will be seen that there was no connecting service from Norwich for the first up train of the day, which reached Kings Lynn at 7.59 am. This service departed from Dereham at 6.55 am and passed the 6.48 am down working from Kings Lynn in the crossing loop at Swaffham. Additional services left Dereham for Norwich at 10.53 am and 8.28 pm, while in the reverse direction other trains left Norwich for Dereham at 4.45 pm and 6.38 pm; both of the latter workings ran through to Wells, with no connections for Kings Lynn travellers (the last service from Dereham to Kings Lynn having departed at 4.16 pm, in connection with the 3.12 pm from Norwich Thorpe).

The locomotives used on the line during World War II consisted of the usual ex-Great Eastern 'Claud Hamilton' 4–4–0s, 'D13' 4–4–0s, 'E4' 2–4–0s, 'J15' 0–6–0s, 'J17' 0–6–0s and 'F3' 2–4–2Ts, together with other types such as the former GNR 'D2' 4–4–0s. Many of these locomotives were fitted with canvas screens which could be lowered at night to eliminate footplate glare, and thereby reduce the threat of air attack. Similar blackout precautions were put into effect at stations and goods depots – all platform lamps being masked or extinguished, while glass roofs were painted black and carriage lights were dimmed.

As a further precautionary measure, all station nameboards were taken down after the Fall of France in May–June 1940 and this, together with the all-pervading nightly blackout, made wartime railway travel a somewhat difficult business. Habitual travellers could usually recognise their stations by reference to familiar landmarks, but visiting strangers were frequently confused by the total absence of nameboards or road signs. There was, furthermore, a widespread fear of spies and 'Fifth Columnists' (especially at the start of the war), and many amusing tales could be told of harmless travellers being reported as 'suspicious characters' simply because they asked which stations they were arriving at!

Dereham station received extra sidings in connection with Air Ministry traffic, a new connection being installed at Dereham South Junction in 1943.[44] This new facility formed an extension from an existing siding on the up side of the line, and it crossed Hall Lane Crossing on the level before terminating in a field. Otherwise, the war produced few alterations in terms of trackwork or infrastructure.

Bombing was not a major feature of the war years as far as the Norwich to Kings Lynn route was concerned, although Norwich itself was badly damaged by enemy air raids. On the other hand, air raids on other parts of the system could cause disruption on all parts of the system, and for this reason delays and other problems were sometimes experienced even in rural areas. Trains were, at this time, frequently packed by servicemen and women from all parts of the world – the uniforms of the US Army Air Force being particularly common to the Lynn & Dereham line.

A further wartime development which might be mentioned here concerns the introduction of armoured trains in coastal areas such as north Norfolk. There were, in fact, around 12 of these trains (together with several 'spares') and they were first introduced in June 1940. Designed to counteract Britain's acute shortage of armoured vehicles in the aftermath of Dunkirk, each train consisted of a heavily-armoured Great Eastern 2–4–2T, flanked by two low sided general purpose wagons and two LMS steel 20-ton coal wagons; the trains were protected by quarter inch steel plate, and they carried crews of 26, including gunners, wireless operators and enginemen. Armament consisted of rifles, machine guns and 6-pounder guns, the latter being mounted in such a way that a 240 degree arc of fire was possible ahead and astern of the train.

The armoured trains were given a distinguishing letter of the alphabet from 'A' to 'M'. 'Train A', powered by 'F4' 2–4–2T No. 7172 being stationed at Hitchen, while 'Train M' ('F5' 2–4–2T No. 7784) was based at Spalding. The train most usually employed on the north Norfolk lines was 'Train G', which was stationed at Heacham, on the Hunstanton branch, from June 1940 until May 1943. 'Train G' was propelled by armoured 'F4' 2–4–2T No. 7189, and it patrolled an area extending from Kings Lynn in the west to Great Yarmouth in the east.

The armoured train made regular trips along the Wells branch, and on one of these forays it collided with some stationary coaches at Wells-next-the-Sea with such force that the engine broke its buffer beam. In another incident, the same train ran through the Gaywood Road level crossing gates at Kings Lynn.

As in World War I, the armoured train patrols were deliberately varied to thwart potential sabotage attempts, and it is likely that 'Train G' ranged widely throughout north Norfolk on its nightly security patrols. The West Norfolk branch was a good place for these patrols to take place, being near the threatened coast but at the same time largely free from other wartime traffic. Similarly, the coastal route between Mundesley and Cromer was regularly visited by the armoured train, but the Lynn & Dereham route and other cross country lines would also have been traversed by 'Train G' on its way to or from the normal patrol areas.

It is possible that other armoured trains – especially 'Train M' from Spalding – may also have visited the Kings Lynn to Norwich lines. However, the movements of 'Trains G' and 'M' were highly secret, and as most patrols took place at night few people would actually have seen (let alone photographed) these trains in operation. It follows that the precise nature of the armoured train patrols are still something of a mystery, and 'Train G' (and its companions) remains one of the most enigmatic aspects of wartime operations on the Kings Lynn to Norwich route.

The war in Europe ended in May 1945, and Japan surrendered unconditionally in the following August. Meanwhile, in July 1945 the wartime coalition government was replaced by Clement Attlee's Labour administration, and this new government lost no time in putting a radical programme of nationalisation into effect. Railways, mines and other vital industries were to be taken into public ownership, but before describing the post-war history of the Kings Lynn to Norwich line in greater detail it would be useful to examine the stations and route of the Lynn & Dereham and Dereham to Norwich sections. The next two chapters will therefore take the reader on an imaginary guided tour of the railway as it would have appeared in the late 1940s and early 1950s.

A platform scene at Kings Lynn during the LNER era with 'Claud Hamilton' 4–4–0s waiting to depart. *Douglas Thompson*

A similar view of Kings Lynn, this time taken on 27th May, 1965. *Douglas Thompson*

The main station building at Kings Lynn was a brick-built design of no particular distinction, though the *porte cochère* seen in this c.1910 view added an element of modest interest to an otherwise plain Victorian façade. *Lens of Sutton*

Chapter Five

Along the Line (1): Kings Lynn to Dereham

Kings Lynn, the western terminus of the former Lynn & Dereham Railway, was a surprisingly busy station used by trains to London, Hunstanton, Peterborough and Spalding as well as those to Dereham and Norwich. When first opened in 1846 the station had been no more than a simple wooden shed flanking what was then known as Friars Road, but in 1871 the Great Eastern, Great Northern and Midland companies joined forces to build a more substantial terminus, and this later station was more than adequate in relation to 19th century traffic needs.

Kings Lynn

The rebuilt Kings Lynn station incorporated twin island platforms with four dead-end roads between them and bays on either side. There were, at one time, engine release facilities at the end of the main arrival platform, but in later years these facilities were removed and the station operated successfully without run-round loops in its platform roads. This mode of operation was possible because of the presence of Kings Lynn engine shed, which meant that spare locomotives were always available to back-on to the end of incoming passenger trains.

Although the station was laid-out as a terminus, many trains continued northwards to Hunstanton, and for this reason Kings Lynn was often a place of considerable activity – especially when restaurant cars or other portions were attached (or detached) to reversing trains *en route* to London or Hunstanton.

Kings Lynn goods depot was situated immediately to the north of the passenger station, though there was no through running connection between the two halves of the terminus – the main entry point to Kings Lynn goods yard being at Lynn Junction, which was well to the east of the passenger station. The goods yard contained a variety of facilities for all kinds of freight traffic, but of equal, if not greater importance (in terms of industrial connections and bulk traffic) was the town's extensive system of dock and harbour lines, the oldest of which – the harbour branch – had been opened by the Lynn & Ely Railway in 1846.

The harbour branch diverged north-westwards from the Cambridge main line at Harbour Branch Junction, some 1 mile 47 chains south of Kings Lynn passenger station. As first constructed it had terminated well away from the main wharves, and this obviously limited its importance as an interchange facility between rail and water transport. Later, however, the opening of a swing bridge across the River Nar enabled the Harbour Branch to play a more useful role in the local transport system, and in subsequent years it became a busy freight link, serving a variety of lineside industries including (in 1938) A. & J. Bowker, the Building Material Company, Dawber Townsley & Co., the East Coast Steamship Company, Kenner Greenwood & Company, the West Norfolk Farmers' Manure & Chemical Co-operative, Gregory & Hampsons, Vynne & Everett and R.W. Paul & Company. Many of these firms were engaged in activities connected with local agriculture – Vynne &

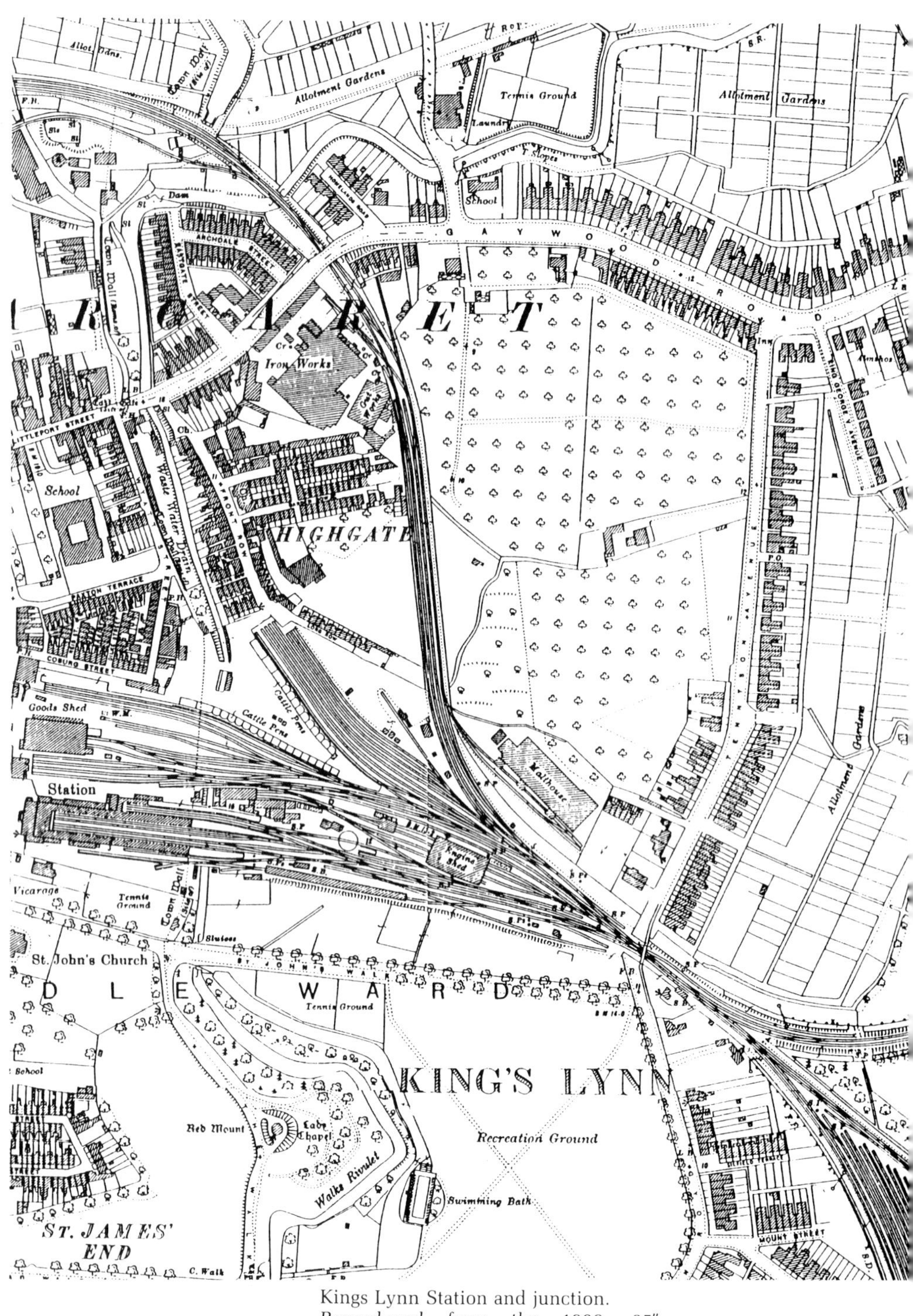

Kings Lynn Station and junction. *Reproduced from the 1906, 25" Ordnance Survey map.*

Everett, for instance, traded in grain and animal feed, and sent much traffic to and from their rail-connected granaries at Narborough, Snettisham and other GER stations.

The Harbour Branch was worked on the 'one engine in steam' system, and although part of the GER, the Midland and Great Northern companies had running powers over this important industrial system.

The Kings Lynn Docks Branch was situated to the north of the Harbour Branch, and entered via Lynn Junction and the main goods yard. Opened on 10th June, 1870 it served the then-new Alexandra Docks, and was later extended to reach the Bentinck Docks. Owned by the Kings Lynn Dock & Railway Company, the docks line was worked by the GER, though the M&GN also had running powers. Like the Harbour Branch, the dock line served numerous local firms and businesses, notably the Anglo-American Oil Company, Kings Lynn Electricity Works, Fison & Sons, the Kings Lynn Co-operative Society, and various smaller firms.

Kings Lynn engine shed was situated on a somewhat cramped site between the goods yard and the passenger station. A 4-road, brick-built structure, the shed provided accommodation for a large assortment of ex-Great Eastern locomotives including (at various times), 'Claud Hamilton' 4–4–0s, 'E4' 2–4–0s, 'F3' 2–4–2Ts, 'J15' 0–6–0s, 'J17' 0–6–0s, 'J19' 0–6–0s, 'J67' 0–6–0Ts, 'J70' 0–6–0Ts, 'Y6' 0–4–0Ts and 'N7' 0–6–2Ts.

Larger locomotives, such as 'B1' and 'B17' class 4–6–0s could also be seen in or around the shed, while from the enthusiasts point of view the presence of specially-groomed 'Royal' locomotives for use to and from Wolferton contributed an additional element of interest.

In the 1930s, 'Claud Hamilton' class 4–4–0s Nos. 8783 and 8787 were the usual Royal engines, and they were both maintained in pristine condition in LNER apple green livery with plenty of polished metalwork. It was usual for some of the ordinary 'Clauds' to be kept polished-up for emergency Royal use, and in the years before World War II Nos. 8868 and 8792 were among the engines so distinguished; both carried black livery, but their burnished smoke box door rings and other embellishments contributed an air of importance to their otherwise plain external appearance.

In 1920 Kings Lynn shed could officially accommodate 12 tender engines and up to 16 tank engines of the 'M15' or similar classes, but by the 1950s its allocation had swelled to no less than 50 locomotives. (The depot was closed to steam in 1959, but 'B1' 4–6–0s and other steam classes continued to use the shed for turning and servicing purposes.)

Access to the four-road shed was via Lynn Junction, or via a headshunt connection from the passenger station; there was also a direct connection from the goods yard, and by this means shunting engines were able to enter the locomotive yard without entering the station proper. The turntable was situated at the west end of the depot, and locomotives were able to take water from a number of strategically-sited water columns.

In general, the buildings in and around Kings Lynn station were undistinguished. The most impressive structure in the vicinity was a large, rail-connected malthouse near the locomotive yard, but the railway buildings themselves were small in scale.

The main station building was a relatively modest brick structure. In earlier days it had boasted a simple *porte-cochère*, but this feature was subsequently removed, an angular canopy being fitted in its place. Further modifications were effected at the northern end of the building, where a large parcels entrance was ruthlessly inserted into the original brick façade – thereby destroying the essential symmetry of the structure (*see photographs*). Other modifications included the removal of ornamental Victorian chimney stacks and the addition of a brick-built extension at the north end of the building; a glazed clerestory above the main passenger entrance was, however, retained, while the station continued to sport a collection of somewhat incongruous decorative urns on its otherwise undistinguished roof.

Other buildings near the passenger terminus included a large brick and concrete goods shed to the north of the platforms, and a long carriage shed to the east. The goods shed was an arc-roofed structure spanning two tracks, and affording ample covered accommodation for the loading or unloading of general merchandise traffic; it was built in 1926 as part of the programme of improvements carried out by the LNER in that year. The carriage shed was specially-built to house the Royal Train, and it spanned just one track.

The station proper was controlled from a two-storey, brick and timber signal cabin which was situated immediately to the east of the platforms. In contrast to most GER signal boxes in the west Norfolk area this cabin was built mainly of brick – the brickwork being carried up to the window sills at the front of the building and to roof level at the rear. It had a two pitch, slated roof, and a brick chimney stack rose from the rear wall of the building; the locking room was originally lit by three large windows, but these were bricked-up to prevent blast damage during World War II.

There were, in addition to these main buildings, a large number of huts, sheds and storage buildings in the goods yard and around the locomotive shed. Few of these minor structures call for special comment, though it is perhaps worth adding that a two road, timber-built engine shed on the periphery of the motive power depot was thought to have dated from the Lynn & Dereham era.

Departing from Kings Lynn, eastbound trains accelerated past Kings Lynn engine shed, and immediately reached Lynn Junction, at which point the Dereham route diverged south-eastwards from the Hunstanton line. The junction was controlled from a standard Great Eastern-style gabled signal cabin standing on the down side of the line; nearby, Tennyson Avenue crossed the railway on the level while, to the west of the box, a substantial footbridge was provided for the benefit of pedestrian road users.

Clattering across the junction points, trains continued roughly south-eastwards, with the Hunstanton branch momentarily visible to the left; a short distance further on, the route divided once again, and from the right hand windows of the train observant travellers could see the GER main line turning sharply towards the south. Running now on the Lynn & Dereham line, trains passed an array of sidings on the up side, but these soon gave way to open country as the single line finally emerged from the outskirts of Kings Lynn and entered the open country beyond.

A glimpse of Kings Lynn station on 11th March, 1961. The *porte cochère* seen in the earlier view has been removed, and the parcels office at the far end of the building has been rebuilt. *R.M. Casserley*

Kings Lynn station in the 1980s, showing the parcels office at the north end of the building. *Douglas Thompson*

The interior of Kings Lynn station, probably photographed around 1948.
Douglas Thompson

A later view of the covered concourse at Kings Lynn. *Douglas Thompson*

‹-Great Eastern 'E4' 2–4–0 No. 62793 ands in the platform at Kings Lynn on 26th ugust, 1950; a 'Claud Hamilton' 4–4–0 is sible to the right. *R.M. Casserley*

:laud Hamilton' 4–4–0 No. 2504 stands ıtside the passenger station at Kings Lynn ı 15th April, 1947; sister engine No. 2518 is ı the nearby turntable. *H.C. Casserley*

att class '4MT' 2–6–0 No. 43142 leaves ings Lynn at the head of a Peterborough to reat Yarmouth excursion. The Hunstanton ·anch can be seen to the right of the loco- otive, while the main line to Cambridge ıd London diverges to the left. *H.N. James*

B.I.S. Ltd 'Planet', 0–4–0 No. 46 propels sand in open wagons, over the weighbridge at the exchange sidings with British Rail at Middleton Towers on the 24th April, 1979. The P.O. wagons on the right have the lettering 'BIS Sand for Rockware Glass Ltd' along the sides. *G. Gamble*

Still in working order on 17th April, 1980 is Motor Rail Simplex No. 24 on the private lines of B.I.S. Ltd at Middleton Towers. *G. Gamble*

Ex BR, class '03' shunter in B.I.S. Ltd livery (with a camel painted on the cab) seen here shunting wagons under the 'wet sand' hoppers at Middleton Towers on 17th April, 1980. *G. Gamble*

Class 31, No. 31 322 seen here arriving at Middleton Towers in charge of a single brake van at 1.30 pm on 15th August, 1979. *G. Gamble*

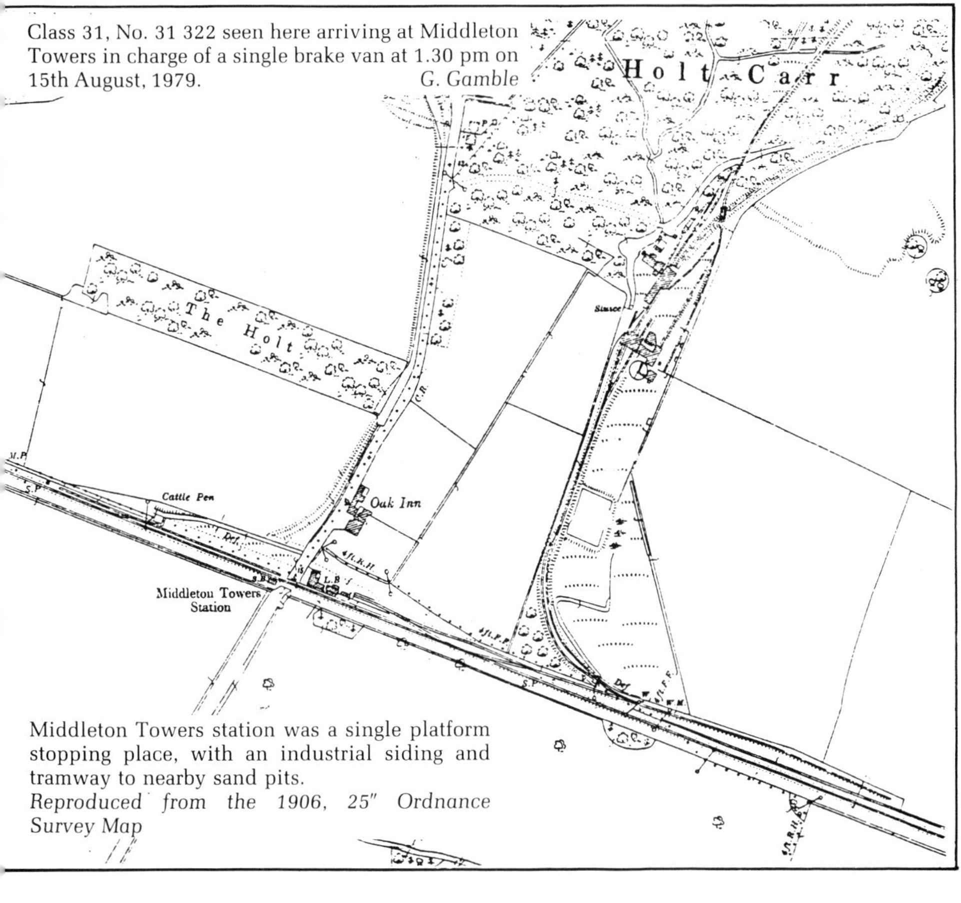

Holt Carr

The Holt

Sluice

Oak Inn

Cattle Pen

Middleton Towers Station

Middleton Towers station was a single platform stopping place, with an industrial siding and tramway to nearby sand pits.

Reproduced from the 1906, 25″ Ordnance Survey Map

Middleton Towers

Maintaining its south-easterly heading, the railway soon passed under the Midland & Great Northern's Kings Lynn cut-off; this was not the *original* Lynn & Fakenham line which (as noted in Chapter Three) had initially left the Hunstanton Railway at Gaywood Junction. As mentioned earlier, Lynn & Fakenham trains shared the Great Eastern station at Kings Lynn, but this arrangement was never entirely amicable, and in 1882 the L&FR decided to build a 4 miles 45 chains 'cut-off' between South Lynn and Bawsey Junction, and when opened to public traffic on 1st January, 1886 the new link became the Eastern & Midlands (later Midland & Great Northern Joint) main line.

Emerging from under the M&GN bridge, Norwich trains passed through a tract of attractively wooded countryside before reaching Middleton Towers, the first intermediate stopping place on the former Lynn & Dereham line.

Originally known simply as Middleton, the station was 3 miles 15 chains from Kings Lynn. Passenger facilities consisted of a single platform on the down side, together with a relatively complex station building which (like many other stations in the area) incorporated two distinct styles of architecture. The main building was situated at right angles to the track, and boasted ornate Tudor-style features, including a bay window which faced directly onto the platform. This interesting old structure was clearly a relic of the Lynn & Dereham Railway, but the adjacent waiting room, with its glazed frontage and projecting canopy, was of somewhat later construction.

When first opened, Middleton station had featured an extremely low platform, and a residual section of this early platform remained *in situ* at the west end; the remainder of the platform was, however, of normal height, and there was for this reason a curious change of levels in front of the station building. Other items of interest at Middleton Towers included some typical Great Eastern type platform lamps, and a level crossing with huge GER-style wooden gates.

Middleton's goods facilities consisted of a dead-end siding to the west of the passenger station, together with a loop siding to the east. A short spur extended from one end of the loop to serve a small loading dock behind the platform, while a further siding diverged north-eastwards to reach important sand pits belonging to J. Boam & Sons (later part of British Industrial Sand Ltd). The high grade silica sand obtained in this part of Norfolk was especially suitable for use in glass-making, and although this important source of bulk traffic will be described in Chapter Seven, it is worth mentioning here that the sand company possessed an extensive internal railway system incorporating both standard and 1 ft 11½ in. gauge track.

Like other country stations, Middleton Towers was a significant employer of labour, and its station master was an important figure in the local community. The station master here, from 1872 until his retirement in October 1899, was William Davis, who had started work on the Eastern Counties Railway back in 1861. Like many GER officials, he had worked his way up 'through the ranks', and prior to taking up his appointment at Middleton he had worked as a goods foreman at Beccles. Mr Davis lived in Kings Lynn after his retirement, and subsequently moved to Norwich, where

An Edwardian scene at Middleton Towers, showing the original Lynn & Dereham buildings (*left*) and the later Great Eastern waiting room (*right*). A 'T26' class 2–4–0 is arriving. Note the tall, GER-style gatepost on the extreme left. *Lens of Sutton*

Middleton Towers, looking west towards Kings Lynn on 2nd September, 1968. Sand wagons occupy the goods siding on the extreme right. *Douglas Thompson*

he died on 7th September, 1920 at the advanced age of eighty-four.[45]

Mr Davis was succeeded by William Nunn, who was himself replaced by Robert Simpson around 1907. By 1912 Mr Simpson had moved to neighbouring Yaxham, his successor at Middleton being Albert Peacock; at the time of the Grouping the station was supervised by George Taylor, and he was still in office during the mid-1920s.

Middleton itself was well over a mile away from the railway, but in the days before motor transport villagers may have enjoyed walking along sunlit lanes to their station. The outlying hamlet of 'Tower End' was, on the other hand, much closer to the railway; nearby, the tall gatehouse of a Medieval house was popularly known as 'Middleton Towers', and this 15th century structure gave its name to both Tower End and the station.

Middleton Towers station was controlled from a two-storey GER style signal cabin which stood beside the level crossing on the up side of the line. Although the station's sidings were worked from this cabin the station was not a block post, and the siding connections could not be worked until the tablet for the Kings Lynn to East Winch section was inserted into a lock provided for that purpose in the signal cabin. When any shunting operations had been completed the single line tablet was handed back to the driver.

East Winch

From Middleton Towers, the single track railway traversed a tract of low-lying but picturesque countryside with an average elevation of about 30 ft. To the north, a range of gentle hills rose to about 100 ft, while on the south side of the line Middleton village occupied an elevated position on a corresponding ridge of higher land.

East Winch, the next station, was 5 miles 15 chains from Kings Lynn. Two platforms were provided, the main station buildings, of brick construction, being on the up side. The down platform, in contrast, was equipped with a simple, timber-built waiting shelter.

The track layout, though simple, was adequate for the needs of a country station serving an agricultural community. The basic configuration consisted of a crossing loop, with a long headshunt at the eastern end and two short, dead-end sidings on the up side. The goods yard contained the usual cattle dock, loading dock and coal wharves, but there was no large goods shed.

The station was bisected by the public road from East Winch to Gayton, which crossed the line on the level between the goods yard and the passenger platforms; this arrangement was fairly common in East Anglia – the idea being that the crossing could be closely supervised by station staff who (until the erection of a signal box) were responsible for opening and closing the heavy wooden gates.

In architectural terms, East Winch reflected Lynn & Dereham practice insofar as the main station buildings were of 'Tudor' or 'Jacobean' appearance, with prominent gables and an array of tall chimney stacks. Close examination of this ornate structure revealed that various modifications had been carried out during the 19th century, though in general the building

East Winch station, looking east towards Norwich during the British Railways era. The platform lamp visible to the left is formed of an upright length of rail with a GER-style glass lantern bolted to the upper end. *Douglas Thompson*

East Winch, looking west towards Kings Lynn on 2nd September, 1968. The simple, timber-built downside shelter can be clearly seen (*right*) while the original Lynn & Dereham building can be glimpsed on the extreme left. *Douglas Thompson*

Narborough and Pentney Station.

Narborough station, looking east towards Norwich, and showing the brick-built waiting room block on the down platform. *Lens of Sutton*

Narborough station, looking west towards Kings Lynn during the 1930s. The station staff appear to be opening the heavy wooden crossing gates – the right-hand gate having been opened while the left-hand gate is still closed against road traffic. *Lens of Sutton*

retained its original Lynn & Dereham character.

The waiting shelter on the down side was probably a later addition; the latter structure incorporated a disproportionately-large canopy that projected out over the platform in order to provide additional shelter for travellers during wet weather. This down side building was clad in vertical match boarding, and its projecting canopy was supported by prominent wooden braces that rose diagonally from the front wall of the structure.

Minor details at East Winch reflected Great Eastern practice – the platform lamps, for example, consisted of somewhat austere glass lanterns supported on upright lengths of rail, or else bolted directly to the station buildings. The signal box, on the down side of the line, was another standard GER structure.

East Winch's station master, around 1888, was William Smith, though by 1896 the local station master was William Fisk; both of these GER employees found subsequent employment at other Norfolk stations, and by 1904 William Smith was serving at Salhouse, on the Cromer branch, while his colleague William Fisk was employed at Docking, on the West Norfolk line.[46]

Later station masters included Edward Jackson, who was at East Winch in the period *circa* 1904–8, and Thomas Hurley, who was in charge of the station around 1912. In 1920, the then station master, Mr L. Raney, left East Winch to take up a new appointment at Silvertown on the busy North Woolwich branch, his replacement being F. Constable – formerly a clerk at Cambridge. Mr Constable evidently regarded East Winch as a 'stepping stone' towards more rewarding appointments elsewhere and in 1921 he transferred to Rye House, to be followed, at East Winch, by William Dines,[47] Three years later, in 1925, the station master was George Taylor, who supervised both Middleton and East Winch stations.

Leaving East Winch, trains continued south-eastwards, running first in cuttings and then emerging to cross a minor road on the level. Beyond, the railway was carried along a low embankment that was pierced, at one point, by a small underbridge. A short distance further on the line passed over the A47 road on an isolated level crossing; there was, at one time, a station in this vicinity, but 'Bilney' was destined to be a short-lived stopping place, and it disappeared from the timetables in the Victorian period.

Narborough & Pentney

Descending towards the Nar valley, trains soon arrived at Narborough & Pentney (8 miles 52 chains), an archetypal country station with up and down platforms, and extensive goods facilities on the down side. Narborough's track layout consisted of a lengthy crossing loop, with a long headshunt extending westwards from one end, and a goods loop running parallel to the running line at the eastern end of the station. The goods loop itself ended in a short headshunt, and four dead-end sidings diverged northwards to serve the goods yard; one of these sidings passed through a substantial goods shed while another served a cattle dock. Further sidings branched south-eastwards to serve Vynne & Everett's granary, and there was, in addition, a short spur on the up side of the line.

The main station buildings were on the up side, in which position the booking office was conveniently situated for the inhabitants of Pentney, but less convenient for Narborough residents – whose village was on the opposite side of the railway. The building was an 'L'-shaped structure, with a one and a half storey, gabled wing in the horizontal stroke of the 'L' and a single storey office wing in the vertical stroke; the gabled east wing was at right angles to the track whereas the station proper was parallel to the platform.

A small, brick building provided additional passenger accommodation on the down side, and the standard, Great Eastern type signal cabin was also situated on the down platform. A minor road from Narborough to Pentney crossed the line at the Norwich end of the platforms, and the resulting level crossing effectively divided the station into two halves, the passenger station being on one side while the main goods yard was situated on the opposite side of the massive GER-type crossing gates.

Narborough & Pentney was, arguably, one of the most attractive stations on the Kings Lynn to Norwich line, and its picturesque qualities were further enhanced by the wooded surroundings in which it stood. Narborough itself was equally attractive, and although only a small village, it could boast a hall, a Perpendicular church, several old houses and a water mill on the banks of the River Nar.

In common with other local stations, Narborough & Pentney was served by a succession of station masters, many of whom were later promoted to other, more prestigious positions on busier GER lines. One of the longest-serving station masters here was Charles Wilby, who remained at Narborough throughout the Edwardian era, but had moved (or retired) by 1922. In East Anglian days the station master had been Mr Nebuchadnezzar Ayres, while around 1890 the station master was James Smith who was subsequently replaced by Thomas Read Nash.[48]

A much later station master was Gabriel Paynter, who had worked at Wells, County School, Kimberley (and possibly other Norfolk stations) before transferring to Narborough after World War I. Like many other railway officials, Gabriel Paynter was a pillar of local society who actively contributed to the social life of the district. He frequently organised staff dinners or other activities, and *The Great Eastern Railway Magazine* took notice of these activities on more than one occasion. In March 1921, for instance, the magazine contained the following brief note:

> Narborough – On New Year's eve the staff at Narborough held a dinner at the Ship Hotel. Mr Paynter, station master, presided and the vice-chair was occupied by Mr Wright. After the loyal toast, the 'Divisional Officers' (Messrs Drury and Hall) were taken, followed by 'The Chairman', 'The Vice-Chairman', and 'The Host and Hostess (Mr and Mrs Crisp). Songs were contributed by all present and Miss Stimpson presided at the piano. It is hoped that this event may become an annual one.

A few weeks later Phillip Holman, who worked at Narborough as a clerk, successfully applied for a new post at Lowestoft and station master Paynter

Swaffham station and junction.
Reproduced from the 1906, 25″ Ordnance Survey Map

Swaffham station in 1964, looking west towards Kings Lynn. *Douglas Thompson*

A two-car Derby 'lightweight' unit pauses in the up platform at Swaffham around 1959. *Mowat Collection*

Swaffham station from the rear, showing the attractive Dutch-style gables and traditional Norfolk brick and flint construction; the station master's house adjoins the main structure (*left*). *Mowat Collection*

evidently arranged a presentation that took place prior to Mr Holman's departure. The presentation was again reported by *The Great Eastern Railway Magazine* which, in August 1921, recorded that:

> On June 4th, in the station master's office, Narborough, Mr Phillip R. Holman, who has been clerk at that station since October 1917 and is removing to a similar position at Lowestoft (North), was presented by Mr G. Paynter, station master, with a pocket wallet as a parting gift from the station staff.
>
> Mr Paynter expressed the good wishes of the subscribers for Mr Holman's future prosperity and happiness and the latter replied in suitable terms thanking his friends for their kind thought.

Departing from Narborough, Norwich-bound trains crossed the River Nar, and with Narborough church visible to the left, the journey through rural Norfolk resumed. Running through well-wooded countryside, the route climbed out of the Nar valley and, about one mile from Narborough, the line was carried over a minor road on a small bridge. Entering a cutting, trains continued their ascent, and as the cuttings gave way to an embankment the single track railway reached an elevation of about 100 feet.

With the exhaust of the labouring engine leaving no doubt that the general direction was now upwards, the railway climbed through further cuttings as it approached Swaffham. Passing under the A1122 road, the route emerged onto a short section of embankment, and with the busy A47 converging from the left, the line entered another cutting. After a further mile, the A47 crossed from the left to the right hand side of the railway, and having surmounted a summit of over 200 ft the route approached Swaffham from a westerly direction.

Swaffham

With the A47 continuing on a parallel course to the right, the railway passed under a minor road bridge, and with sidings now visible on either side, trains slowed as they entered the important intermediate station at Swaffham.

Situated some 14 miles 37 chains from Kings Lynn, Swaffham served a small country town which, in the 1950s, had a population of about 3,000. In railway terms, its importance stemmed from its status as the junction for branch services to Thetford, and this importance was underlined by the presence of a two-road engine shed and a 45 ft diameter locomotive turntable. The main station buildings were on the up side, and access to the down platform was by means of a pedestrian footbridge.

Swaffham station building was a large and particularly ornate structure; like other stations on the Lynn & Dereham line, it was built in a 'Tudor' style, with decorative windows, grotesque chimney stacks and other features commonly found on 16th century manor houses. The platform frontage was protected by a large platform canopy which was supported by huge, curved brackets with trefoil *motiffs* in their spandrels.

The station building was built to the familiar 'hall and cross wings' plan, with a centrally-placed ticket office flanked by two projecting cross wings.

Approaching the station from the rear, travellers were able to enter the building by means of a central doorway in the recessed middle part of the structure; this doorway was flanked by two rectangular windows, and by the two cross wings which, between them, provided support for a small canopy. The platform frontage, in contrast, was entirely flush – the idea being that its slab-like façade would provide a convenient support for the main platform canopy. (For this reason the building was not a true 'hall and cross wings' structure because the two cross wings did not extend through the full width of the structure.)

Apart from its tall and decorative chimney stacks, the station building was distinguished by the provision of ornate 'Dutch' gables at the rear, and by the use of traditional Norfolk brick and flint construction methods. Flint was extensively used at the rear of the building, though as this material was not suitable for use at square corners, brick was employed as a reinforcement (the windows, however, were dressed with stone lintels and quoins). The station building was, by any definition, a substantial and well-built Victorian structure which was, in truth, an ornament to the town in which it stood.

Swaffham's main passenger facilities were concentrated in the up side buildings, and travellers waiting for eastbound trains on the down platform had to be content with a small waiting room and an open-fronted shelter. The latter structure had brick-built rear and side walls, and a single-pitch roof that extended out towards the platform edge as a protective canopy. Internally, the shelter was equipped with simple wooden seats and a display of timetables and railway travel posters. The sloping wooden roof was supported by braces extending diagonally from the brick side walls, and by a central post which prevented the timber roof structure from sagging; the brick walls were constructed of 'English bond' brickwork.

Swaffham's track layout was unusually complex by normal branch line standards. The line through the station was double track, and, with additional loops on each side of the main running lines, the layout seemed, at first glance to be part of a multiple track main line rather than a country branch. The main goods sidings were on the down side, the good yard proper having three sidings, one of which served a large goods shed. There were two further dead-end sidings to the west of the main yard, together with an array of storage sidings to the east.

The basic track configuration was made more complicated by the presence of a multiplicity of slips and crossovers, some of which crossed the up main line in order to reach the engine sidings or other facilities on the south side of the station.

The engine shed and attendant installations occupied an elevated position above Pool Lane, and the two-road shed itself could only be reached via the locomotive turntable. An additional siding branched away from the turntable and, turning sharply onto a westerly alignment, it then continued westwards along the back of the locomotive yard. A water tank stood beside the engine shed, and watering facilities were available in the depot.

Swaffham engine shed was a cheaply-built timber-structure, and, perhaps for this reason, it did not survive into the diesel era. The shed was closed in the 1950s, and in its last years the depot consisted of little more than an engine siding, coaling stage and ashpit.

As mentioned above, the engine shed and turntable were situated on an embankment, and this caused particular problems after a Worsdell 'G14' 2–4–0 derailed itself in the yard on 2nd September, 1894; the engine concerned – No. 567 – tumbled over the edge of the bank and crashed into the road below. Recovery was, needless to say, a difficult operation, but the casualty was eventually winched back to rail level. (On a footnote, it is perhaps worth noting that this former main line locomotive had clearly been demoted to branch line work after barely a decade in main line use.)

The station was controlled from two signal boxes, one of which stood on the up side near the footbridge, while the other was situated further to the east at Swaffham Junction. Other features of interest at Swaffham included an assortment of private sidings serving granaries or other premises belonging to local firms such as Vynne & Everitt, W. Preston, Jeffrey & Co., and Chamberlayne & Company; in 1897 the Great Eastern Way & Works committee agreed that £29 would be expended on an extension of 'Mr Preston's Siding'.

A comparatively large station such as Swaffham provided employment for a large labour force of clerks, goods porters, passenger porters, signalmen, foremen and other grades in the locomotive and permanent way departments. This large staffing establishment was supervised, for many years, by station master John Coker, whose tenure of office spanned the Edwardian era, World War I and the Grouping – a period of at least 25 years, representing a quarter century of continuous service to the local community.

Among those employed at Swaffham in station master's Coker's time was signalman R. Barker – a keen arts and crafts enthusiast who specialised in the production of hand-made brushes. His son, Mr R.J. Barker, was disabled as a result of sustaining no less than 43 wounds during World War I. Another local casualty in that terrible conflict was former porter-gateman Edwin Ward, who joined the Royal Field Artillery in January 1917 and died in October 1918 as a result of wounds received in action.[49]

Swaffham town centre was within easy walking distance of the railway, and a pleasant stroll down Station Street soon brought the appreciative visitor to a spacious market area dominated by elegant Georgian houses and an unusual market cross surmounted – appropriately enough – by a representation of Ceres, the Roman Goddess of harvest and fruitfulness.

Dunham

Leaving Swaffham station, trains quickly reached Swaffham Junction, at which point the former Watton & Swaffham line diverged to the south-east. Curving gradually north-eastwards, the Dereham route climbed steadily towards its summit.

Cuttings alternated with embankments as the line traversed an area of rolling hills, and with Palgrave to the left and Sporle to the right, down trains passed the site of Sporle station where, in 1847, the line from Kings

An interesting Edwardian view of Dunham station, looking west towards Kings Lynn. The wagon turntable visible behind the three cattle wagons gave access to the goods shed which was (unusually) sited at right angles to the running line. *Lens of Sutton*

Lynn had ended in a temporary terminus. Beyond this point, the route turned imperceptibly towards the east, and running along an embankment trains skirted the village of Little Dunham; to the right, Little Dunham's parish church could be glimpsed from the gently swaying carriages.

Dunham station (18 miles 36 chains) was a passing place with up and down platforms and a long goods loop on the up side, together with an array of three sidings to the west of the passenger station. The main 'Tudor gothic'-style station building was on the up side, and facilities on the opposite platform consisted of a waiting room and a standard Great Eastern-type signal cabin. The waiting room was a turn-of-the-century brick-built GER structure, while the neighbouring signal cabin was a typical brick and timber design with a glazed upper floor and a brick-built rear wall.

One of the first station masters here was Mr C. Underhill, who was assisted in the 1860s, by his son Francis. Having served a sort of 'apprenticeship' under his father's tutelage, Francis Underhill enjoyed a long and happy association with the Great Eastern Railway, and when he retired in 1918 he had served the company for no less than 51 years (much of the time was spent at Wroxham, on the neighbouring Cromer branch). Mr Underhill (Senior) remained in charge at Dunham until about 1890, and there were, thereafter, a succession of station masters, among them Alfred Page and Herbert Youell (thought to have been a relative of Harry Youell, who served at several other Norfolk stations).

In 1908 Dunham's station master was James Andrews, who replaced Herbert Youell in the early 1900s and was content to remain at this idyllic country station throughout World War I, the Grouping, and for several years after that; he was still working at Dunham in 1925, having supervised the station for a period of at least 20 years.

The longest-serving railwayman at Dunham was not station master Andrews but William Ellis, a porter, who started work at the station in September 1872 and retired in April 1921 after half-a-century of continuous service; he was 74 years old at the time of his retirement. Commenting on Mr Ellis's retirement, *The Great Eastern Railway Magazine* pointed out that William Ellis had joined the GER 'at a period when railway hours knew no limit', and this veteran railwayman could 'tell many interesting tales of the time previous to the introduction of the block telegraph . . . when he had to wait patiently, often until after midnight, for the arrival of special cattle trains'. His 'familiar face and powerful voice' would, added the GER magazine, 'be greatly missed by the travelling public, many of whom looked upon Mr Ellis as a station landmark'.

One reason for the exceptionally-long working lives of men such as William Ellis was of course the 1914–18 war, which produced severe labour shortages on the Home Front. With large numbers of able-bodied men serving in HM forces older employees were encouraged to remain at work long after they would otherwise have retired, while in a further effort to sustain the war effort, women were employed in jobs that had traditionally been regarded as 'men's work'. One of these female employees was Miss Gertrude Porter who worked at Dunham for 4½ years as a booking clerk. During that time she formed a friendship with John Etheridge, a porter, and

A view eastwards from the down platform at Dunham – which was, by the late 1960s, used for all traffic. The signal cabin had been demolished, and all points and connections had been removed. *Douglas Thompson*

Reproduced from the 1906, 25″ Ordnance Survey Map

on 30th April, 1921 the couple were married in Swaffham parish church. Two days previously, on 28th April, the staffs of Dunham and Fransham stations had gathered to see station master Andrews present the happy couple with an 'electro-plated teapot'; Mr Andrews wished the couple many years of happiness of behalf of himself and the rest of the station staff. Electro-plated teapots seem to have been the usual form of wedding present at Dunham, and in August 1919 signalman Sydney Betts was the recipient of a similar gift on the occasion of his own marriage![50]

Others employed at Dunham in the early 20th century included porters Harry Minns and John Sidney Neale, both of whom joined the Norfolk Regiment. Harry Minns volunteered for service at the start of the 1914–18 war, while John Neale also joined the army at the very start of the conflict; they were, at that time, serving at Wroxham and North Walsham respectively. Sadly both men perished in the war, together with Harry Neale's brother Charles – the latter had worked as a gate lad at Harleston prior to joining the Norfolk Regiment.

Fransham

Departing from Dunham, down trains passed beneath a road overbridge and immediately plunged into the line's summit cutting; Fransham, the next station, was only 1 mile 23 chains further on.

The smallest, and perhaps least important station on the Lynn & Dereham line, Fransham was 19 miles 59 chains from Kings Lynn. There was just one platform on the down side, and the station was not a block post – though a small signal box was provided in connection with the adjacent level crossing. Goods facilities were confined to a single siding on the up side of the line, and no goods shed or cattle dock was provided.

Fransham was not, in later years, considered important enough to have its own station master, and in the early LNER period it was placed under the control of James Andrews at nearby Dunham. Previous to this, Fransham seems to have had a bewildering succession of station masters, few of whom remained for more than a few months. In 1888 the station master was a Mr Durrant, but *Kelly's Directory of Norfolk* shows that in 1896 the station was supervised by Alfred Page. By 1900 Mr Page had been replaced by William Thomas, while in 1908 the station master was Harry Youell. This lack of continuity suggests that Fransham may have been regarded as an ideal 'first post' for young station masters, and in this context it is interesting to find that Harry Youell soon transferred to North Walsham, on the busy Cromer branch, where he remained for several years before moving into a more prestigious job as station master at Cromer (GER). Meanwhile, back at Fransham, Thomas Newall had taken over as station master by 1908, and he was still in office at the end of the Great Eastern period around 1923. Mr Newall was assisted, at the end of World War I, by Sydney Betts – who carried out a variety of duties in the capacity of porter-signalman; Mr Betts subsequently transferred to Dunham to take up a new post as a signalman.

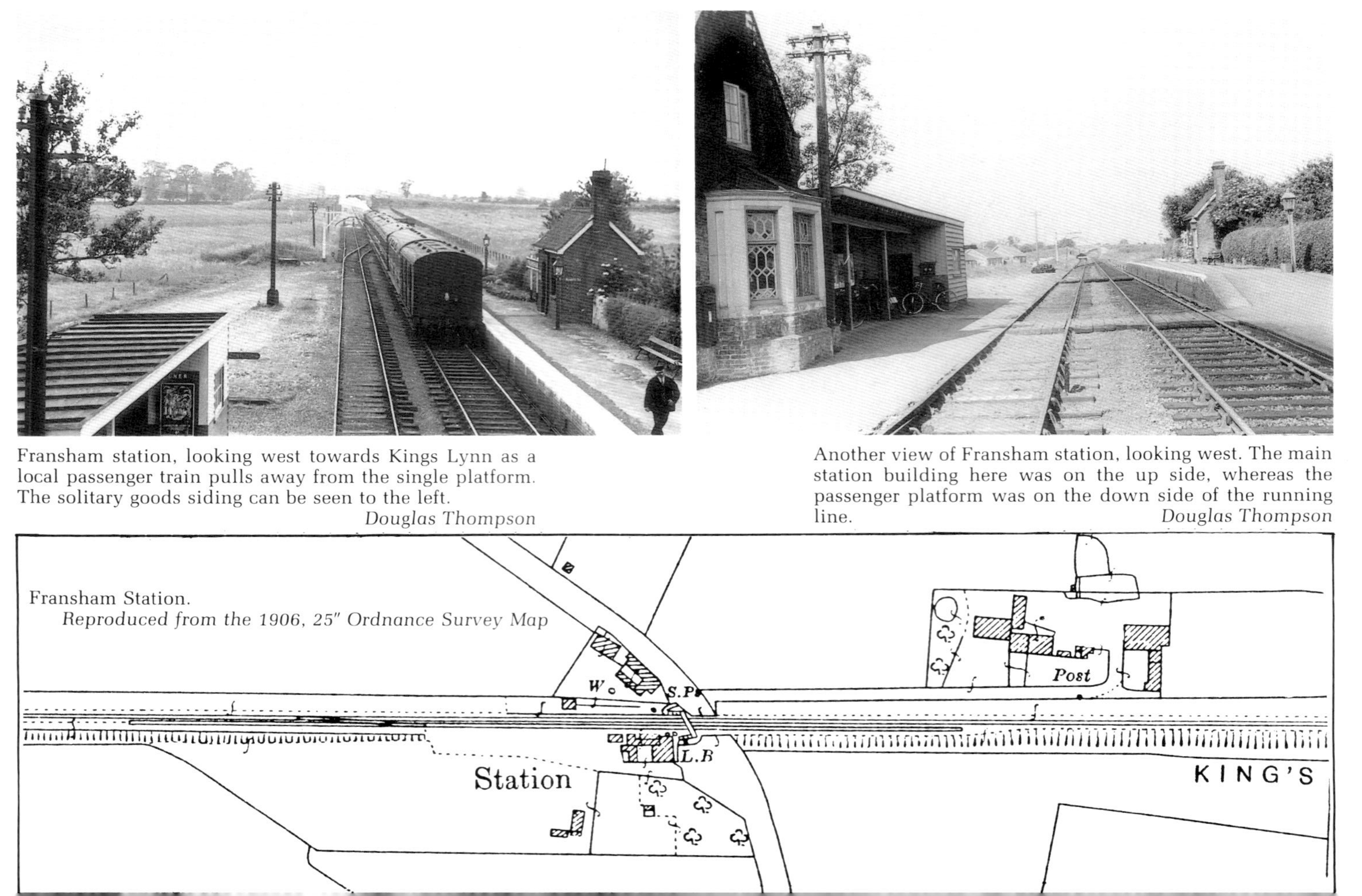

Fransham station, looking west towards Kings Lynn as a local passenger train pulls away from the single platform. The solitary goods siding can be seen to the left.
Douglas Thompson

Another view of Fransham station, looking west. The main station building here was on the up side, whereas the passenger platform was on the down side of the running line.
Douglas Thompson

Fransham Station.
Reproduced from the 1906, 25" Ordnance Survey Map

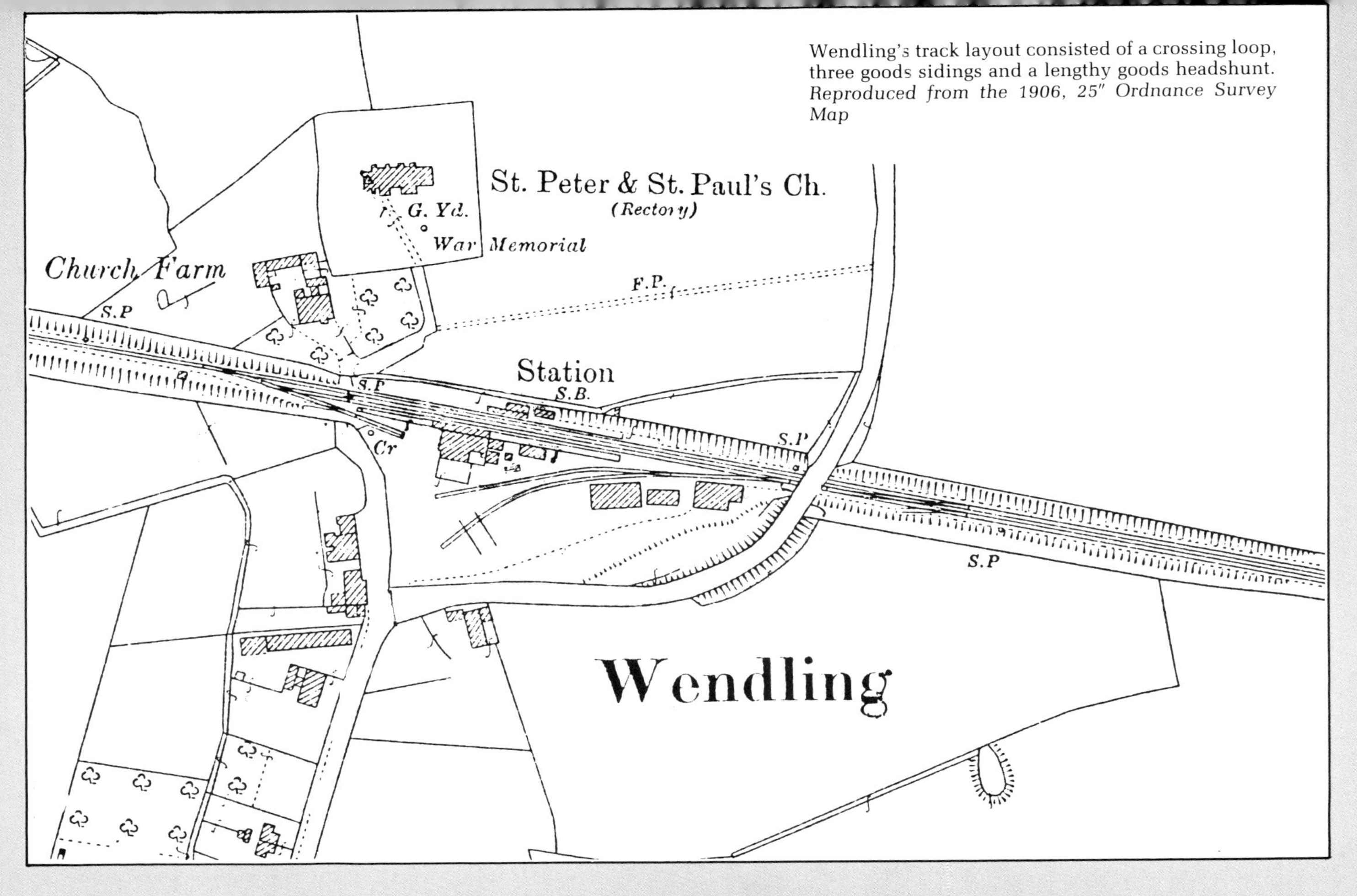

Wendling's track layout consisted of a crossing loop, three goods sidings and a lengthy goods headshunt. *Reproduced from the 1906, 25″ Ordnance Survey Map*

Wendling station, looking east towards Norwich; the lengthy goods headshunt can be glimpsed beneath the road overbridge, and the substantial station buildings are prominent to the right. *Douglas Thompson*

A view looking west from the overbridge seen in the previous photograph, showing the two-siding goods yard to the left. There was a third goods siding on the far side of the station building (*see plan*). *Douglas Thompson*

Wendling

From Frensham, the route continued due east, passing through a shallow cutting and then traversing an embankment that was pierced by a succession of small underbridges, by means of which a country lane and two farm tracks passed beneath the railway. With a minor road running parallel to the south, the line descended towards the village of Wendling and, about five minutes after leaving Fransham, trains came to a stand in the down platform at Wendling station.

A much larger place than neigbouring Fransham, Wendling was a two platform station, situated 22 miles 35 chains from Kings Lynn. Its station buildings and goods sidings were on the up side, facilities on the down platform being confined to a waiting shelter and GER type signal box.

Wendling's track plan incorporated a short dead-end spur at the west end of the up platform, together with two further sidings to the east and a long headshunt which extended eastwards beside the main line. The road from Wendling village to Longham was carried across the railway on an arched bridge to the east of the platform, and Wendling parish church was embowered in trees to the north of the station.

The main station building here was very similar to its counterpart at Dunham, both buildings being Tudor-gothic style stations incorporating domestic accommodation for the station master and his family. These two buildings both featured a two-storey domestic block, with a single-storey lean-to to the left (at Wendling) or to the right (at Dunham); the platform frontages were protected by substantial wooden canopies, supported by large curving brackets with trefoil spandrels (as at Swaffham).

Wendling station building had probably changed little since Lynn & Dereham days, though it was noticeable that the Great Eastern had added an additional, single-storey building to the east of the original L&DR structure; this later building – which was physically detached from its neighbour – was presumably needed to cater for growing traffic at the end of the 19th century.

The down side buildings were more complex than those at Swaffham or Dunham. As originally constructed, the down platform had probably been equipped with a simple open-fronted waiting shed like that at East Winch, but at the end of the 19th century this austere structure had clearly been regarded as inadequate, and the Great Eastern therefore added a more substantial waiting shed to the east of the original. At about the same time, a brick-built gentlemen's urinal was erected to the west of the original waiting shelter, and the accretion of buildings on the down platform was finally completed when the GER added a signal cabin beside the new waiting room extension.

The signal cabin was another typical Great Eastern Railway two-storey design with a fully glazed upper floor and a brick rear wall that extended to roof level; the front and side walls of the locking room were of timber construction, with a large 'double' window at platform level.

At night, Wendling's platforms were lit by oil lamps resting in Great Eastern style glass lanterns – one of which was bolted to the front of the signal cabin. The crossing loop was signalled by up home and starting signals and down home and starters, and it is interesting to note that some of these signals retained their GER wooden posts until the diesel era; the down home signal, for example, was a wooden posted specimen with an upper quadrant arm, while the up home retained its lower quadrant arm until the BR period!

Like all country railways, the Kings Lynn to Norwich line was very much a 'family' affair; staff and travellers were often personal friends, and in these happy circumstances GER employees sometimes spent their entire working lives at one place. Others served at different stations on the same line, starting, perhaps, as a lad porter or other junior employee and then moving to a more responsible job at a neighbouring station. Station masters moved from station to station in a similar search for higher pay or status; Charles Wilby, for example, was station master at Wendling before transferring to Narborough, while his predecessor (at Wendling) subsequently became station master at Dunham. The station master at Wendling during the Edwardian period was John Walpole, and his immediate successors included William Coman (c.1920) and Mr H. Pallintine, who was in charge of the station during the early LNER era.

Eastwards from Wendling, the line passed the site of Wendling Abbey – a Premonstratensian house belonging to the 'White Canons', who were supposed to devote themselves to preaching and theology (but were, in reality, as addicted to comfortable living as any other Medieval religious orders). The abbey was abolished at the Reformation and, apart from a few lumps and indentations in the surrounding fields, there were no visible signs of this Medieval religious establishment.

Continuing eastwards the railway crossed a tiny stream and, descending gradually, trains coasted through further cuttings before crossing the A47 road on an overbridge. Curving onto a north-easterly heading the single line then passed over a country lane on another overbridge as it approached its junction with the Norfolk Railway in the market town of East Dereham.

A later view of Wendling, taken on 24th August, 1968. All trains used the up platform following the removal of the crossing loop. *E. Wilmshurst*

The original wooden engine shed at Dereham. This ramshackle timber-framed structure was demolished around 1926 and a new shed, of brick construction, was erected in its place. The Norwich line can be seen to the left, while the north-to-west curve is visible to the right. *National Railway Museum*

Another view of the two-road engine shed at Dereham. A GER 'T26' class 2–4–0 is standing on the north-to-west curve, and some of Dereham's extensive agricultural factories can be seen in the background. *National Railway Museum*

Dereham West Junction, looking west towards Kings Lynn. The signal box was later moved to a new position, beyond the level crossing.

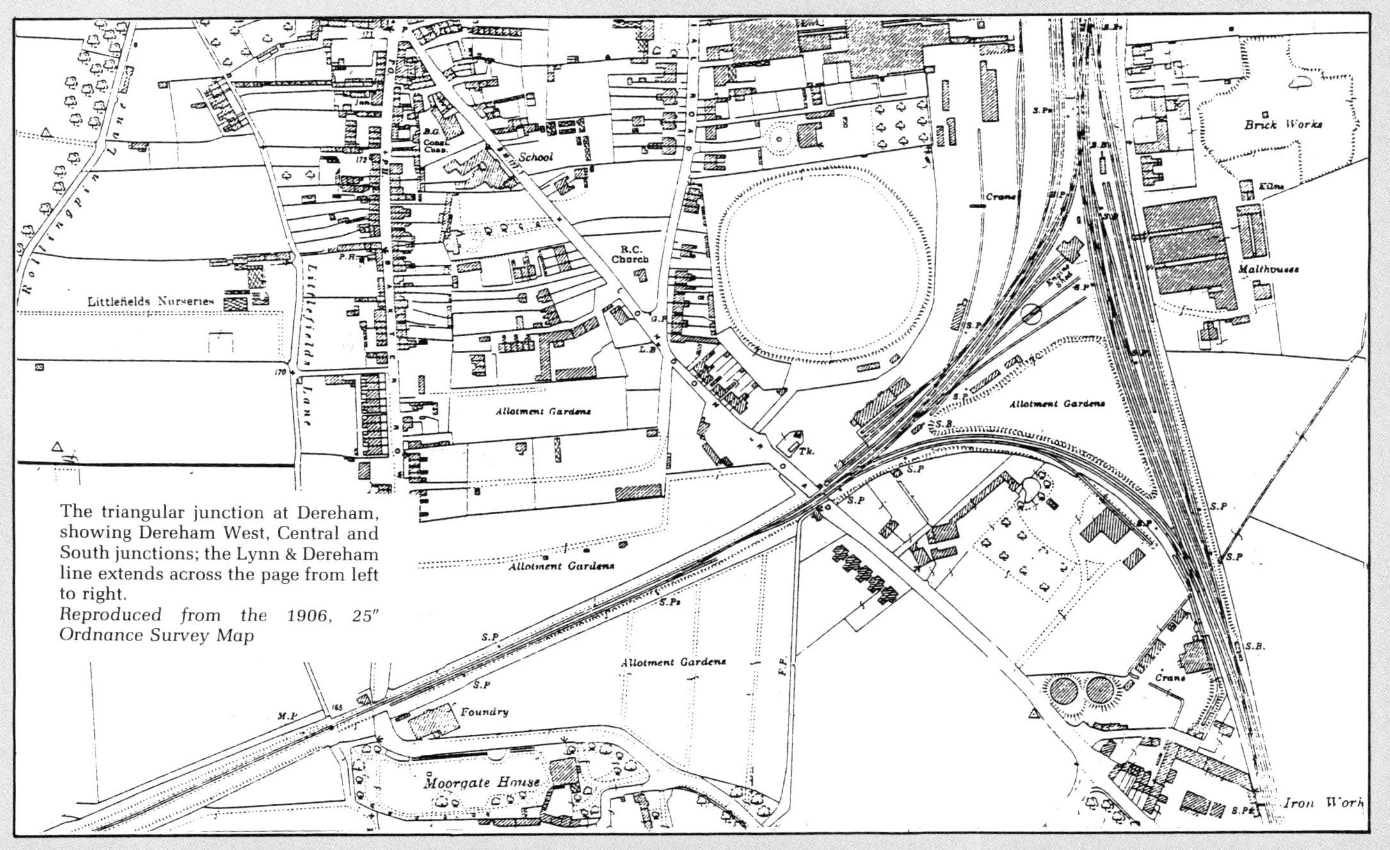

The triangular junction at Dereham, showing Dereham West, Central and South junctions; the Lynn & Dereham line extends across the page from left to right.

Reproduced from the 1906, 25" Ordnance Survey Map

Dereham station, looking north towards Wells-next-the-Sea during the early 1900s; the Kings Lynn branch bay is to the left of the picture, while the goods shed can be seen to the right of the main up and down platforms. *National Railway Museum*

DEREHAM. G.E.R.

The main station buildings at Dereham, seen from the rear in this *c*.1910 view. The decorative 'Tudor' chimney stacks can be clearly seen. *Lens of Sutton*

The platforms at Dereham, looking north towards Wells-next-the-Sea during the LNER era. A Kings Lynn branch train occupies the bay platform (*left*) while a Great Eastern tender locomotive takes water in the distance. *Lens of Sutton*

A two-car multiple unit train leaves Dereham in October 1969. *E. Wilmshurst*

Dereham Central box was a relatively large cabin with a 50-lever McKenzie & Holland frame. It was built around 1880. *Douglas Thompson*

Chapter Six

Along the Line (2): Dereham to Norwich

Opened by the Norfolk Railway in February 1847, Dereham station was orientated on a north-to-south alignment, and Kings Lynn trains, having arrived from the west, were faced with a sharp curve before they could enter the station proper. Before this, however, the railway passed over two closely-spaced level crossings prior to reaching Dereham West Junction, where the direct curve to Norwich (used mainly by freight and excursion trains) diverged to the right. The junction was controlled from a 36-lever signal box that had first been opened (as 'Dereham D Box') in April 1880, but was later rebuilt on a new site to the west of the junction points.

As their train negotiated the west-to-north curve travellers could, by glancing to the right, see Dereham's two-road engine shed, with its 45 ft diameter turntable; originally a wooden structure with a prominent clerestory along the apex of its roof, the shed was later rebuilt in more durable brick. The rebuilt shed was slightly longer than its wooden predecessor, with a total length of about 52 ft. The usual allocation included 'E4' 2–4–0s, 'F3' 2–4–2Ts and other typical Great Eastern classes, and these locomotives could often be seen in the shed or alongside the primitive coaling stage. Messroom and office facilities were sited in a small extension that adjoined the southern wall of the shed, and additional storage space was available in a single storey shed on the far side of the locomotive turntable.

Having passed the locomotive shed trains joined the former Norfolk Railway in Dereham station, and here, in a busy junction station some 26 miles 43 chains from Kings Lynn, the first part of the cross-country journey to Norwich came to an end.

Although Dereham was merely a small country town with a population (around 1950) of just 8,000, its station was a place of some importance, shared by trains to Wroxham, Norwich, Kings Lynn and Wells-next-the-Sea. Long up and down platforms were provided, the down platform being much longer than its counterpart on the up side. There was an additional, dead-end bay on the down side, and this bay had run-round facilities for the benefit of trains which terminated their journeys here.

The main station building was on the down side, and in common with the stations on the Lynn & Dereham line, its flamboyant architectural features exhibited pronounced 'Tudor' features. There were, nevertheless, many differences between Dereham and the stations *en route* to Kings Lynn – which was, after all, only to be expected when one recalls that Dereham was a Norfolk Railway station and not part of the Lynn & Dereham Railway. The station's long platforms were partially covered by extensive canopies, and a privately-run refreshment room catered for the needs of hungry travellers.

To casual observers, the most noticeable architectural feature of Dereham's Tudor-style station buildings were the tall, cylindrical chimney stacks with their ornate helical mouldings. In later years, some of these chimneys were rebuilt in plain brickwork, but several of the original 'Tudor'-style examples remained *in situ* until closure.

Some trains were divided at Dereham, the usual practice, around 1930, being for the front portions of northbound workings to run through to Wells, while the rearmost vehicles were taken to Kings Lynn by another locomotive. In the opposite direction, a few trains from Kings Lynn were combined with services from Wells-next-the-Sea, and the two portions would then go forward to Norwich as one working.

Dereham's goods facilities were lavish, and consisted of a large goods shed on the up side, plus several loops and various private sidings which branched out to serve Dereham gas works, Whitbread's maltings, Fison & Son, Stammers' mill, and other lineside agricultural premises.

The goods shed was situated immediately behind the up platform – in which position it formed a convenient support for a length of platform canopy. The goods shed was built of brick, and it incorporated an internal loading platform so that small freight and sundries traffic could be unloaded undercover. An office extended from the south gable as a sort of lean-to addition; on closer examination this part of the structure appeared to have been a modern addition, and photographs confirm that it dated from a rebuilding of the goods shed that had been carried out by the LNER around 1939.[51]

Dereham's up and down platforms were linked by a lattice girder footbridge, and a similar bridge was provided beyond the platforms for the benefit of pedestrians using Norwich Street. Other details at this end of the station included a substantial brick water tower, beyond which, a water column was available for engines heading north towards Wells-next-the-Sea. Locomotives needing water were detached from their trains and run 'light' for the short distance to the watering point, this movement being controlled by a raised disc signal near the water tower; when their tanks were replenished, the engines were then returned to the down platform, where they were re-coupled to their trains prior to resuming the northwards journey to Wells-next-the-Sea.

Minor structures in and around Dereham station included the usual diverse collection of huts, sheds and stores. There was, for instance, a small brick-built hut at the north end of the up platform, while platelayers' huts and storage facilities were scattered around the station and goods yard area. A diminutive brick-built structure on the up platform housed a gentlemen's urinal, and, nearby, a swan-necked water crane provided watering facilities for southbound trains.

The station was liberally-supplied with signal cabins and, in addition to the 'West' box at Dereham West Junction there were three other cabins. Dereham North Box was a 24-lever cabin at the north end of the up platform. It had first been installed in April 1888,[52] and like most of the other signal boxes between Kings Lynn and Norwich it was a standard Great Eastern structure, with a glazed upper floor and a two-pitch gabled roof. All of Dereham's signal cabins were timber-framed buildings clad in horizontal weather boarding; they were heated by stoves, and tall stovepipe chimneys extended vertically from their slated roofs.

The station proper was controlled from Dereham Central Box, a large, 50-lever cabin dating from about 1880 and incorporating a McKenzie & Holland

Dereham station, looking south with the Kings Lynn line to the right and the Wymondham line to the left; the signal incorporates an interesting mixture of GER, LNER and BR components. Dereham Central box can be seen to the left of the running lines. *C.L. Mowat Collection*

A busy scene at Dereham during the early 1960s. Up and down Wells trains wait in the main platform while a class '101' Metro-Cammell unit waits in the Kings Lynn bay. A class '31' A1A-A1A locomotive stands in the goods yard during a break in shunting operations (*right*). Note the swan-necked water crane on the up platform. *N.E. Stead*

frame. A separate box, known as Dereham South, controlled the southernmost extremity of the station layout – including the eastern end of the Dereham avoiding line, which converged from Dereham West Junction at a point some 16 chains south of Dereham Central Box.

Dereham itself could be seen to the west and north of the station; this prosperous country town contained many attractive old houses, including some thatched cottages near the church which were associated with Bishop Edmund Bonner, who burned many unfortunate Protestants during the notorious reign of Mary I. Nearby, the detached bell-tower of East Dereham church was once used as a prison for French prisoners-of-war – one of whom was shot while trying to escape and is buried in the church yard.

In operational terms, Dereham was of significance in that down trains from Kings Lynn became 'up' workings for the remainder of their journeys to Wymondham, while in the opposite direction, westbound services became 'up' trains at this point! There was some logic behind this apparent change of direction in that most passenger trains did in fact reverse in Dereham station – it should be added, however, that a similar situation pertained in the case of trains using the Dereham avoiding line, even though these workings passed from the Lynn & Dereham Railway and onto the Norfolk line *without* changing direction!

Dereham was, even more than Swaffham, an important rural junction which in its heyday provided employment for large numbers of clerks, porters, signalmen, permanent way men, engine crews and supervisory staff. The local station master was, needless to say, an important figure who would today be regarded as a 'middle manager' in his own right; Mr Charles Eastaugh supervised the station during the later Victorian period, but Francis Arthur Easton had taken over by 1904, and he remained in office for several years thereafter.

The station master in 1922 was Frederick Young, while others working at Dereham in the post-World War I period included signalmen C. Carter and G. Clarke, porter T. Bone, shunter T. London, and chief goods clerk R. Syder – who had worked at the station for at least 25 years.

The pages of *The Great Eastern Railway Magazine* provide many glimpses of life at Dereham station, and show that GER employees indulged in a wide range of social activities. Railwaymen were, for example, encouraged to study first aid, and in February 1920 the GER magazine revealed that Messrs E.G. Cocker, H.F. Cocker, W. Wells, W. Salmon, S. Howell, P. Douglas, H. Sales and C. Carter had received their ambulance certificates from Dr J.K. Howlett, (the Hon. Surgeon) while E. Bellchamber and R. Graveling had received vouchers. Station master Young had also presented Dr Howlett with 'a gold-mounted briar pipe and tobacco pouch which had been purchased by the members to show their appreciation of the great interest he had taken in their work'.

In May 1921 the magazine printed an essay by signalman C. Carter entitled 'My Holiday', while the same edition featured an item on goods clerk R. Syder, who had recently been presented with 'a silver-mounted walking stick' in recognition of his services as auditor to the staff coal club. A further item, in August 1921, reported that Dereham railwaymen had attended the

Dereham South Junction in GER days, looking north towards the station; the direct line to Kings Lynn diverges to the left, and the engine shed is visible in the distance. *National Railway Museum*

Dereham South Junction in GER days, looking towards Norwich. Dereham South Box stands on the up side of the main line, while the gas works siding can be seen on the opposite side of the railway. *National Railway Museum*

unveiling of a war memorial in the parish church, and placed a wreath 'in remembrance of colleagues who had made the supreme sacrifice'.

Leaving Dereham passenger station eastbound trains proceeded – as 'up' workings – past Dereham Central Box and over a complex web of pointwork. With the rear wall of Dereham engine shed visible to the right, the route curved gradually south-eastwards as it approached Dereham South Junction and the converging west-to-south curve.

Dereham South Box was situated on the east side of the line. Added around 1880 (ie shortly before the opening of the west-to-south avoiding line) it had originally been known as 'Dereham A Box'. A 30-lever frame was initially installed, but the box was rebuilt by the LNER with a 32-lever frame. The Dereham triangle was severely speed restricted, and working timetables reveal that trains passing between the West and Central, and West and South junctions were subject to a strict 15 mph speed limit in each direction.

Yaxham

From Dereham, the route continued due south towards the quaintly-named hamlet of Dumpling Green where, in 1813, the writer George Borrow had been born. Cuttings prevented a clear view, though a few houses could be glimpsed as trains crossed the B1135 road on the level. Emerging from the cutting, the railway dipped slightly into the Tud Valley before crossing the River Tudd on a small bridge; Yaxham, the next stop, was only a short distance further on.

Situated some 28 miles 35 chains from Kings Lynn (via Dereham station), Yaxham was a two platform station, with picturesque Tudor-style buildings on the down side. Architecturally, Yaxham was, like the rest of the stations between Kings Lynn and Norwich, of great interest and charm, and indeed its ornate Victorian buildings would not have been out of place at a much larger station. The main building, of Norfolk Railway vintage, incorporated a two storey station master's dwelling, while an adjacent, glass-fronted waiting room was clearly of Great Eastern origin.

The goods yard contained a large, gabled goods shed, together with an end-loading dock and a coal wharf. Other sidings diverged from the down side of the line in order to serve a neighbouring granary, and it was possible – via a connection between the up main line and the granary headshunt – for southbound goods trains to reverse across the down main line in order to pick-up loaded vehicles from this private siding.

Yaxham's relatively complex track layout was controlled from a standard Great Eastern wooden signal cabin, which was (unusually) attached to a range of brick-and-timber waiting rooms on the up platform. The box itself was of typical Great Eastern appearance, and it contained a 26-lever McKenzie & Holland frame.

A minor road crossed the line on the level at the north end of the platforms, and the resulting level crossing was also of typical GER design, with a single set of gates which – being of great size and weight – needed sturdy diagonal bracing and massive white-painted gate posts (although primarily a structural feature these prominent white posts gave drivers a useful visual

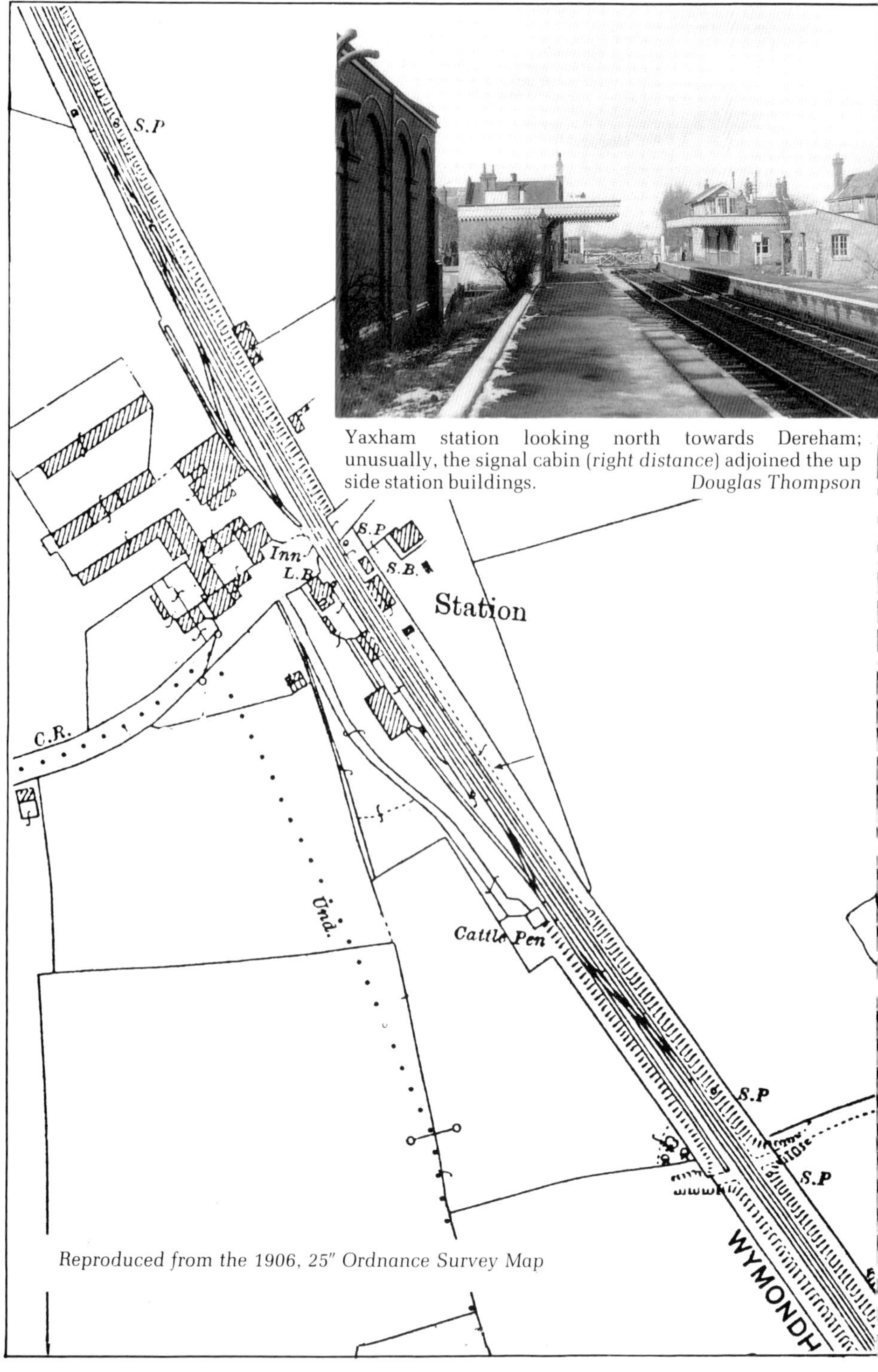

Yaxham station looking north towards Dereham; unusually, the signal cabin (*right distance*) adjoined the up side station buildings. *Douglas Thompson*

Reproduced from the 1906, 25" Ordnance Survey Map

identification when approaching each crossing).

The station master in 1888, and indeed for many years thereafter, was Harry Stokes, but by 1912 Mr Stokes had been replaced by Robert Simpson who came to Yaxham from Middleton and remained for 11 years before moving to Wroxham in 1922. Little is known of those employed at Yaxham during the Norfolk Railway's independent existence, though *Kelly's Directory of Norfolk* provides useful details of the earliest station masters, among them John Playford, who supervised the station during the 1850s.

Thuxton

Leaving Yaxham, southbound trains ran south-eastwards, running first in cuttings and then on a further stretch of embankment. With the B1135 running parallel to the right, the route passed close by the villages of Whinburgh and Garveston, but no stations were provided at these places – the villages concerned being conveniently close to Yaxham or Thuxton stations.

One of the smaller intermediate stations, Thuxton was 37 miles 4 chains from Kings Lynn. There was a level crossing to the south of the platforms, and the main station buildings were on the down side. Like their counterparts elsewhere on the line, these structures exhibited an interesting mixture of architectural styles, and whereas the main block, with its two storey station master's house and quaint 'Tudor' details was of Norfolk Railway origin, the detached brick-and-timber waiting room was of obvious Great Eastern appearance and displayed the letters 'GER' in its iron canopy supports.

Goods facilities here were, in later years at least, suitable only for coal class traffic and general merchandise; there was no cattle dock or end-loading dock, and no goods shed or fixed crane was provided. The single siding goods yard was situated on the down side, and to the north of the platforms; the siding was linked to the down main via a trailing connection, while a crossover/single slip arrangement allowed access from the up main line. Thuxton was not a block post, the signal box having been reduced to ground frame status in 1933.[53]

As we have seen, some of the stations between Kings Lynn and Norwich had several different station masters in a relatively short space of time, while others enjoyed the services of long-serving railwaymen such as James Andrews at Dunham; a similar situation pertained at Thuxton in that station master William Barker remained in office for a period of at least 30 years from the early 1890s until the 1920s.

In contrast to certain other country stations, Thuxton was well-sited in relation to the small settlement that it purported to serve, and Thuxton village was within easy walking distance of the railway; the parish church, with its Perpendicular nave and Decorated tower, was on the south side of the line.

Hardingham

Departing from Thuxton, trains continued south-eastwards, with the River Yare to the left and the B1135 away to the right. After about half a mile, the

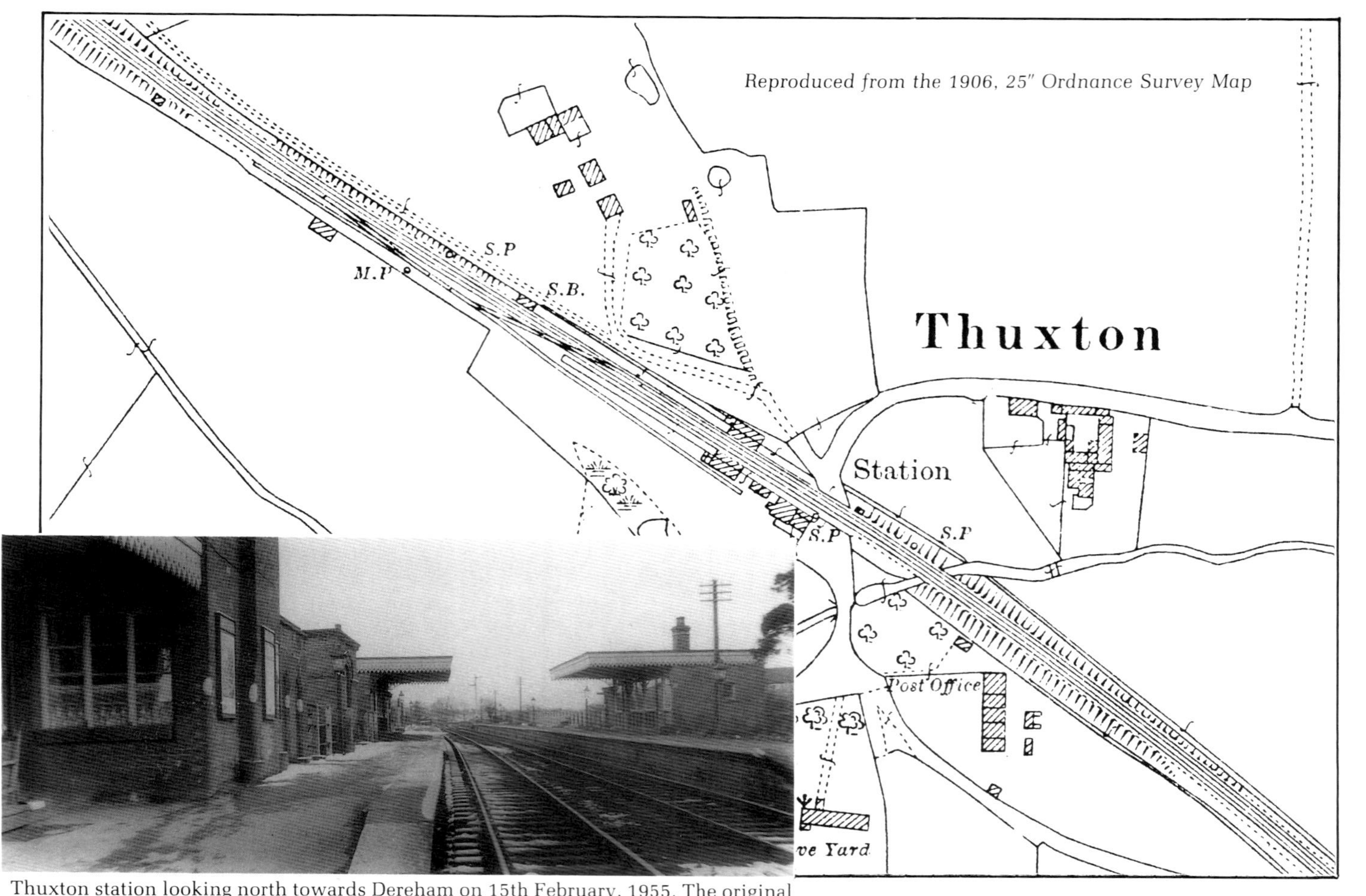

Thuxton station looking north towards Dereham on 15th February, 1955. The original Norfolk Railway station buildings here were much altered during the Great Eastern

route emerged from a cutting and, running on a long embankment, the double track railway approached Hardingham, crossing first the sparkling River Blackwater, and then the lane from Runhall to Hardingham village.

Hardingham station was 32 miles 34 chains from Kings Lynn and, like most of the other stopping places *en route* to Norwich, this two-platform station was lavishly-equipped, with extensive station buildings and a relatively complex track layout incorporating most of the facilities needed at a local railhead serving a wide rural area.

The main station building was on the down side. Of Tudoresque appearance, it was similar to other station buildings between Wymondham and Dereham, with prominent gables, ornate chimneys and *cottage ornée* windows. The building was an 'L' shaped structure, with a two storey domestic wing (incorporating the station master's house) and a single storey waiting room block. The platform frontage was protected by a projecting canopy which, on closer examination, was really *two* canopies placed side-by-side; the southernmost section was of GER vintage, but the northern half, with its plain saw tooth decoration, was possibly of Norfolk Railway origin.

Facilities on the up platform were more primitive, and consisted of nothing more than a simple waiting room; this structure had a Great Eastern type canopy, and probably dated from the doubling of the line in 1882. The nearby signal cabin was a standard GER design with 21 levers.

The goods yard here was on the down side; only two sidings were available, but each of these had its own headshunt, and the resulting configuration was more complex than might be imagined. A wagon turntable gave access to three short spurs, and the yard layout was made more complex by the presence of a double slip. An additional siding was sited to the north of the down platform, and this siding was linked to both the up and down running lines.

Other facilities at Hardingham included the usual cattle pens, loading dock, and a rail-connected granary belonging to J. Baly & Sons. Hardingham village was over a mile to the south of the railway, but like other rural stations Hardingham functioned as a railhead, not for one, but for a group of dispersed villages. Moreover the presence of a station often became a focus for Victorian building development, and something of this nature took place at Hardingham – where an inn, a chapel and several houses grew up around the station during the 19th century.

Hardingham's longest-serving station master was probably Charles Howard Smith, who entered GER service in 1867 and retired in 1917 after a career spanning 50 years. Mr Smith's very first appointment was as a clerk at Yarmouth Vauxhall, and he became a station master in 1878, serving first at Buckenham before moving on to Ashwellthorpe, Brundall and finally Hardingham; he arrived at the latter station around 1887 and stayed for no less than three decades. (After his retirement, Mr Smith lived for several years at 'Venetian House', Wymondham.)

One of Charles Smith's immediate successors was Walter Tallent, who had served at County School, Kimberley and other Norfolk stations before transferring to Hardingham after World War I.[54]

A detailed view of Hardingham signal box. This standard GER cabin had a 21-lever McKenzie & Holland frame. *Douglas Thompson*

Hardingham station, looking west during the British Railways period. The goods loading docks to the left have been filled-in by building materials, but otherwise the station is still more or less intact. *Douglas Thompson*

A rear view of Kimberley station, showing characteristic 'brick-and-flint' walling on the original Norfolk Railway buiding; the canopy visible here was probably a Great Eastern addition. *G.R. Mortimer*

A useful shot of the platform at Kimberley Park. Items of interest include the 'GER' spandrels (*right*) and the varied collection of two-wheeled platform trolleys (left). *Douglas Thompson*

Kimberley Park

From Hardingham the route entered a succession of cuttings which continued for well over a mile. Beyond, the line emerged onto an embankment and, passing over an occupation bridge, trains descended towards the next stop at Kimberley Park (34 miles 17 chains).

Until 1923 this station was known simply at 'Kimberley', but after the Grouping its name was changed to Kimberley Park in order to avoid confusion with a former GNR station at Kimberley in Nottinghamshire. Up and down platforms were provided, the main buildings being on the down side, while a smaller waiting room was situated on the up platform. A minor road crossed the line on the level at the Dereham end of the station, and there was a standard Great Eastern signal cabin at the southern end of the down platform.

The goods yard, situated on the down side of the line, consisted of a single siding linked by trailing connections to both the up and down main lines; loading docks and a cattle pen were provided, but Kimberley had no goods shed or yard crane.

The station master here at the end of the 19th century was James Raney, and his successors included Gabriel Paynter and Walter Tallent, both of whom found subsequent employment at neighbouring GER stations such as County School and Narborough. A later station master, Mr F. Bloom, left Kimberley in 1920 to take up a new position at Silver Street; he was replaced at Kimberley by Francis Belton, who was still in office around 1925.[55]

Wymondham

Accelerating from Kimberley, trains descended, through cuttings, towards the village of Crownthorpe, but no station was provided here and the railway curved round the village in a great arc. Nearing Wymondham, the line first passed beneath the B1135 road, and then, a short distance further on, trains rattled over Church Lane level crossing; to the right, an ornate crossing keeper's cottage was a reminder of the early days of the Norfolk Railway, while to the left the lofty towers of Wymondham Abbey church rose impressively above the line. In 1920 a siding was installed at this point to serve a nearby brush factory and a new signal box, known as Church Lane, was erected to control this new facility.

Entering a cutting, the line approached Wymondham South Junction, where a standard GER signal box controlled the converging Dereham and Ely routes. Gaining the down main line, trains then entered Wymondham station, coming to rest in the down platform.

Situated on the busy Norwich to Cambridge main line, Wymondham was 37 miles 76 chains from Kings Lynn. The station seemed, at first glance, to have been designed as a three platform junction, the up side being an island with tracks on either side. The outermost platform face was, however, fenced off, and in later years the station functioned as a two platform stopping place, the 'third line' behind the up platform being used as a goods loop.

Wymondham station in the Edwardian era. Railwaymen and travellers pose in the sunshine on a summer afternoon, and the distinctive brick and flint buildings can be seen to advantage. *Lens of Sutton*

A platform scene at Wymondham. The platform to the left of the main line is thought to have been designed as an island, though for most of its life it functioned as a side platform – the outer line (*left*) being used as a bypass line for goods trains. *Douglas Thompson*

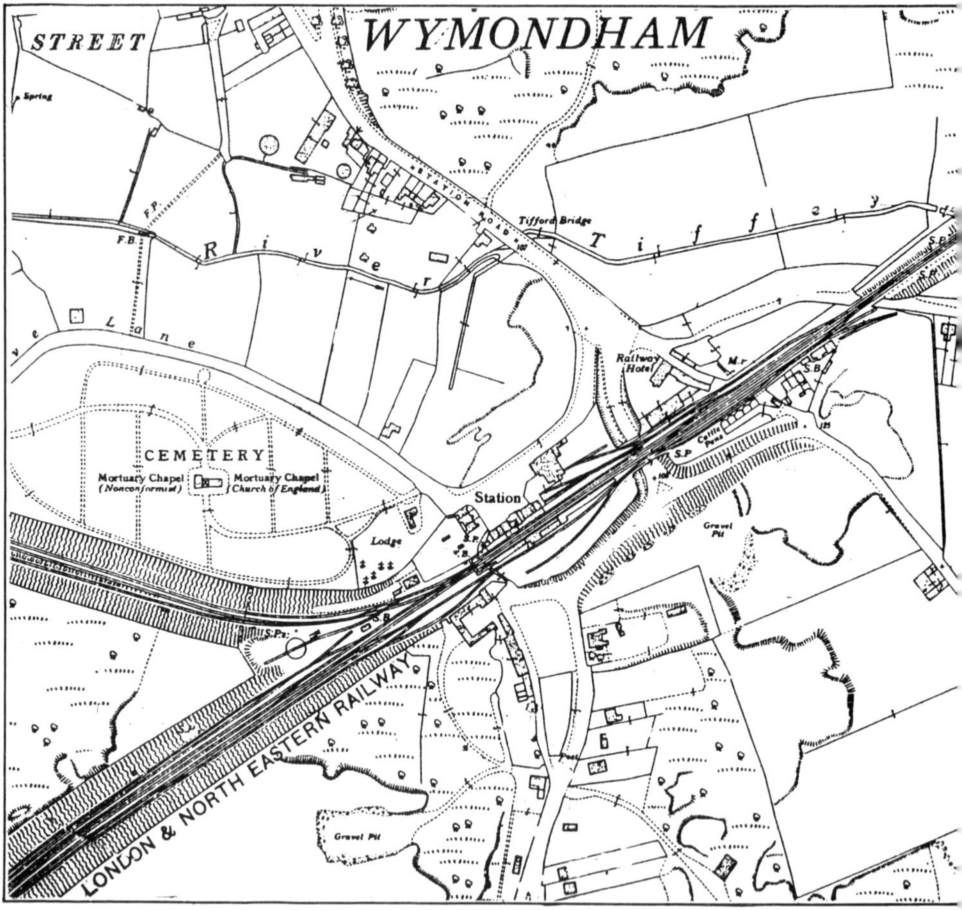

Wymondham station and junction.

Reproduced from the 1906, 25″ Ordnance Survey map

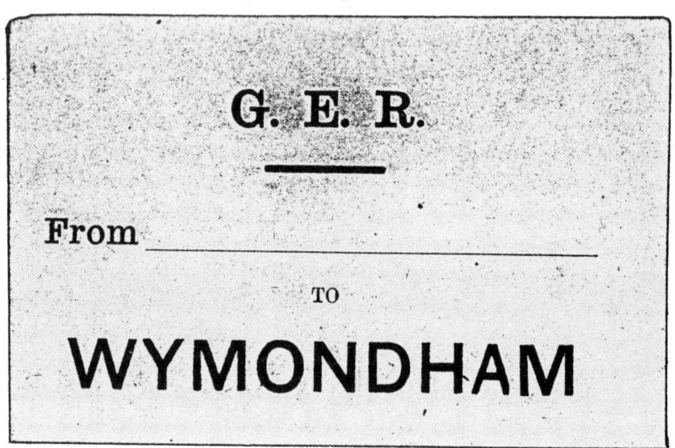

G. E. R.

From

TO

WYMONDHAM

Courtesy John Strange

The main station buildings were on the down side, but there were substantial passenger facilities on the up platform in addition to the main booking office and waiting rooms. The up and down platforms were linked by a lattice girder footbridge, from which those with an interest in railway operation could obtain a good view of Wymondham's extensive goods sidings. The main goods yard was situated on the down side, to the north of the passenger station, but there were additional loops and sidings on both sides of the running lines, together with several private sidings which served nearby roadstone quarries.

The layout was large enough to justify the provision of two signal boxes, although the North box was reduced to ground frame status during the BR period; the larger, South box, had a 42-lever McKenzie & Holland frame.

Wymondham's importance stemmed from its role as a junction, not only for the Kings Lynn and Wells lines, but also for the Forncett branch, which diverged south-eastwards from the main line at Wymondham North Junction. Opened on 2nd May, 1881, the Forncett line formed a useful link between the Cambridge and Ipswich main lines, and although there were very few through trains between Dereham and Forncett, there was, at one time, a useful local service to and from Wymondham, and travellers wishing to avoid an intermediate change at Norwich were sometimes able to reach London in good time by changing at Wymondham and Forncett.

In emergencies, the Forncett line formed an alternative path for London to Norwich traffic, and when, in 1912, the main line was blocked by flooding at Flordon, Norwich expresses were re-routed via Wymondham from where, after reversal, they were able to reach their destination via the Cambridge main line.

Wymondham's junction facilities included a locomotive siding and a 45 ft diameter turntable. Situated in the 'V' of the junction between the Dereham and Ely lines, the turntable was useful when tender engines were employed on the Forncett branch service, but (as far as can be ascertained) Wymondham was not an engine 'shed' in the accepted sense of the term. It is conceivable that, in Norfolk Railway days, a proper shed had been available, but in later years Wymondham might more accurately have been described as a stabling point.

In the mid-1950s, Wymondham's usual allocation was a 'J69' 0–6–0T or a 'J15' 0–6–0, one of the engines noted at Wymondham around 1956 being 'J69' 0–6–0T No. 68616. These locomotives were used for local shunting duties, for which purpose an 0–6–0T or 0–6–0 would be sent out from Norwich and stabled overnight in the engine siding. (Later still, around 1968, these duties were performed by an '08' class 0–6–0 diesel shunter.)

Having reached the London to Norwich main line, Kings Lynn to Norwich workings became 'down' trains for the remainder of their journey to Norwich Thorpe – this theoretical change of direction (the second since leaving Kings Lynn!) being necessary because, after leaving the branch, trains gained the down main line for the final leg of their journey to Norwich.

From Wymondham, through trains proceeded north-eastwards towards Norwich, passing the site of Wymondham North Junction, and entering the

Wymondham South Junction signal box had a 42-lever McKenzie & Holland frame; the Dereham line passes behind the box, while the Norwich to Cambridge main line is visible in the foreground. *Douglas Thompson*

A general view of the west end of Wymondham station, looking towards Wymondham South Junction; the Dereham route diverges to the right. *C. L. Mowat Collection*

open country beyond. The junction was of some interest in that it was once formed of interlaced trackwork; the pointwork was situated at the northernmost extremity of the station layout, the main line and branch being interlaced from that point to the bifurcation of the two routes. In 1917 the junction was moved to the actual point of divergence, and the interlaced trackwork was removed.[56]

Norwich Thorpe

Heading north-eastwards along the Ely to Norwich main line, most trains passed through the wayside station at Hethersett without stopping, and soon reached a deep cutting over which the Norwich to London route passed on an impressive arched viaduct. Beyond, the route continued to Trowse Lower Junction, where the London route converged from the left. Curving north-westwards, trains passed over the pointwork at Thorpe Junction, and with a vast array of sidings now visible to the left, the 48 mile 14 chain journey from Kings Lynn drew to a close.

Opened in 1844 as the western terminus of the Yarmouth & Norwich Railway, Norwich Thorpe was used by Norwich & Brandon trains from 15th December, 1845. Although the Eastern Union Railway opened a separate terminus at Norwich Victoria in 1849, Norwich Thorpe became the city's main terminal station after the formation of the Great Eastern Railway in 1862.

The station was substantially rebuilt in 1886, as a result of which it acquired an impressive brick and stone façade of somewhat 'Central European' appearance. Designed by W. Ashbee, the GER architect, this stylish, two storey building incorporated a centrally-placed dome, with a *porte-cochère* in front, and long wings on either side. Behind its towering dome, the station was an essentially simple affair, with three island platforms providing just six main platform faces. There were large numbers of goods sidings to the south of the passenger station, while numerous other sidings branched out to serve the former Norfolk Railway locomotive works which, in later years, became part of one of the GER's largest engine sheds.

A triangular junction at the southern end of the station enabled through passenger or freight workings to avoid the station entirely, and this avoiding line (known as the Wensum Curve) was regularly used by prestige trains such as 'The Norfolk Coast Express' on its summer schedules.

Norwich Thorpe was controlled from separate passenger and goods boxes, together with Norwich Junction box at the north end of the triangular junction, and Trowse Swing Bridge Junction and Wensum Junction boxes at the west and east ends of the Wensum Curve respectively.

Much of Norwich's freight traffic was handled in the goods sidings at Norwich Victoria, but Norwich Thorpe was (until comparatively recently) a very busy freight centre. Other goods facilities were situated at Norwich Trowse, the most important traffic handled at the latter station being in connection with Messrs Colman's vast mustard works, which was served by its own siding connection from Trowse goods yard.

Hethersett station, some 6¼ miles from Norwich, was served by most Dereham trains in GER and LNER days, though in the BR period many trains passed through this wayside station without stopping. *Douglas Thompson*

Although it occupied the approximate site of the original Norfolk Railway terminus, Norwich Thorpe was a relatively modern station, dating from 1886. The station was bombed by the Luftwaffe in World War II, and evidence of the resulting damage can be seen in this c.1952 view. *Lens of Sutton*

An earlier view of Norwich Thorpe station, taken *c*.1921. *Photomatic*

'Claud Hamilton' 4–4–0 No. 62604 awaits the 'right away' at Norwich Thorpe during the early 1950s. *Douglas Thompson*

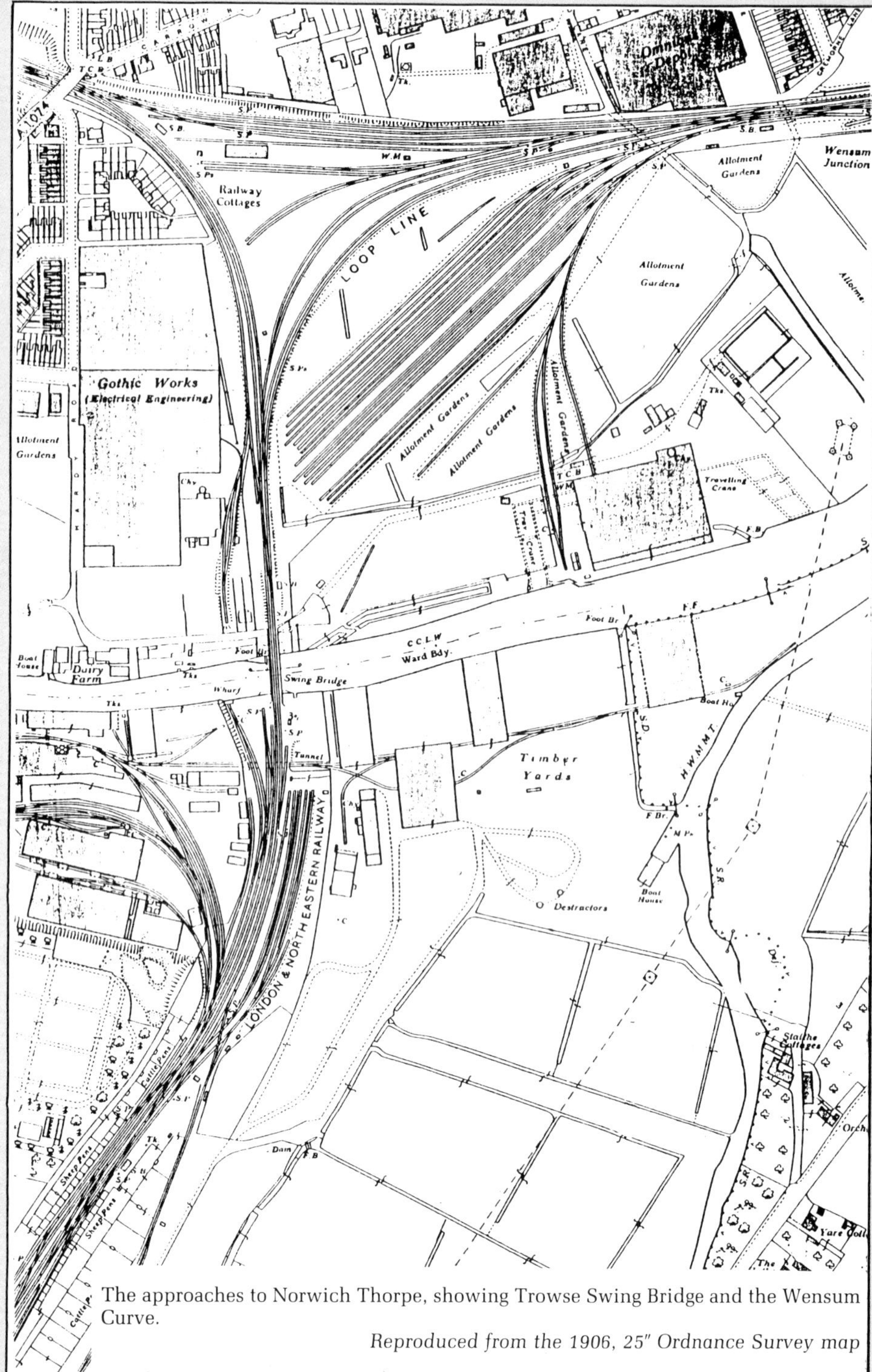

The approaches to Norwich Thorpe, showing Trowse Swing Bridge and the Wensum Curve.

Reproduced from the 1906, 25" Ordnance Survey map

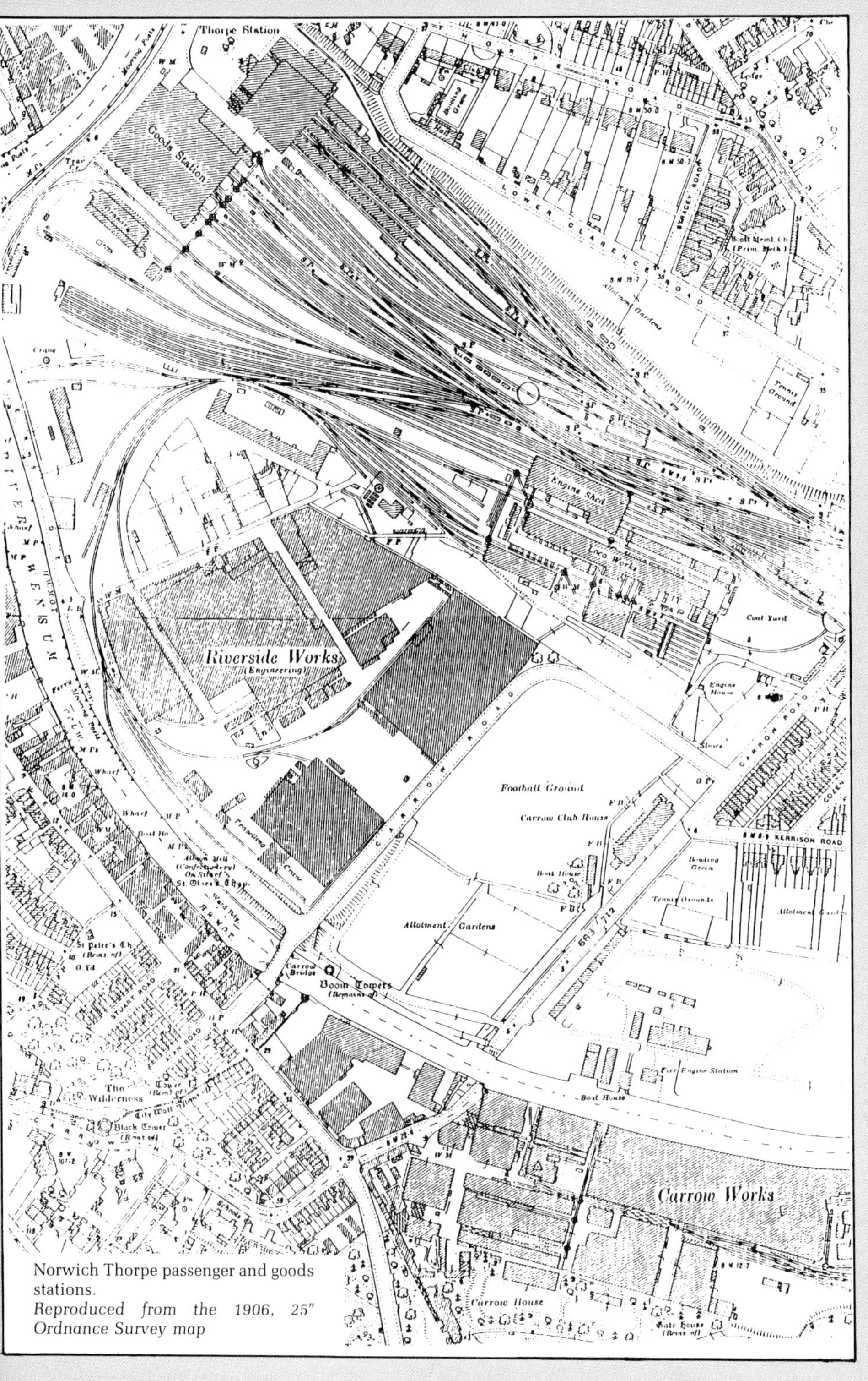

Norwich Thorpe passenger and goods stations.
Reproduced from the 1906, 25" Ordnance Survey map

A *c*.1950s view of the concourse at Norwich Thorpe station. The belted 'gaberdine' raincoats and traditional W.H. Smith & Son bookstall contribute a decided 'period' feeling to this everyday scene. *Douglas Thompson*

Another atmospheric shot of Norwich Thorpe, during the 1950s. An ex-GNR 0–6–0 stands in platform 5, while an ex-LMS 2–6–4T blows off steam in platform 3. *Douglas Thompson*

Norwich Thorpe station was situated away from the city centre, though the terminus was within easy walking distance of the famous cathedral and other historic buildings such as Norwich Castle. For railway travellers, the ornate domed station buildings at Norwich Thorpe served as a worthy introduction to the architectural splendours of a thousand year old city, and from our point of view this bustling, ex-Great Eastern Railway terminus forms a grand, and fitting finale for our imaginary journey along the Lynn & Dereham Railway and its eastwards continuation from Dereham to Norwich.

A Swindon class '120' multiple unit (car No. 53708 leading) crosses Trowse swing bridge, near Norwich Thorpe, on 19th September, 1983, forming a cross-country service to Peterborough via Thetford and Ely. *Brian Morrison*

'Claud Hamilton' 4–4–0 No. 2502 stands outside the engine shed at Kings Lynn.
N.E. Stead Collection

The later, brick-built shed at Dereham, with a typical collection of ex-Great Eastern motive power.
N.E. Stead Collection

Chapter Seven

The British Railways Era (1948–1989)

The end of the war in Europe was followed by the election of a Labour government, pledged to nationalise rail transport and other vital industries. This electoral pledge was rapidly carried out, and at midnight on 31st December, 1947 the LNER, LMS, GWR and SR railway companies were taken into public ownership. Henceforth the Kings Lynn to Norwich route would be part of a new, state-owned transport organisation known as British Railways.

In the short term, the immediate results of this momentous change of ownership were remarkably few, and in retrospect it would probably be true to say that nationalisation made no difference at all to rural lines such as the Norwich to Kings Lynn route. The one noticeable sign that the 'BR era' had commenced was the application of new liveries to locomotives and rolling stock. Until the late 1940s the engines seen on these north Norfolk lines had carried the rather dreary black livery favoured by the LNER, but after nationalisation 'mixed traffic' locomotives such as the 'B12' 4–6–0s started to appear in an attractive lined-black livery that recalled the colour scheme made famous by the London & North Western Railway.

As far as coaches were concerned, the change of appearance was even more striking in that non-corridor stock was given an overall maroon livery in place of the drab browns of the LNER period. Corridor vehicles, meanwhile, received a striking red and cream livery which did much to brighten-up the rundown appearance of post-war Britain – although it should be noted that many ex-LNER coaches remained in brown or varnished teak liveries until the early 1950s![57]

Motive Power

In locomotive terms, the Norwich to Kings Lynn route had changed little since the Great Eastern period. Many passenger services were handled by former GER 'Claud Hamilton' 4–4–0s, which were still active in the Norfolk area. Large numbers of these engines were still shedded at Kings Lynn and in 1950 the local allocations includes 'D15s' Nos. 62501, 62502, 62505, 62506, 62507 and 'D16s' Nos. 62513, 62514, 62518, 62559, 62575 and 62588.

Freight traffic was handled by a variety of ex-GER six-coupled types including 'J15', 'J17' and 'J19' class 0–6–0s and, on a less regular basis, 'N7' class 0–6–2Ts. Locally based 'J15s' included Nos. 65359 and 65378 at Kings Lynn and Nos. 65373, 65390, 65398, 65404, 65417, 65422, 65426, 65469 and 65479 at Norwich. At the same time, Kings Lynn had a large allocation of 'J17' 0–6–0s – among them Nos. 65519, 65527, 65530, 65544, 65548, 65549 and 65572, while Norwich housed sister-locomotives Nos. 65507, 65509, 65512, 65513, 65516, 65553, 65469, and 65479. Local 'J19s' included Nos. 64640, 64642, 64654, 64668 and 64672 at Kings Lynn and Nos. 64644 and 64674 at Norwich. It was usual for several engines to be sub-shedded at Dereham, and in the early 1950s Dereham's allocation included 'J15' 0–6–0s Nos. 65469 and 65460, together with 'Claud Hamilton' 4–4–0 No. 62584.

Other types used on the Norwich to Kings Lynn line during the early British Railways period included 'F6' 2–4–2Ts, 'E4' 2–4–0s and former Great Central 'C12' 4–4–2Ts. The latter were used on the Kings Lynn to South Lynn (M&GN) shuttle service, and they also worked on the Swaffham to Thetford branch; in 1953, for instance, 'C12' 4–4–2T No. 67360 often worked on this bucolic route, and on 15th October, 1953 this same engine was noted double-heading the morning train from Thetford in tandem with 'Claud Hamilton' 4–4–0 No. 62564!

Engines used on the Kings Lynn to Norwich line were also out-stationed at Swaffham and Wells-next-the-Sea. In general, there were usually two engines at these sheds at any one time, and in 1956 Swaffham housed 'J15' 0–6–0 No. 65460 and an 0–6–0 diesel shunter which was used on pilot duties. Wells normally had two 'D16' 4–4–0s for use on the Norwich line, together with a veteran 'E4' 2–4–0 for use on the cross country branch to Heacham. Mr W.J. Sutton, who knew the Wells–Dereham–Norwich line in the late 1940s and early 1950s, recalled that the regular Wells-based engines were 'D16s' Nos. 62540, 62561, 62570 and 62577; No. 62561 was kept in immaculate condition, but its less fortunate companions were seldom cleaned.

Post-War Excursion and Freight Traffic

Excursions and other special workings introduced an element of variety, 'pilgrimage' trains to Walsingham (on the Wells branch) being a special feature. These workings were often headed by 'B12' 4–6–0s, which worked through to Wells after setting down passengers at Walsingham. Excursions were sometimes double-headed, and Mr Sutton remembered one such train that ran from Wells to London at the time of the 1953 Coronation; two 'Claud Hamilton' 4–4–0s were required to lift the lengthy train up the steep inclines between Wells and Dereham, though on arrival at Wymondham the 4–4–0s were replaced by a 'B17' 4–6–0 which took over for the remainder of the trip to London.

Other excursions were regularly provided between Norwich and Hunstanton, and these were also headed by 'D16' 4–4–0s or 'B12' 4–6–0s. Similar trains were run on summer Sundays between Thetford and Hunstanton, while in the eastbound direction there was a regular flow of summer excursion traffic between Peterborough and Great Yarmouth; interestingly, the Thetford excursions were routed via Watton and Swaffham – though the Norwich and Peterborough trains travelled on the 'main line' between Kings Lynn and Wymondham.

Post war freight services consisted of two up and two down trains on the Lynn & Dereham line, together with two up and two down workings between Norwich and Wells-next-the-Sea (later reduced to just one working in each direction). On the Lynn & Dereham section, the first freight working of the day left Kings Lynn at about 6.20 am while the second departed at around 11.28 am. The first train ran through to Dereham, but the later train left the Lynn & Dereham route at Swaffham and proceeded along the Thetford line to Watton. In the afternoon, the first train left Dereham at 1.10 pm, while the second up working travelled back to Kings Lynn at around 5.00 pm.

If necessary, extra freight services were provided on both the Lynn & Dereham and Norwich–Dereham–Wells lines during the busy sugar beet season, though in general there was less freight traffic during the 1950s than in previous years.

One new form of bulk freight did, however, appear during the early 1950s. As we have seen, the sand pits at Middleton Towers had been important as a source of traffic for the railway for many years, but in 1951 a new and more sophisticated treatment plant was installed by British Industrial Sand Ltd (successors to Joseph Boam Ltd). By 1958, sand traffic had grown to such an extent that three loaded trains were being despatched from Middleton Towers every day. These workings – which often consisted of up to 45 fully-loaded wagons – departed at 10.48 am, 3.48 and 10.10 pm, while in the reverse direction trains of empties left Kings Lynn at 10.48 am and 3.48 pm.

The sand trains were often double-headed, and in addition to the usual ex-GER 4–4–0 and 0–6–0 locomotives this lucrative form of traffic was also handled by an 'N7' 0–6–2T (0–6–2Ts were comparatively rare in north Norfolk, although it is interesting to note that an 'N7' was occasionally employed on freight duties between Norwich, Dereham and Wells-next-the-Sea). A summary of some of the most widely-used locomotive classes used on the Kings Lynn to Norwich route is given in *Table Five* below.

Table Five

PRINCIPAL LOCOMOTIVE CLASSES USED ON THE KINGS LYNN–DEREHAM–NORWICH LINE

GER Class	*LNER Class*	*Type*	*Typical Numbers*
'Y' class	–	2–4–0	328
No. 1 class	–	2–4–0	2/4/6/26/30/31/33/34/35/44/45/49/50/107/108
'T19' class	–	2–4–0	
'T26' class	'E4'	2–4–0	439/440/441/442/443/445/446/447/448/449/450
'G14'	–	2–4–0	562/563/564/565/567
'D13' (ex-'T19')	'D13'	4–4–0	
'Claud Hamilton'	'D16/2/3'	4–4–0	62513/62514/62518/62559/62588
Worsdell 'Y14'	'J15'	0–6–0	65359/65373/65378/65390/65398/65404/65417
Holden	'J17'	0–6–0	65507/65509/65512/65519/65527/65553/65569
Hill '1000'	'N7'	0–6–2T	69694/69707
	'B12'	4–6–0	
–	'C12'	4–4–2T	67360
–	'D2'	4–4–0	

The coaching stock used on the Lynn & Dereham line and connecting routes during the early British Railways period still exhibited a distinctly pre-grouping flavour, and many trains between Kings Lynn, Dereham, Wells and Norwich were invariably composed of antiquated wooden vehicles from the former Great Eastern, Great Northern, North Eastern or Great Central companies. Modern LNER coaches also appeared, but as these Gresley-designed vehicles were modelled on earlier Great Northern stock their comparative modernity would not have been apparent to ordinary travellers!

Passenger Services in the 1950s

Post-war passenger train services were similar to those provided during the LNER period, with a basic pattern of six up and six down workings each way between Kings Lynn and Dereham. In July 1950 the first up and first down trains left Dereham and Kings Lynn at 6.55 and 6.50 am respectively, and having passed each other in the crossing loop at Swaffham, these services reached their destinations a few minutes before 8.00 am.

In the up direction, further trains left Dereham at 8.12, 11.05 am, 4.10 and 7.40 pm, while balancing down workings departed from Kings Lynn at 9.55 am, 12.45, 3.5, 5.40 and 6.20 pm. Additional trains ran on Tuesdays, Wednesdays and Saturdays, and in term time a school train left Swaffham at 8.25 am for the benefit of pupils attending Dereham High School.

Some trains continued through to Norwich after reversal at Dereham, and at other times there were good connections with Wells-next-the-Sea branch services – by means of which through travellers could reach Norwich from Kings Lynn in two hours. On the Wells branch, local travellers had a choice of six up and six down trains, while the Dereham to Wymondham section was served by eight up and seven down services.

In September 1955 British Railways introduced a fleet of brand new diesel multiple units into the area, and at the same time the entire timetable was radically altered. Taking full advantage of the new multiple unit trains, BR provided what was undoubtedly the best passenger service ever seen on the Kings Lynn to Dereham route, with 12 trains in each direction between Kings Lynn and Dereham, and 10 each way between Dereham and Wells-next-the-Sea. One train ran through from Kings Lynn to Norwich, and two worked back from Norwich to Kings Lynn.

Journey times varied between 50 and 60 minutes for the 26½ mile trip from Kings Lynn to Dereham, while through journeys to Norwich were accomplished in about 1½ hours (though the 9.03 am down service from Kings Lynn omitted several stops after Dereham, and reached Norwich in just 85 minutes).

The new trains were disliked by steam enthusiasts, but everyday travellers appreciated their companionable 'open plan' interiors and novel 'all round' windows – which afforded an excellent view of the line ahead for people seated in the front saloons.

The trains themselves were of two distinct types, some sets being two-car 'Derby' units, while others were the familiar Metro-Cammell sets (later class

Table 45 NORWICH, DEREHAM, KING'S LYNN and WELLS-ON-SEA

Second class only between Norwich and King's Lynn and Wells-on-Sea except where otherwise shown

Miles	Week Days	am	am	am	am		am	am	am	am	am	am	am	am		pm	pm	pm	pm ¶	pm	pm	pm
—	**Norwich** (Thorpe) dep	..	..	6 35	..	..	7 48	..	..	9 21	1030	..	1039	..	..	12 5	12 11	..	..	1 8	..	2 10
6¼	Hethersett	...	...	...	...	...	...	...	...	...	...	...	1050	...	...	...	...	...	...	1 19	...	2 21
10¼	**Wymondham** arr	..	..	6 50	..	..	8 6	..	..	9 36	1048	..	1056	..	..	1219	12 25	..	..	1 25	..	2 27
—	6 **London** (L'pool St) 5 dep	...	...	...	...	...	...	4 24	...	4A35	...	6 51	6e54	...	...	9A30	9B47	...	Saturdays only	10P30	...	10V30
—	**Wymondham** dep	..	..	6 51	..	..	..	8 13	..	9 37	..	1057	1057	..	..	1220	12 28	..		1 28	..	2 28
14	Kimberley Park	...	...	6 57	...	...	...	8 19	...	9 43	...	11 3	11 3	...	...	1226	12 34	...		1 34	...	2 34
15¾	Hardingham	..	..	7 1	..	..	..	8 24	..	9 48	..	11 8	11 8	..	..	1231	12 39	..		1 39	..	2 39
17½	Thuxton	...	...	7 5	...	...	...	8 28	...	9 52	...	1112	1112	...	...	1235	12 43	...		1 43	...	2 43
19¾	Yaxham	..	..	7 11	..	..	..	8 34	..	9 58	..	1118	1118	..	..	1241	12 49	..		1 49	..	2 49
21½	**Dereham** arr	...	...	7 15	...	...	...	8 38	...	10 2	...	1122	1122	...	...	1245	12 53	...		1 53	...	2 53
—	**Dereham** dep	..	6 47	..	8 6	..	..	..	8 46	..	..	..	..	1127	..	..	..	1 1	..	..	2 12	3 2
25¾	Wendling	...	6 55	...	8 14	...	...	...	8 53	...	...	Saturdays only	Except Saturdays	1135	...	Except Saturdays	Saturdays only	1 9	...	...	2 20	3 10
28¼	Fransham	..	7 1	..	8 20	..	..	..	8 59	..	..			1141	..			1 15	..	..	2 26	3 16
29¾	Dunham	...	7 5	...	8 24	...	...	...	9 3	...	...			1145	...			1 19	...	...	2 30	3 20
33¼	**Swaffham**	..	7U17	..	8 31	..	..	..	9 10	..	..			1152	..			1 25	1 35	..	2 38	3 28
39¼	Narborough & Pentney	...	7 26	...	8 40	...	...	...	9 22	...	...			12 5	...			...	1 47	...	2 47	3 37
43	East Winch	..	7 33	..	8 47	..	..	..	9 29	..	..			1212	..			..	1 55	..	2 54	3 44
45	Middleton Towers	...	7 38	...	8 52	...	...	...	9 34	...	...			1217	...			...	2 0	...	2 59	3 49
48¼	**King's Lynn** arr	..	7 43	..	8 58	..	..	..	9 41	..	..	..	..	1224	..	..	..	..	2 8	..	3 6	3 58
89½	43 Cambridge arr	...	9 56	...	10C 7	...	...	...	12H7	...	...	...	...	2 45	...	...	...	...	3J50	...	4L39	6D50
145¼	43 **London** (L'pool St) "	..	1121	..	11C28	..	..	..	1Y37	..	..	..	..	4 52	..	..	..	..	5J12	..	6L 2	..
—	**Dereham** dep	6 4	...	7 17	...	...	...	8 54	...	10 6	...	1123	1124	...	...	1254	12 54	...	...	2 3	...	...
26¼	North Elmham	6 13	..	7 26	..	..	..	9 3	..	1015	..	1131	1132	..	..	1 3	1 3	..	..	2 11	..	..
27¾	County School	6 17	...	7 30	...	...	...	9 7	...	1022	...	1136	1136	...	...	1 7	1 7	...	...	2 18	...	...
31¼	Ryburgh	6 24	..	7 37	..	..	..	9 14	..	1029	..	1141	1142	..	..	1 14	1 14	..	..	2 25	..	..
33¾	**Fakenham** (East)	6 29	...	7 43	...	...	...	9 19	...	1034	...	1146	1147	...	...	1 19	1 19	...	...	2 30	...	...
38¾	Walsingham	6 38	..	7 52	..	..	..	9 28	..	1043	..	1154	1155	..	..	1 28	1 28	..	..	2 39	..	..
40¼	Wighton Halt	...	...	7 57	...	...	...	9 33	...	1048	...	1158	1159	...	...	1 33	1 33	...	...	2 44	...	...
43¼	**Wells-on-Sea** arr	6 47	..	8 3	..	..	..	9 39	..	1054	..	12 4	12 5	..	..	1 39	1 39	..	..	2 50	..	..

	Week Days—*continued*																Sundays					
	pm	pm	pm	pm	pm	pm	pm	pm	pm	pm	pm		pm	pm	pm		am	am	pm	pm	pm	
Norwich (Thorpe) dep	3 5	3 22	..	..	4 56	5 35	..	6 10	6 20	..	..	..	8 56	9 32	..	..	9 51	..	..	5 45	8 15	..
Hethersett	3 16	3 33	...	...	5 8	...	...	6 21	6 31	...	...	...	...	9 42	...	...	10 2	...	...	...	8 26	...
Wymondham arr	3 23	3 40	..	..	5 15	5 50	..	6 28	6 38	..	..	..	9 11	9 48	..	..	10 9	..	..	6 0	8 33	..
6 **London** (L'pool St) 5 dep	12A30	12A30	...	...	1A30	3G30	...	3A30	...	...	...	...	6K30	6K30	Saturdays only	...	...	...	...	2 24	...	...
Wymondham dep	3 26	3 41	..	..	5 16	5 51	..	6 29	6 39	..	..	..	9 12	9 49		..	1010	..	..	6 1	8 34	..
Kimberley Park	3 32	3 47	...	...	5 22	5 57	...	6 35	6 45	...	...	...	9 18	9 55		...	1016	...	...	6 7	8 40	...
Hardingham	3 37	3 52	..	..	5 27	6 2	..	6 40	6 50	..	..	..	9 23	10 0		..	1021	..	..	6 12	8 45	..
Thuxton	3 41	3 56	...	...	5 31	6 6	...	6 44	6 54	...	...	...	9 27	10 4		...	1025	...	...	6 16	8 49	...
Yaxham	3 47	4 2	..	..	5 37	6 12	..	6 50	7 0	..	..	..	9 33	1010		..	1031	..	..	6 22	8 55	..
Dereham arr	3 51	4 6	...	...	5 41	6 16	...	6 54	7 4	...	...	...	9 37	1014		...	1035	...	...	6 26	8 59	...
Dereham dep	Except Saturdays	Saturdays only	4 17	5 14	..	..	6 18	Saturdays only	Except Saturdays	7 18	8 19	..	9 43	Saturdays only	1018	..	..	..	..	..	From Yarmouth (Vauxhall) dep 7 33 pm (Table 48)	..
Wendling			4 25	5 22	...	...	6 26			7 26	8 27	...	9 51		1026	...	...	...	...	...		...
Fransham			4 31	5 28	..	..	6 32			7 32	8 33	..	9 57		1032	..	..	..	..	..		..
Dunham			4 35	5 32	...	...	6 36			7 36	8 37	...	10 1		1036	...	...	...	...	...		...
Swaffham			4 42	5d43	..	..	6 44			7d47	8d48	..	10 9		1044	..	..	..	..	..		..
Narborough & Pentney			4 52	5 52	...	...	6 54			7 56	8 57	...	1019		1054	...	...	...	...	...		...
East Winch			4 59	5 59	..	..	7 2			8 3	9 4	..	1026		11 1	..	..	..	..	..		..
Middleton Towers			5 4	6 4	...	...	7 7			8 8	9 9	...	1031		11 6	...	...	...	...	...		...
King's Lynn arr			5 10	6 10	..	..	7 14			8 14	9 15	..	1038		1113	..	..	..	..	..		..
43 Cambridge arr	...	...	7 7	7N32	...	...	8R36	...	...	...	12F46	...		...	...	...	...	...	...	...		...
43 **London** (L'pool St) "	..	..	8 40	11Q23	..	..	9T58	..	..	..	a2F23	..		..	..	..	..	..	..	..		..
Dereham dep	4 15	4 15	...	...	5 42	...	...	7 12	7 12	...	...	...	Except Saturdays	1016	...	...	1037	1047	1 20	6 30		...
North Elmham	4 24	4 24	..	..	5 50	..	..	7 21	7 21	..	..	..		1025	..	..	..	1056	1 29	6 39		..
County School	4 28	4 28	...	...	5 57	...	...	7 25	7 25	...	...	...		1029	...	...	...	11 1	1 33	6 46		...
Ryburgh	4 35	4 35	..	..	6 4	..	..	7 32	7 32	..	..	..		1036	..	..	..	11 8	1 40	6 53		..
Fakenham (East)	4 40	4 40	...	...	6 9	...	...	7 37	7 37	...	...	...		1041	...	...	...	1113	1 46	6 58		...
Walsingham	4 49	4 49	..	..	6 18	..	..	7 49	7 49	..	..	..		1050	..	..	11 7	1122	1 55	7 7		..
Wighton Halt	4 54	4 54	...	...	6 23	...	...	7 54	7 54	...	...	...		1055	...	...	...	1127	2 0	7 12		...
Wells-on-Sea arr	5 0	5 0	..	..	6 29	..	..	8 0	8 0	..	..	..	...	11 1	..	..	1116	1133	2 6	7 18	..	..

- **¶** First and Second class
- **A** Via Norwich (Thorpe)
- *a* am
- **B** On 16th June, 8th and 15th September departs Liverpool Street 9 30 am via Norwich
- **C** Fridays and Saturdays only. Runs 30th June to 8th September inclusive
- **D** Via March and St. Ives
- **d** Arrives 4 minutes *earlier*
- **E** Except Saturdays
- **e** Via Norwich (Thorpe). Second class only Ipswich to Norwich
- **F** Via March. On Saturday nights via Downham
- **G** Via Norwich. On Saturdays departs Liverpool Street 2 24 pm via Ely
- **H** On Fridays and Saturdays 29th June to 8th September inclusive arrives Cambridge 12 18 pm
- **J** Saturdays only. Runs 14th July to 1st September inclusive
- **K** Via Norwich (Thorpe). The East Anglian. Limited accommodation
- **L** On Fridays and Saturdays 7th July to 1st September inclusive arrives Cambridge 4 48 pm and Liverpool Street 6 10 (6 13 pm on Saturdays)
- **N** Not after 8th September. On Saturdays arrives Cambridge 7 40 pm. Also runs on Wednesday 12th and Saturday 15th September Cambridge arrive 9 16 pm via St. Ives
- **P** Saturdays only. Via Norwich (Thorpe)
- **Q** Runs Mondays to Fridays until 6th July and from 3rd to 7th September. Also runs every Saturday until 8th September Liverpool St. arr 9 53 pm
- **R** Mondays to Fridays. Runs 9th July to 31st August inclusive. Also runs on Saturdays 28th July to 1st September inclusive Cambridge arrive 9 18 pm
- **S** Saturdays only
- **T** Except Saturdays. Runs 9th July to 31st August inclusive
- **U** Arrives 5 minutes *earlier*
- **V** Except Sats. Via Norwich (Thorpe)
- **Y** On Fridays and Saturdays 29th June to 8th September inclusive arrives Liverpool St. 1 42 pm and on Saturdays 16th, 23rd June & 15th Sept. 1 33 pm

For OTHER TRAINS between Norwich and Wymondham, see Table 6

The May 1956 passenger timetable.

Table 45—*continued* WELLS-ON-SEA, KING'S LYNN, DEREHAM, and NORWICH

Second class only between Wells-on-Sea and King's Lynn and Norwich except where otherwise shown

Miles	Mls		Week Days																				
			am		am	am		am	am		am		am	am		am	am	am ¶	pm	pm	pm	pm	pm
–		**Wells-on-Sea** .. .. dep	..	..	..	**6 55**	..	..	**8 8**	..	..	..	..	**9 49**	..	**11 2**	**11 2**	Saturdays only	From Thetford dep 11E31 am (Table 37) 11S38 am	**1210**	**1234**	..	**1 44**
2¼		Wighton Halt				7 1			8 14					9 55		11 8	11 8			1216	1240		1 50
4¼		Walsingham				7 6			8 19					10 0		11 13	11 13			1221	1245		1 55
9½		**Fakenham** (East)				**7 16**			**8 29**					**1010**		**11 23**	**11 23**			**1230**	**1254**		**2 5**
12		Ryburgh				7 21			8 34					1015		11 28	11 28			1235	1259		2 10
15½		County School				7 32			8 40					1021		11 37	11 37			1241	1 8		2 17
17		North Elmham				7 36			8 44					1025		11 41	11 41			1245	1 12		2 21
21½		**Dereham** arr				**7 44**			**8 52**					**1033**		**11 49**	**11 49**			**1252**	**1 19**		**2 28**
—	Mls	**43 London** (L St) dep	..	..	..	..	..	..	..	..	..	..	**5 54**	..	..	..	..	**8C27**		..	..	**8R24**	..
—		43 Cambridge ... „											8H 2					10C 3				10T15	
—	–	**King's Lynn** .. dep	..	..	**6 48**	..	..	**7 48**	..	..	**9 3**	..	**9 52**	..	..	Except Saturdays	Saturdays only	**11 42**		Except Saturdays	Saturdays only	**1 5**	..
—	3¼	Middleton Towers			6 54			7 54			9 9		9 58					11 49				1 12	
—	5¼	East Winch			6 59			7 59			9 14		10 3					11 55				1 17	
—	8¾	Narborough & Pentney			7 6			8 6			9 21		1010					12 3				1 24	
—	14¼	**Swaffham**			**7h20**			**8 15**			**9 30**		**1019**					**12 15**	**1225**			**1 34**	
—	18¼	Dunham			7 28			8 25			9 37		1026					..	1233			1 42	
—	19¾	Fransham			7 32			8 29			..		1030					..	1237			1 46	
—	22¼	Wendling			7 38			8 35			9 45		1036					..	1243			1 52	
—	26¼	**Dereham** .. .. arr			**7 45**			**8 41**			**9 51**		**1043**					..	**1250**			**1 59**	
—		**Dereham** dep	**6 50**			**7 50**			**8 58**		**9 56**			**1047**		**11 50**	**11 54**			**1253**	**1 20**		**2 29**
23½		Yaxham	6 54			7 55			9 3		..			1051		11 54	11 58			1257	1 24		2 33
26		Thuxton	7 0			8 1			9 9					1057		12 0	12 4			1 3	1 30		2 39
27½		Hardingham	7 4			8 5			9 13		..			11 1		12 4	12 8			1 7	1 34		2 43
29½		Kimberley Park	7 8			8 9			9 17					11 5		12 9	12 12			1 11	1 38		2 47
33		**Wymondham** .. .. arr	**7 13**			**8 14**			**9 22**		**1014**			**1110**		**12 13**	**12 17**			**1 16**	**1 43**		**2 52**
146½		**6 London** (L'pool St) 5 arr	**10A0**			**1121**			**12J35**		**1V37**			**1K55**		**3A30**	**3A30**			**4A34**	**5 0**		**6A39**
—		**Wymondham** dep	**7 14**			**8 16**			**9 24**		**1015**			**1112**		**12 15**	**12 19**			**1 17**	**1 44**		**2 53**
37		Hethersett				8 24								1120							1 52		3 1
43½		**Norwich** (Thorpe) .... arr	**7 31**			**8 34**			**9 39**		**1028**			**1130**		**12 29**	**12 37**			**1 31**	**2 3**		**3 10**

	Week Days—*continued*																Sundays					
	pm	pm	pm	pm	pm		pm	pm	pm	pm	pm	pm	pm	pm			am	am	pm	pm	pm	
Wells-on-Sea .. .. dep	..	**3 15**	..	..	**5 24**	..	..	..	**7 18**	..	**8 18**	Saturdays only	Except Saturdays	**11 6**	..	..	..	**1145**	**4 0**	**6 12**	**7 26**	..
Wighton Halt		3 21			5 30				7 24		8 24			1112				1151	4 6	6 18		
Walsingham		3 26			5 35				7 29		8 29			1117				1156	4 11	6 23	7 36	
Fakenham (East)		**3 36**			**5 45**				**7d42**		**8 39**			**1127**				**12 7**	**4 21**	**6 34**		
Ryburgh		3 41			5 50				7 47		8 45			1132				1212	4 26	6 39		
County School		3 47			5 56				7 53		8 51			1138				1218	4 33	6 45		
North Elmham		3 51			6 0				7 57		8 55			1142				1222	4 37	6 49		
Dereham arr		**3 59**			**6 8**				**8 5**		**9 3**			**1150**				**1230**	**4 45**	**6 57**	**8 4**	
43 London (L St.) dep	**12B24**	..	..	**12S27**	..	..	**2U24**	**4G30**	..	..	..	**5 54**	**5 54**	Saturdays only	..	..	To Yarmouth (Vauxhall) arr 11 2 am (Table 48)	..	..	..	..	..
43 Cambridge ... „	1B49		1D53	2 35			3U56	5G46				7 22	7 22									
King's Lynn .. dep	**3 14**	..	**4 8**	**5 15**	..	..	**6 15**	**7 19**	..	**8 19**	..	**9 20**	**9 20**		..	..		..	..	..	..	..
Middleton Towers	3 21		4 15	5 21			6 21	7 25		8 26		9 26	9 26									
East Winch	3 26	..	4 20	5 26			6 26	7 30		8 31		9 31	9 31									
Narborough & Pentney	3 38		4 31	5 33			6 33	7 37		8 38		9 38	9 38									
Swaffham	**3 48**	..	**4d43**	**5 42**			**6d45**	**7 46**		**8 47**		**9k51**	**9k51**									
Dunham	3 56		4 51	5 49			6 52	7 53		8 54		9 58	10d2									
Fransham	4 0		4 55	5 53			6 56	7 56		8 58		10 1	10 6									
Wendling	4 6		5 1	5 59			7 2	8 2		9 4		10 7	1012									
Dereham .. .. arr	**4 12**	..	**5 8**	**6 6**	..	..	**7 9**	**8 9**	..	**9 11**	..	**1013**	**1019**		..	..		..	..	..	..	..
Dereham dep		**4 16**			**6 10**				**8 12**		**9 15**						**9 38**		**4 47**	**6 59**	**8 6**	
Yaxham		4 20			6 14				8 16		9 19						9 42		4 51	7 3	8 10	
Thuxton		4 26			6 20				8 22		9 25						9 48		4 57	7 9	8 16	
Hardingham		4 30			6 24				8 26		9 29						9 52		5 1	7 13	8 20	
Kimberley Park		4 34			6 28				8 30		9 33						9 56		5 5	7 17	8 24	
Wymondham .. .. arr		**4 39**			**6 33**				**8 35**		**9 38**						**10 1**		**5 10**	**7 22**	**8 29**	
6 London (L'pool St) 5 arr		**7N55**			**11Q56**						**2a23**						**1A 4**		**8 19**	**12A14**	**2a18**	
Wymondham dep	..	**4 44**	..	..	**6 35**	..	..	..	**8 36**	..	**9 39**	..	..	..	..	..	**10 3**	..	**5 12**	**7 24**	**8 31**	..
Hethersett		4 52			6 43												1011			7 32	8 39	
Norwich (Thorpe) .... arr	..	**5 4**	..	..	**6 56**	..	..	..	**8 49**	..	**9 52**	..	..	..	..	..	**1020**	..	**5 27**	**7 41**	**8 48**	..

¶ First and Second class
A Via Norwich (Thorpe)
a am
B On Saturdays departs Liverpool Street 12 14 and Cambridge 1 47 pm (12 10 and 1 35 pm respectively on 16th, 23rd June and 15th September)
C On 8th and 15th September departs Liverpool Street 8 24 and Cambridge 9 53 am
D Via St. Ives and March
d Arrives 4 minutes *earlier*
E Except Saturdays
G On Saturdays departs Liverpool Street 4 27 and Cambridge 5 56 pm
H From 23rd July to 1st September inclusive departs Cambridge 8 37 pm
h Arrives 6 minutes *earlier*
J Via Norwich (Thorpe) On Saturdays arrives Liverpool St. 12 45 pm
K Via Norwich (Thorpe). The East Anglian. Limited accommodation On Fridays and Saturdays arrives Liverpool Street 2 6 pm
k Arr 5 minutes *earlier*
N Via Norwich (Thorpe). On Saturdays arrives Liverpool Street 8 6 pm
Q Via Norwich (Thorpe). On Saturdays arrives Liverpool St. 9 53 pm via Ely
R Mondays to Fridays. Also Runs Saturdays 14th July to 25th August Liverpool Street departs 9 50 am
S Saturdays only
T Via St. Ives and March. On Saturdays 14th July to 25th August departs Cambridge 11 14 am via Ely
U On Fridays and Saturdays 29th June to 8th September departs Liverpool Street 2 27 and Cambridge 4 9 pm
V On Saturdays arrives Liverpool Street 1 33 pm (1 21 pm via Norwich (Thorpe))

For OTHER TRAINS between Wymondham and Norwich, see Table 6

May 1956 (continued).

'101s'). Norwich's allocation, by April 1956, included 13 'Derby' units and 11 Metro-Cammell sets. The Metro-Cammell vehicles included motor brake seconds Nos. 79048, 79047, 79054, 79065, 79066 and 79075, together with driving trailer seconds Nos. 79263, 79281, 79282 and 79291, while the Derby twin units included motor brake seconds Nos. 79034 and 79046, and driving trailer composite No. 79250.

Half a dozen sets were usually stabled at Dereham for work on the routes to Kings Lynn and Wells-next-the-Sea, while another unit was normally stabled overnight at Kings Lynn to work the first down service to Dereham. The new trains were also used on the Swaffham to Thetford route, and in this capacity they worked a daily through train between Thetford and Dereham.

The June 1956 passenger timetable provides ample evidence of the very real improvements resulting from the introduction of new rolling stock on the Kings Lynn to Norwich route. On the Lynn & Dereham section, operations began with the departure of the first up and down trains from Dereham and Kings Lynn at 6.47 am and 6.48 am respectively. These services passed each other in the crossing loop at Swaffham, and the two multiple units then worked a series of return trips between Kings Lynn and Dereham. In the up direction, westbound services departed from Dereham at 8.06, 8.46, 11.27 am, 2.12, 3.02, 4.17, 5.14, 6.18, 7.18, 8.19 and 9.43 pm, while balancing eastbound workings left Kings Lynn at 7.48, 9.03, 9.52 am, 1.05, 3.14, 4.08, 5.15, 6.15, 7.19, 8.19 and 9.20 pm. The 9.43 am and 3.02 pm up services were through workings between Norwich and Kings Lynn, while in the down direction the 9.03 am from Kings Lynn ran through to Norwich Thorpe.

The basic weekday train services between Norwich and Dereham in the summer of 1956 provided 12 trains in each direction, most of these workings being through trips between Norwich and Wells. On Sundays, the Norwich–Dereham–Wells section was served by two out and back trains between Norwich and Wells, one short distance working between Dereham and Wells-next-the-Sea, one unbalanced evening service from Wells to Norwich, and a return through working between Dereham and Great Yarmouth. (There were, however, no Sunday services on the Lynn & Dereham line.)

In retrospect, it must be said that the new dieselised train services were introduced at a time when government policies and road competition were poised to do irreparable harm to the railway system. In 1956, most people still assumed that the newly-nationalised railways would be maintained in perpetuity as a vital part of the infrastructure of a modern industrial state. Sadly, the government of the day appeared to view the railways as an expensive anachronism, and from the later 1950s onwards more and more state resources were directed into massive road building programmes and away from the cash-starved railways.

A Derby 'lightweight' two-car multiple unit departs from Wendling during the middle 1950s. The upper quadrant home signal (*left*) is mounted on a much older post.

Oakwood Collection

A class '08' shunter stands at Kings Lynn station stabling point. Note the spilt sand on the tracks from the numerous sand trams from Middleton Towers. Taken 17th April, 1980.

G. Gamble

The Run-down Begins

Railway closures were hardly a new phenomenon. The 'Big Four' companies had embarked upon a major closure programme during the depression years of the early 1930s, and in the years following nationalisation BR carried out a number of minor closures. In general, these early withdrawals were designed to eliminate hopelessly uneconomic rural lines that could never hope to pay their way; the West Norfolk branch between Heacham and Wells-next-the-Sea, for instance, lost its passenger services on Saturday 31st May, 1952 – but this modest rationalisation had little impact on the more important lines between Kings Lynn, Dereham, Wells and Norwich.

There was, in the 1950s, an inevitable desire to prune competing routes – after all, the railway system was now under unified management, and it made sense for scarce resources to be concentrated on the most viable lines. In this context the Midland & Great Northern Joint line became an obvious candidate for rationalisation. Built to challenge the GER, this east-to-west cross-country route was duplicated by other lines between Leicester, Kings Lynn and Norwich. The problem of over-capacity between the Midlands and East Anglia was worsened by the condition of three large bridges on the M&GN route which were said to be difficult to maintain, and it was perhaps inevitable that the Midland & Great Northern Joint route would be deleted from the British Railways system. Accordingly, on Saturday 28th February, 1959 the M&GNJR was closed in its entirety, leaving a few truncated stubs for local passenger and freight traffic.

The demise of the Midland & Great Northern Joint line meant that, in the short term at least, additional traffic was diverted onto former Great Eastern lines such as the Kings Lynn to Norwich route – this extra traffic being mainly in the form of summer excursion trains and holiday relief workings between the Midlands and East Anglian holiday resorts such as Great Yarmouth.

Unfortunately, the era of mass railway closures was not yet over. Indeed, in 1959 it had hardly begun, and those who thought that the Kings Lynn to Dereham line would escape the government's axe were mistaken; in the next few years railways began to close in increasing numbers, and it soon became clear that official policy was now directed away from rail transport, and towards the promotion of roads and motoring at the expense of all other considerations.

Beeching and After

Government bias against rail transport reached its peak in March 1963 when the publication of Dr Richard Beeching's controversial report entitled *The Reshaping of British Railways* recommended the withdrawal of railway passenger services from 5,000 miles of line and the closure of 2,363 stations. An appendix to the main report listed the lines which would be closed and, ominously, the report warned that these intended victims were only the 'most hopelessly uneconomic ones'; the remaining branch lines would be 'dealt with' [*sic*] after the first wave of closures had been carried out.

The Beeching Plan presaged doom for many lines in East Anglia, two notable victims being the Dereham to Wells-next-the-Sea branch and the Swaffham to Thetford route. The Beeching closures were rushed into effect, and the Wells branch was closed on Saturday 3rd October, 1964, leaving a revised passenger service on what was now seen as the 'main line' between Kings Lynn, Dereham and Norwich. Goods services to and from Wells lingered on for another month, but by 31st October the line had been closed completely beyond Fakenham. The Swaffham to Thetford line suffered a similar fate, losing its passenger services in June 1964 and its remaining goods services in April 1965.

On the face of it, north Norfolk had escaped the worst effects of the Beeching axe, and the election of a new, less anti-railway government in 1964 seemed to guarantee the survival of those rural lines that had survived the initial pruning. The railway trade unions predicted that the incoming Labour government would herald a period of stability for the state-owned railways, and in 1967 Transport Minister Barbara Castle presented what appeared to be a blueprint for future railway development. A so-called 'basic railway network' of about 11,000 route miles was envisaged, and although some closures were still contemplated, the 'Castle Plan' was much better than the final Beeching proposals which (if fully implemented) would have reduced the national railway system to a pitiful 3,000 route miles.

The Labour proposals enabled 'socially-necessary' lines to be subsidised by national or local government, but – perhaps significantly – most of these 'socially-necessary' lines were concentrated in urban areas where Labour voters predominated. The future for loss-making branch lines in rural (and predominantly Tory) areas remained bleak – especially in Norfolk, where the lines from Kings Lynn to Hunstanton, Kings Lynn to Norwich and Norwich to Cromer had all been excluded from Mrs Castle's basic network for development.[58]

With closure drawing ever nearer, the threatened lines in north Norfolk became mere shadows of their former selves as economies and rationalisation of facilities took effect. In August 1966, for example, all stations between Wymondham, Dereham and Kings Lynn became unstaffed halts, while the withdrawal of goods facilities from intermediate stations was carried out progressively between 1964 and 1966. Dereham remained a relatively busy freight centre, and private siding traffic on what was left of the Wells-next-the-Sea branch ensured that goods train still ran between Wymondham and Fakenham. At the western end of the line the sand quarries at Middleton continued to provide a useful source of bulk freight traffic, but otherwise the elimination of local freight traffic had been completed by April 1966.

Further economies were put into effect at Dereham, where the lavish facilities that had grown up in Great Eastern days were gradually simplified. The Dereham avoiding line was taken out of use in 1965, and conventional up and down working through the station was abolished. The former down platform became a dead-end road used by up and down services, while the former up line became a freight-only line used by the surviving goods workings to Fakenham. Southwards, the line to Wymondham was reduced to single track in June 1965, while train services were reduced in response to falling passenger loadings.

It was clear that the Kings Lynn to Norwich route had not prospered – one problem being loss of connecting lines such as the Swaffham to Thetford and Dereham to Wells lines. These routes may not have been profitable in themselves, but they had acted as 'feeders' to the main Kings Lynn to Norwich route, and although BR may have hoped that passengers would travel to railheads such as Swaffham or Dereham by car or bus, what actually happened was somewhat different. In reality, once travellers to places such as Norwich or Kings Lynn had transferred to road transport they showed little desire to change from road to rail at some intermediate point such as Dereham. Thus, traffic that had hitherto flowed by rail was permanently transferred to the roads, and the surviving lines in north Norfolk became locked into a relentless spiral of decline.

In the meantime, rationalisation of facilities had continued apace on both the Lynn & Dereham and Dereham to Wymondham sections, and by 1968 many of the smaller stations between Kings Lynn and Norwich had lost all of their loops, sidings and connections. At Yaxham, all trains used the former down (westbound) platform, while on the Lynn & Dereham line the crossing loops at Wendling, Dunham and Narborough & Pentney had been removed, leaving just one platform in use at each of these stations. At Wendling and Narborough the former up (westbound) platforms remained in use, though at Dunham the former down (eastbound) platform was used by all trains.

Most of the intermediate signal boxes were now closed, and with goods sidings lifted and signalling dismantled the rationalised stations fell victim to vandalism and decay. Platforms became covered with weeds, and abandoned buildings became increasingly decrepid as the combined effects of weather and malicious damage took their toll.

In places, BR demolished some of the redundant buildings completely – at Dunham, for example, the signal cabin was removed, while at Dereham the up side platform canopy was taken down. Other stations, in contrast, managed to retain much of their original infrastructure; at Swaffham, the passing loop remained in use, together with the associated signal box and signalling, and at neighbouring East Winch a similar situation pertained in that the crossing loop was still needed for passing purposes.

The line was not yet regarded as a 'basic railway', and with a few passing loops still in use the Kings Lynn to Norwich route managed to retain at least some of the atmosphere of a Victorian railway. The trains provided in these last, twilight years, were usually two-car class '101' sets, though some of the Kings Lynn to Norwich through workings were worked by four-car formations. The surviving freight services were, by this time, usually worked by class '31' A1A-A1As – typical numbers, during the late 1960s and early 1970s being Nos. D5531 and D5533 (both of which worked on the Norwich to Dereham line at various times).

Closure of the Lynn & Dereham Line

With significant quantities of freight still being handled at Dereham, North Elmham, Ryburgh and Fakenham the Wymondham to Dereham line remained fairly busy throughout the 1960s, but with less freight traffic to sustain it (apart from the flourishing sand traffic at Middleton Towners) the western part of the Kings Lynn to Norwich route seemed to have little future.

In the late 1960s BR decided that the former Lynn & Dereham section was no longer able to cover its costs, and with expenses running at twice the level of receipts it was announced that the railway would be closed between Kings Lynn and Dereham (exclusive) with effect from 9th September, 1968. As this was a Monday, the last trains were scheduled to run on Saturday 7th September, 1968 and on that historic day 120 years of railway history were brought to a close on the Lynn & Dereham line.

The last day was marked by the running of a Midland & Great Northern Railway Society 'East Anglian Branch Line Farewell' special, and in this way local enthusiasts marked the virtual extinction of one of Norfolk's most attractive rural lines.

On a footnote, it is perhaps worth mentioning that the former East Anglian Railways' branch from Kings Lynn to Wisbech was also closed on 7th September, 1968, and in this way two closely-related lines were wiped out together. As originally planned, the Lynn & Dereham line and the Kings Lynn to Wisbech line would have formed part of a major east-to-west cross country route, and although this ambitious scheme was never brought to fruition the Dereham and Wisbech lines shared a complex and inextricably-linked early history (see *Chapters One and Two*). It was, in many ways, sad but entirely appropriate that BR should have chosen to eliminate both of these ex-EAR lines on the same weekend. Their simultaneous demise wiped out 12 local stations from the BR passenger network, leaving only the Lynn & Ely main line as a monument to the ambitions of Victorian pioneers such as Henry Bruce, Edward Self and the other entrepreneurs who had struggled to bring railway communication to this north-west corner of East Anglia.

Closure of the Dereham Branch

The closure of the Lynn & Dereham line was not quite the end of the story because the former Norfolk Railway branch from Wymondham to Dereham continued to operate. Regrettably, in the early months of 1968 British Railways had already published withdrawal notices for four supposedly uneconomic Norfolk lines – among them the Norwich to Dereham route. Before giving her consent to this new round of closure and rationalisation, Transport Minister Barbara Castle 'sought the advice' of the East Anglian Transport Users' Consultative Committee, though most Dereham rail users knew full well that the decision to close the line was probably a foregone conclusion.

As usual, the pre-closure consultative process was little more than a formality. Some people argued that the costs of the Wymondham to Dereham line were surely covered by its freight revenues, but this argument had little effect because TUCC enquiries were only empowered to discuss *passenger* traffic. In the end, the only real grounds for objection to the closure of this 11¼ mile line concerned the level of 'hardship' that would result, and as additional bus services were proposed, it appeared that little real hardship would be caused. Accordingly, in April 1968 the Transport Minister gave her consent to the withdrawal of passenger services between Norwich and Dereham, subject to the provision of extra bus services.

The proposed closure was not immediately implemented, and on 15th September, 1968 the doomed branch became involved in a serious flooding incident. It had rained more or less continuously for several days, and the rain persisted for a full 24 hours on 14th–15th September, creating utter chaos in the Norwich area. Norwich itself became completely cut off by earth slips on the Ely, Ipswich and Great Yarmouth lines, and until these lines could be brought back into use the only spare ballast and permanent way materials were on the Dereham line. Two engineer's trains were hastily assembled and sent onto the branch, and passenger services were temporarily suspended while surplus ballast and other much-needed permanent way materials were recovered from the recently-singled Wymondham to Dereham line.

The Dereham branch remained popular locally, but in September 1969 the Eastern Region finally announced that the surviving passenger services between Wymondham and Dereham would be withdrawn with effect from 6th October, 1969, and as this was a Monday, the final trains would be run on Saturday 4th October. The stations at Kimberley Park, Hardingham, Thuxton, Yaxham and Dereham would be closed, but goods services would continue to run between Wymondham, Dereham and Fakenham.

The last day was, as usual, marked by the appearance of numerous extra travellers – among them many railway enthusiasts who turned up to photograph the final hours of operation. The closure of the line was however, conducted with decorum, and the few regular travellers were not swamped by hordes of 'last day' revellers. Only towards the end of the day did that final Saturday assume an especial historical significance, and as the very last up and down trains proceeded along the line little knots of people gathered to pay their last respects. This was indeed the end of an era, and at the cessation of the day's operation those who had participated in the finalities sensed that an old and much-loved local institution had passed away. In truth, the Kings Lynn to Norwich railway was no more.

The Final Years

The withdrawal of regular passenger services enabled BR to implement further economies, and the line from Wymondham to Fakenham was soon reduced to a long siding, worked on the 'one engine in steam' system. The remaining signal boxes were abolished, and most level crossings were then worked by train crews, resulting in extended journey times for the surviving freight workings.

Continuing rationalisation resulted in a further decline in facilities – notably at Wymondham, where the junction was remodelled to allow access via a simple turnout. Trains from the Norwich direction were, in consequence, unable to proceed directly onto the branch, and a reversal along the down main line became necessary before the northwards journey to Dereham could continue. (Later still, in 1981, the main line through Wymondham station was itself singled, and this further simplification allowed Dereham trains to run straight onto the branch without reversal.)

At Dereham, many sidings remained *in situ*, but with crossovers removed the operation of the station and goods yard was much simplified. The former Lynn & Dereham route remained intact for a short distance from the bay platform on the down side of the station to the site of the A1075 level crossing, this residual section of the L&DR route being needed as a headshunt for the nearby coal yard.

Coal class traffic was handled at Dereham for several more years, though the main form of traffic in later years was grain and fertilizer. Public goods traffic was accepted at North Elmham and Ryburgh until July 1971, and both of these Wells branch stations continued to handle private siding traffic after that date.

In 1978, the branch from Wymondham was continuing to deal with about 55,000 tons of freight a year, but BR claimed that the line was unable to cover its operating costs, and in a further contraction the route was cut back from Fakenham to Ryburgh in 1979. The Ryburgh to North Elmham section lingered on until 1981, but in that year the line was closed beyond North Elmham (although the redundant track from Ryburgh to North Elmham was not immediately lifted).

North Elmham had remained the end of the line for several years, the main traffic during the 1980s being grain and fertilizers. At the end of 1988, rumours began to circulate in the Dereham area to the effect that the whole line would soon be closed, and following enquiries made by the transport pressure group Transport 2000, BR admitted that the 4½ mile section between Dereham and North Elmham would be closed to all traffic with effect from 25th January, 1989. The future of the Wymondham to Dereham line was, by this time, also in considerable doubt, and in announcing the impending demise of the North Elmham service, BR added that the Dereham line was scheduled to close in June 1989 – thereby forcing the last regular rail users (UKF at Dereham) onto the already-crowded roads.

Re-opening of the Line?

In the interim, there had been much pressure and lobbying for a reinstatement of some form of passenger service between Norwich and Dereham. In 1975, the 'Wymondham, Dereham & Fakenham Railway Action Committee' had been formed as a result of a meeting called by the East Anglian branch of the Railway Invigoration Society, and these two related organisations commenced a vigorous campaign for the re-introduction of passenger services over the Dereham branch. Pointing out that the line was (at that time) still required as a freight route, the campaigners argued that a railbus or diesel multiple unit service could have been provided at little extra cost, while the population growth in Dereham and the surrounding area would (they suggested) ensure the longer term future of the Wymondham to Dereham route.

On 8th April, 1978 the campaigners organised a special train service between Norwich and Dereham, and over 600 people took the opportunity to travel on the otherwise freight-only branch. A six-car multiple unit formation made two return trips over the line, and large numbers of well-wishers turned out to welcome the train at intermediate stations such as Yaxham and Hardingham. The journey to and from Norwich took about 80 minutes each way, inclusive of five stops at unmanned level crossings. In all, the two special trips were regarded as an overwhelming success, and local travellers were encouraged in their belief that the line could one day be revived as a commuter route.

Growing interest in rural lines such as the Dereham branch brought a series of further special trains to the route during the ensuing years. On 21st April, 1979 the Wymondham, Dereham & Fakenham Rail Action Committee repeated its earlier success by providing a shuttle dmu service between Norwich, Dereham and Fakenham. On this occasion the Action Committee joined forces with the Railway Development Society and the newly-formed Fakenham & Dereham Railway Society to organise the aptly-named 'Fakenham Flyer'; again, the chartered train was an instant success, and plans were made for similar trips in the years ahead.

On Sunday, 23rd April, 1981 the Fakenham & Dereham Railway Society organised a seaside special from Ryburgh, North Elmham, Dereham, Yaxham, Thuxton, Kimberley Park and Wymondham to Clacton, Frinton and Walton-on-the-Naze, the return fare for this attractive excursion being just £6.50. A few months later, on Saturday 19th September, 1981, the Wymondham, Dereham & Fakenham Rail Action Committee arranged another chartered dmu service between Norwich and Dereham. Four up and four down trains were provided and, with stops at Yaxham, Hardingham and the other intermediate stations, the Action Committee effectively brought the Wymondham to Dereham line back to life – albeit for only a day!

These special excursions became something of an institution on the Dereham line. On 28th September, 1985, for instance, the branch was brought back to life for another day's passenger operation, while on 25th May, 1986 the Railway Development Association joined forces with the Wymondham, Dereham & Fakenham Action Committee to run a seaside excursion from Dereham to Sheringham. The fare, for this dmu trip, was £5 per head.

Post-Closure Developments on the Lynn & Dereham Line

The work of local pressure groups did much to keep the Dereham branch in the news in the years following closure, and while this was clearly a good thing the attention focussed on the Wymondham to Dereham route inevitably meant that the Lynn & Dereham line became regarded as a somewhat marginal appendage to the 'Dereham main line'. There was no longer any physical connection between the eastern and western sections of the ertswhile Kings Lynn to Norwich cross country route – the Lynn &

Dereham section having been lifted between Middleton Towers and the A1075 level crossing at Dereham. Some of the former L&DR stations remained more or less intact, but a section of the former trackbed had been obliterated by new road works between Dereham and Wendling, and at Swaffham the abandoned line had been covered by building developments.

Only at its western extremity did the Lynn & Dereham Railway continue to function as a working freight line, and indeed the 3½ miles section between Kings Lynn and Middleton Towers was so busy that, by 1980, there were four sand trains each day. Loaded trains left Middleton at 5.30, 9.00 am, 1.35 and 4.00 pm, and after re-marshalling at Kings Lynn the sand wagons were sent forward to factories in Yorkshire at 7.38, 8.44 and 9.16 pm. Much of the Middleton sand output was used for glass making by firms such as Rockware Glass of Knottingly.

The sand was conveyed either in 24-ton bulk powder wagons or in open wagons or hopper vehicles, though in November 1980 the Ministry of Transport announced that British Industrial Sand had been offered a grant of £624,000 towards the cost of 60 high-capacity hopper wagons and improved loading facilities at Middleton Towers.

Locomotives seen on the Middleton sand workings were usually class '31' A1A-A1As, or class '37' Co-Cos – the latter being permitted to haul 940 ton loads whereas the class '31s' were limited to 870 ton maximum loads.

British Industrial Sand maintained a small fleet of 0–4–0 or 0–6–0 diesel shunters for use on the firm's privately-owned system at Middleton, and in 1980 one of these engines was ex-BR '03' shunter No. D2054. Until 1978 the sand company had also operated an extensive 1 ft 11½ in. gauge internal narrow gauge system; 15 'Simplex' shunting locomotives were available to work this industrial network, and when the narrow gauge system was replaced by conveyors some of the BIS shunters were transferred to the Leighton Buzzard narrow gauge railway.

As intimated earlier, special passenger trains were frequently run on the Wymondham to Dereham line after the cessation of regular services, but the Lynn & Dereham section did not enjoy the support of a pro-railway pressure group, and perhaps for this reason the line did not feature in many enthusiasts' tours. On the other hand, the 3½ mile branch from Kings Lynn to Middleton Towers was not entirely neglected in this respect, and on 12th July, 1986 the Southern Electric Group's 'Fenland Tiger' railtour brought a dmu special onto the L&DR route, giving London-based enthusiasts an opportunity to travel over the line.

Latest Developments

The news that the Dereham branch would be closed completely in June 1989 led to renewed pressure for a reinstatement of the line for passenger services. Public attitudes towards railway closure had changed dramatically since the 1960s, and whereas in the 'Beeching era' the general public had repeatedly been told that railways were 'old fashioned' and 'Victorian', the oil crisis of 1974 had effectively tipped the balance back towards energy-efficient forms of transport and away from road transport. There was, moreover, greater interest in the whole concept of privately owned and operated branch lines, and against this background a new company known as the Great Eastern Railway Company (1989) Holdings Ltd was formed with the aim of purchasing 16 miles of line between Wymondham, Dereham and North Elmham.

It was suggested that one and a quarter million pounds would be enough to purchase and re-open the branch, and the company planned to raise this sum by a mixture of share issues, EEC and local grants, and public donations. Further cash could be generated by development of the 13 acre station site at Dereham, the intention being that, in addition to a fully-revived GER-style station, there might also be shops, a hotel and a museum or heritage centre. Feasibility studies indicated that 500 Dereham residents worked in Norwich, while 700 Norwich residents commuted to work in Dereham, and it seemed that a regular commuter service would be welcomed by increasingly frustrated road users.

The line would be worked mainly by diesel multiple units, though it was envisaged that tourist traffic would be catered for by the provision of steam-operated services.

The Mid-Norfolk Railway Society – which had already established an operating base in the goods yard at County School – supported the re-opening scheme, and it was hoped that other railway socieities would provide steam locomotives or vintage rolling stock for use on the proposed tourist services. In the early months of 1991, *The Railway Magazine* stated that the work needed to bring the line up to passenger-carrying standards would 'take around two years', and at the time of writing the project is still at an early stage.

Postscript

The remaining portion of the Kings Lynn to Wymondham line is, at present, intact but out of use, though the activities of the Mid-Norfolk Railway Society have ensured that the Dereham branch is not yet extinct. New rolling stock has from time to time been delivered to the line, one of the first arrivals being a Ruston diesel-hydraulic shunter from the British Sugar factory at Bury St Edmunds, which was delivered by road to Hardingham on 15th October, 1983.

More recently, in the summer of 1992, it was announced that class '20' Bo-Bo No. 20069 would be sent to the Dereham line as soon as it had been stripped of asbestos. The engine would, on arrival in Norfolk, be restored to its original green livery as No. D8069.

In July 1992 the Conservative government published its White Paper on the privatisation of British Railways. It remains to be seen what effect this proposal will have on the promotion and operation of preserved lines, though one must hope that – whatever changes take place on the BR system – the new proposals will ultimately benefit the Wymondham to Dereham line and other privately-owned lines.

Notes and References

Lack of space precludes the use of footnotes, but the following brief notes may be of help to those seeking further sources of information on the Kings Lynn to Dereham line.

1. *The House of Commons Journal*, March–June 1845.
2. *The House of Commons Journal*, 21st July, 1845.
3. *The House of Commons Journal*, 20th March, 1845, p. 169.
4. *The House of Lords Journal*, 17th July, 1845.
5. *Proceedings of the Institute of Civil Engineers*, 1898 (obituary notice).
6. Lynn & Dereham Railway, half-year reports.
7. *The Railway Times*, 5th December, 1846.
8. *The Railway Chronicle*, 27th February, 1847.
9. *The House of Lords Journal*, 17th July, 1845, p. 754.
10. *The Railway Chronicle*, 14th November, 1846, p. 1110.
11. *The Railway Chronicle*, 27th February, 1847, p. 201.
12. *The Railway Times*, 2nd March, 1850.
13. Lynn & Dereham Railway, half-year reports.
14. *The Railway Times*, 17th March, 1849, p. 277.
15. *Ibid.* p. 277.
16. *Ibid.* p. 277.
17. *Ibid.* p. 278.
18. *Ibid.* p. 278.
19. The Cope Report, quoted in *The Railway Times*, 18th August, 1849, p. 943.
20. *Ibid.* p. 943.
21. *Ibid.* p. 943.
22. *Ibid.* p. 943.
23. *The Railway Times*, 18th August, 1849, pp. 943–4.
24. *Ibid.* p. 944.
25. See *The Wells-next-the-Sea Branch* (The Oakwood Press – 1988) for further details.
26. Lynn & Hunstanton Railway Act of Incorporation, 1st August, 1861.
27. *The Railway Times*, 1st February, 1862, pp. 101–2.
28. *The Railway Times*, 12th September, 1875.
29. PRO MT6 334/7.
30. PRO MT6 248/10.
31. PRO MT6 417/3.
32. PRO MT6 417/3.
33. E.L. Ahrons, Locomotives of the Great Eastern Railway, *Railway Magazine*, 1915, *passim*,
34. *Ibid.*
35. *Ibid.*
36. Official reports held at The Fleet Air Arm Museum, RNAS Yeovilton.
37. PRO MT6 2426/2.
38. PRO MT6 2461/9.
39. E.L. Ahrons, Locomotives of the Great Eastern Railway, *Railway Magazine*, 1915, p. 302.
40. Great Western coaches had been painted crimson lake in the years before, during and after World War I, but chocolate and cream livery was re-introduced around the time of the grouping.
41. *The Railway Magazine*, June 1936.

42. The 'Aylsham traffic' referred to in the working timetable was destined for stations on the Wroxham to County School cross country line, which provided a connection between the Cromer and Wells-next-the-Sea routes.
43. Peter Corbell, The RAF on D-Day, *Air Pictorial*, October 1972, pp. 396–401.
44. PRO MT29.
45. *The Great Eastern Railway Magazine.*
46. *Ibid.*
47. *Ibid.*
48. *Kelly's Directory of Norfolk.*
49. *The Great Eastern Railway Magazine.*
50. *Ibid.*
51. The rebuilt office was similar to its predecessor, but of more generous proportions.
52. PRO MT6 248/10.
53. PRO MT29.
54. *Kelly's Directory of Norfolk.*
55. *Ibid.*
56. PRO MT6 2461/9.
57. LNER coaches were, in fact, still being turned out in varnished teak livery in 1953, and for this reason Eastern Region coaching stock retained the old liveries long after the other BR regions had adopted the new red or red and cream colour schemes.
58. In the event, the Cromer branch escaped closure, and it remains part of the present-day BR system; the Hunstanton branch, in contrast, was closed to all traffic on Saturday 3rd May, 1969.

A Note on Sources

Other sources are, in general, mentioned in the text. These include Acts of Parliament, official documents, official reports and contemporary journals such as *The Railway Times, The Railway Chronicle, The Locomotive Magazine, The Great Eastern Railway Magazine* and *The Railway Magazine.* Also GER, LNER and BR working timetables and notices, *Kelly's Directories of Norfolk, The Journal of the House of Commons, The Journal of the House of Lords,* and various editions of the standard 25-inch, 6-inch and 1-inch Ordnance Survey maps. This written evidence was supplemented by field work carried out at the sites of bridges, stations, etc., and by extra details supplied by local people or enthusiasts such as Nigel Angelbeck, Nick Moore, John Strange, W.J. Sutton and Canon Charles Bayes

Acts of Parliament – Further Notes

The early history of the Lynn & Dereham and its contemporaries was unusually complicated, and numerous Acts, plans and other documents were consulted in an effort to judge the relationships that existed between the Lynn & Dereham, Lynn & Ely, Eastern Counties, and other constituents of the GER. The following list of Acts may be of interest to those with a deeper interest in East Anglian railway history.

Eastern Counties Railway, 4th July, 1836 (6 & 7 Wllm. cap. 106); incorporation.
Northern & Eastern Railway, 4th July, 1836 (6 & 7 Wllm. cap. 103); incorporation.
Yarmouth & Norwich Railway, 18th June, 1842 (5 & 6 Vic. cap. 82); incorporation.
Norwich & Brandon Railway, 10th May, 1884 (7 & 8 Vic. cap. 15); incorporation.
Norfolk Railway, 30th June, 1845 (8 & 9 Vic. cap. 41); incorporation.

Lynn & Ely Railway, 30th June, 1845 (8 & 9 Vic. cap. 55); incorporation.
Lynn & Dereham Railway, 21st July, 1845 (8 & 9 Vic. cap. 126); incorporation.
Ely & Huntingdon Railway, (8 & 9 Vic. cap. 48); incorporation.
East Anglian Railway, 22nd July, 1847 (10 & 11 Vic. cap. 275); incorporation.
Norfolk Railway, 31st July, 1845; Dereham branch, etc.
Lynn & Fakenham Railway, 13th July, 1876; incorporation.
Wells & Fakenham Railway, 24th July, 1854 (17 & 18 Vic. cap. 180); incorporation.
Lynn & Hunstanton Railway, 1st August, 1861 (24 & 25 Vic. cap. 199); incorporation.
Great Eastern Railway, 7th August, 1862 (25 & 26 Vic. cap. 223); incorporation.

Further Reading

Some of the following books or articles contain specific references to the Kings Lynn to Norwich line, while others are of a more peripheral nature. All of the titles listed should, however, contain material of interest to railway modellers or other enthusiasts.

Cecil J. Allen, *The Great Eastern Railway* (1955) *passim*.
J.F. Gairns, The Norfolk Lines of the London & North Eastern Railway, *The Railway Magazine*, February 1929, pp. 85–90, 181–86, 366–70.
H.H. Meik, The East Anglian Railway, *The Railway Magazine*, 1910, pp. 330–34, 401–404.
Donald Gordon, The Lynn & Dereham Railway, *The Railway Magazine*, June 1958, pp. 376–380.
B.D.J. Walsh, Branch Lines to Thetford, *The Railway Magazine*, June 1953, pp. 373–79.
E. Tuddenham, A Journey to Wells-next-the-Sea, *Railway World*, March 1965, pp. 82–87.
W.R. Jenkinson, The Predecessors of the Great Eastern Railway, *The Great Eastern Railway Magazine*, 1913–15, *passim*.
David Bosher, Norfolk Postscript, *The Railway Magazine*, February 1980, pp. 56–59.
G. Gamble, Sand From Middleton, *The Railway Magazine*, December 1980, pp. 559–562.
H.G.E. Ellis, The Royal Link at Kings Lynn, *Railway World*, February 1984.
N. Crump, *By Rail to Victory*, LNER (1947).
Stanley C. Jenkins, *The Wells-next-the-Sea Branch*, The Oakwood Press (1988) *passim*.
Stanley C. Jenkins, *The Lynn & Hunstanton Branch*, The Oakwood Press (1987) *passim*.
Stanley C. Jenkins, *The Melton Constable to Cromer Branch*, The Oakwood Press (1991) pp. 9–19.
Stanley C. Jenkins, *The Cromer Branch*, The Oakwood Press (1989) *passim*.
Iain Scotchman, The Dereham Branch, GERS Journal, January 1979.
W.A. Dutt, *The Little Guide to Norfolk*, (1903).
E.L. Ahrons, Locomotive and Train Working in the Latter Part of the 19th Century: The Great Eastern Railway, *The Railway Magazine*, 1918, *passim*.
C.B. Carter, LNER Coach Cascading in the 1930s, *British Railway Journal*, Summer 1986, pp. 101–105.
John Watling, GER Carriages in Crimson Lake, *British Railway Journal*, Spring 1986, pp. 77–81.

Appendix One

Chronological List of Important Dates

1845 Lynn & Dereham Railway incorporated with Powers to build a railway from Kings Lynn to Dereham (21st July).

Norfolk Railway empowered to construct a branch line from Wymondham to Dereham (31st July).

1846 Lynn & Dereham Railway opened from Kings Lynn to Narborough (26th October).

1847 Norfolk Railway branch opened from Wymondham to Dereham (15th February).

Lynn & Dereham, Lynn & Ely and Ely & Huntingdon railways amalgamated to form the East Anglian Railways (22nd July).

Lynn & Dereham line opened from Narborough to Swaffham (10th August).

Lynn & Dereham line opened from Swaffham to Sporle (26th October).

1848 Lynn & Dereham line completed throughout to Dereham (11th September).

Eastern Counties Railway assumes control of the Wymondham–Dereham line.

1849 Dereham branch extended from Dereham to Fakenham (20th March).

The East Anglian proprietors disagree with the EAR Directors over the conduct and management of the company's affairs.

1851 After many vicissitudes, the East Anglian Railways attempt to form an alliance with the Great Northern Railway.

1852 The East Anglian company is taken over by the Eastern Counties Railway, the proposed GNR alliance having been rejected.

1857 The Wymondham to Fakenham line is extended to Wells-next-the-Sea.

1862 The East Anglian Railways and the Norfolk Railway are both absorbed into the newly-created Great Eastern Railway (7th August).

The Lynn & Hunstanton Railway is opened to Hunstanton (3rd October).

1869 Incorporation of Watton & Swaffham Railway (12th July).

1870 Opening of Kings Lynn Docks branch (10th June).

1871 New station built at Kings Lynn.

1875 Watton & Swaffham line opened to passenger traffic (15th November).

1879 Lynn & Fakenham line opened from Kings Lynn to Massingham Road (16th August).

1880 Major re-signalling scheme at Dereham (April).

1881 Wells branch train involved in accident at Norwich (21st January).

Opening of Wymondham to Forncett cut-off (2nd May).

1882 Wymondham to Dereham line doubled between Wymondham and Dereham (November).

1886 Cut-off line at Kings Lynn provided for Eastern & Midlands (originally Lynn & Fakenham) traffic (1st January).

Dereham avoiding line opened between Dereham West and Dereham South junctions (June).

1894 Accident at Swaffham (2nd September).

1914 Start of World War I (4th August).

1915 Zeppelin L4 bombs Kings Lynn (19th January).

1916 New siding installed at Dereham (February).

1917 Zeppelins drop bombs near Wells and Dereham (19th October).

1918 End of World War I (11th November).

1923 Grouping of railways and creation of LNER (1st January).

Kimberley renamed Kimberley Park.

1926 New offices and goods shed provided at Kings Lynn.

1933 Economies put into effect at Thuxton and Dereham West.

1939 Start of World War II (3rd September).
1940 Station nameboards taken down to confuse German invaders.
1943 New siding at Dereham for Air Ministry.
1945 End of World War II.
1948 Nationalisation of railways (1st January).
1955 Introduction of diesel multiple unit fleet, and closure of Dereham shed to steam engines (September).
1959 Kings Lynn shed closed to steam.
1963 Publication of the Beeching Plan heralds period of major railway closures.
1964 Wells-next-the-Sea branch closed to passenger traffic (3rd October).
Wells-next-the-Sea closed to freight traffic (31st October).
1965 Wymondham to Dereham line reduced to single track; Dereham avoiding line taken out of use.
1966 Withdrawal of local goods services.
Stations between Kings Lynn and Wymondham become unstaffed halts (August).
1968 Closure of the Lynn & Dereham line (7th September).
Wymondham to Dereham line closed during flood emergency (15th September).
1969 Passenger services withdrawn between Wymondham and Dereham (4th October).
1971 Withdrawal of freight services between North Elmham and Ryburgh (July).
1978 Special passenger train run on Dereham line (8th April).
Closure of narrow gauge lines at Middleton Towers.
1979 Closure of Fakenham to Ryburgh freight line.
1980 British Industrial Sand offered government grant towards improved sand loading facilities at Middleton Towers.
1981 Further simplification of trackwork at Wymondham.
Closure of North Elmham to Ryburgh freight line.
Special trains run on Dereham line in April and September.
1986 Special train run from Dereham to Sheringham (25th May).
Special train runs to Middleton Towers (12th July).
1989 Closure of freight line from Dereham to North Elmham.
Closure of Wymondham to Dereham line announced by BR.
Formation of the Great Eastern Railway (1989).
1991 Re-opening scheme announced at meeting held in Dereham station.

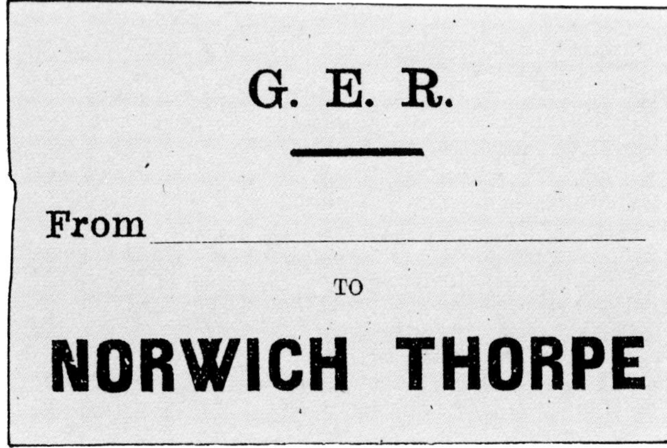
G. E. R.

From

TO

NORWICH THORPE

Courtesy John Strange

Appendix Two

Some GER Station Masters on the Kings Lynn to Norwich Line

Station	*1862*	*1888*	*1896*	*1904*	*1908*	*1912*	*1922*
Middleton	unknown	William Davis	William Davis	William Nunn	Robert Simpson	Albert Peacock	George Taylor
East Winch	John Smallhouse	William Smith	William Fisk	Edward William Jackson	Edward William Jackson	Thomas Hurley	William Dines
Narborough	Nebuchadnezzar Ayres	James Smith	Thomas Read Nash	Charles Wilby	Charles Wilby	Charles Wilby	Gabriel Paynter
Swaffham	unknown	Charles Saintby	Charles Saintby	John Coker	John Coker	John Coker	John Coker
Dunham	Charles Underhill	Charles Underhill	Alfred Page	Harbert Youell	James Andrews	James Andrews	James Andrews
Fransham	Edgar Skeet	Mr Durrant	Richard Jesse Read	Harry Youell	Thomas Newall	Thomas Newall	Thomas Newall
Wendling	unknown	Alfred Page	Charles Wilby	John Walpole	John Walpole	John Walpole	William Coman
Dereham	John Playford	Charles Eastaugh	Charles Eastaugh	Francis Arthur Easton	Francis Arthur Easton	Francis Arthur Easton	Frederick Young
Yaxham	unknown	Harry Stokes	Harry Stokes	Harry Stokes	Harry Stokes	Robert Simpson	Robert Simpson
Thuxton	Mr Mills	Thomas Spicer	William Barker	William Barker	William Barker	William Barker	William Barket
Hardingham	unknown	Charles H. Smith	Charles H. Smith	Charles H. Smith	Charles H. Smith	Charles H. Smith	Walter Tallent
Kimberley	Henry Cheney	James Raney	James Raney	James Raney	Gabriel Paynter	Walter Tallent	F. Bloom

Index

NORWICH THORPE STATION